DATE DUE

THE POLITICS OF CHILD DAYCARE IN BRITAIN

The Politics of
Child Daycare in Britain

VICKY RANDALL

OXFORD
UNIVERSITY PRESS

OXFORD

UNIVERSITY PRESS

Great Clarendon Street, Oxford OX2 6DP

Oxford University Press is a department of the University of Oxford.
It furthers the University's objective of excellence in research, scholarship,
and education by publishing worldwide in

Oxford New York

Athens Auckland Bangkok Bogotá Buenos Aires Calcutta
Cape Town Chennai Dar es Salaam Delhi Florence Hong Kong Istanbul
Karachi Kuala Lumpur Madrid Melbourne Mexico City Mumbai
Nairobi Paris São Paulo Shanghai Singapore Taipei Tokyo Toronto Warsaw
and associated companies in Berlin Ibadan

Oxford is a registered trade mark of Oxford University Press
in the UK and certain other countries

Published in the United States
by Oxford University Press Inc., New York

© Vicky Randall 2000

The moral rights of the author have been asserted
Database right Oxford University Press (maker)

First published 2000

British Library Cataloguing in Publication Data

Data available

Library of Congress Cataloging in Publication Data
Randall, Vicky.
The politics of child daycare in Britain / by Vicky Randall.
p. cm.
Includes bibliographical references and index.
1. Child care—Government policy—Great Britian. I. Title.
HQ778.7.G7 R36 2000 362.71′2′0941—dc21 00-031349

ISBN 0-19-828048-3

1 3 5 7 9 10 8 6 4 2

Typeset by Best-set Typesetter Ltd., Hong Kong
Printed in Great Britain
on acid-free paper by
Biddles Ltd
Guildford & Kings Lynn

CONTENTS

LIST OF TABLES

1

Introducing Childcare: Questions and Themes

This book is about the politics of childcare in Britain in the post-war era. As such its ambit is broad-ranging, covering different forms of child-care provision, different time-periods, different decision-making levels and contexts. Even so it is informed, and to an extent inspired, by a single overriding question, concerning why it is that the state's contri-bution, whether in terms of direct provision, or direct or indirect subsidy, to child daycare in this country has been so meagre. Although at one level, and from a feminist perspective, this might not seem so sur-prising—men have dominated the political process so what do you expect?—viewed another way it is more of a puzzle: that is, when this record of public neglect is considered alongside the growing percentage of women in paid employment, the upsurge and impact of second-wave feminism, and the much more generous provision in a range of other European countries.

What is meant by child daycare in this discussion? In a generic sense child daycare must mean looking after or watching over children during the day, or a part of it, and in whatever context. So it includes care by parents, relatives, or friends; it also includes paid care by nannies, and even babysitters. However, the focus of interest here is on kinds of childcare based outside the child's home and somewhat more formalized. In Britain this has meant day nurseries, childminders (registered and unregistered), nursery schools, nursery classes, and playgroups. Although the need for childcare does not cease when children go to school, and the need for after-school and holiday provi-sion is an important issue, the emphasis in this text is on provision for the under-fives.

Our subject, then, is the making of child daycare policy in Britain. However, the extent to which there has actually *been* a national policy, meaning an explicitly and systematically elaborated government approach to childcare, until quite recently, must be questioned. Policy instead has been implicit, evident retrospectively in the sequence of official decisions or non-decisions, actions or inertia that touch on child-care provision. More specifically regarding public sector provision, as

TABLE 1. *Daycare and nursery education provision in UK, 1988*

Form of provision	Percentage and category of children provided for
Local authority day nurseries	0.9 (of under-5s)
Private and voluntary day nurseries	1.1 (of under-5s)
Registered childminders	5 (of under-5s)
Local authority nursery school and classes (full- and part-time)	25 (3–4-year-olds)
Local authority primary schools	20 (3–4-year-olds)

Source: Bronwen Cohen, *Caring for Children: The 1990 Report* (Edinburgh: Family Policy Studies Centre, 1990), 19.

compared with a (growing) number of European countries (as well as New Zealand and Australia), in Britain this has been sensationally low.

As Table 1 shows, in 1988 local authority day nursery places were available for just 0.9 per cent of under-fives, generally those prioritized on grounds of social need. Private and voluntary nurseries only brought the total coverage of day nursery provision up to 2 per cent of the age range. Registered childminders accounted for a further 5 per cent. In addition, with some limited local authority funding support, playgroups catered for approximately 50 per cent of children aged 3 and 4 but typically this was for only two or three half-day sessions a week. At the same time 25 per cent of 3- and 4-year-olds were attending nursery school or classes but for 84 per cent of them, this was part-day, and of course limited to school term time.[1] Inevitably comparisons are complicated by differences in the forms of provision, the age range for which they are provided, and the age at which children start school, but the broad contrast between Britain's record and that of other European countries is clear. By the end of the 1980s Britain was one of the four EC countries scoring lowest on provision for the under-threes and, with Portugal, the lowest in provision for children between 3 and school age.[2]

By 1995, the number of part-time nursery education places had grown.[3] There had also been further expansion of private daycare

---

[1] See Bronwen Cohen, *Caring for the Family* (Edinburgh: Family Policy Studies Centre, 1990).

[2] See European Commission Childcare Network, *Childcare in the European Communities 1985-1990* (Brussels: Commission of the European Communities, 1990).

[3] By the late nineties, as described in Chs. 4 and 7, it had expanded further. The Labour government's Early Years Development Partnership initiative, launched in 1997, which in turn builds on a foundation laid through the Conservative government's voucher scheme, aims to cover the eligible age group of 3- and 4-year-olds, although it remains part-day and there are concerns about the quality and suitability of provision in some of the different relevant 'settings'.

provision but the number of local authority day nursery places had actually fallen slightly and there was still no governmental recognition of the need for a national policy. Rather than catching up with some of its more progressive EC partners Britain had virtually stood still.[4] How is this to be explained?

While the focus of this discussion is on the amount of publicly provided or funded care, we shall encounter a number of related problems. Although increasingly policy-makers have come to realize in principle the need to integrate educational and care aspects of childcare, their continuing fragmentation in practice has placed real difficulties in the way of reform. The (day)care aspect has moreover been seen as particularly low-status work, with correspondingly low levels of pay. Fragmentation has been both a cause and an effect of the continuing 'training muddle', with insufficient access to training for many daycare workers and on the other hand an unsystematized plethora of training qualifications being offered.[5]

THE GENERAL APPROACH—GENDERED INSTITUTIONALISM?

The discussion that follows does not offer a systematic critique of policy, important as that would be. It aims rather to shed light on the kind of politics and policy processes that have led to these policy outcomes. In so doing it uses more than one strategy of enquiry. Besides tracing the *historical* development of British childcare policy and the (changing) policy process associated with it, it looks to the implications of *comparative* analysis. This is at two levels: variations amongst British local authorities are referred to at different points and there is a more extended consideration of cross-national differences.[6]

To the extent that the study is characterized by an underlying

---

[4] For a more systematic 1995 comparison with other European countries see Ch. 6.

[5] See Denise Hevey, *The Continuing Under-fives Training Muddle* (London: VOLCUF, 1986).

[6] The analysis draws on a range of primary and secondary sources. Chs. 2 and 6, on the historical roots of childcare policy and cross-national comparisons respectively, rely very largely on secondary material, the main exception being reference to Hansard for the 1945 parliamentary debate. Other chapters make use of a wide range of documentary material, including PRO papers, Hansard, women's movement literature, government reports, and TUC records. They also draw on around forty interviews with officials in central and local government, councillors, an MP, a trade union women's officer, representatives of childcare-related pressure groups, and childcare researchers and academics.

theoretical approach it could be described as gendered institutionalism: that is, a combination of a feminist perspective with what has become popularly known as the 'new institutionalism', especially its 'historical' variant. Historical institutionalism has been defined as the approach that emphasizes the way in which political struggles 'are mediated by the institutional setting in which [they] take place'.[7] It focuses upon how institutions interact and more generally 'the process of politics and policy-making within given institutional parameters'.[8] Finally, its adherents, while tending to emphasize institutional continuity, recognize the part played by historical contingency, by 'accidents of timing and circumstance'[9] and the extent to which social development is in consequence 'path-dependent'.

Apart from the inevitable debate as to how 'new' the new institutionalism is,[10] critics of this perspective have warned of two particular potential weaknesses. One is to do with falsifiability.[11] Without some broader comparative frame of reference, it will be difficult either to refute such a historical narrative or to estimate the extent of its uniqueness. This is one reason why the present study employs both historical and comparative analysis.

Second, there is the danger that an excessive concentration upon institutions will understate or obscure the role of broader contextual

[7] G. John Ikenberry, cited in Kathleen Thelen and Sven Steinmo, 'Historical Institutionalism in Comparative Perspective', in S. Steinmo, K. Thelen, and F. Longstreth (eds.), *Structuring Politics* (Cambridge: Cambridge University Press, 1992), 2.

[8] Ibid. 7. In so doing, however, it recognizes the significance of power, and especially unequal power relations, to the extent that Hall and Taylor suggest this approach 'can usefully be read as an effort to elucidate the 'second' and 'third' dimensions of power identified some years ago in the community power debate'. See Peter A. Hall and Rosemary C. R. Taylor, 'Political Science and the Three New Institutionalisms', *Political Studies*, 44:5 (1996), 940–1.

[9] Ellen M. Immergut, 'The Theoretical Core of the New Institutionalism', *Politics and Society*, 26:1 (1998), 23.

[10] Historical institutionalism emerged partly in reaction to the earlier emphasis on political behaviour, or, in Marxist approaches, on social class structure. While in some respects drawing on the 'old', legalistic and descriptive, institutionalism, whose limitations had prompted the behavourial revolution in the first place, it is 'new' in several important respects. Though stressing the role of institutions, it is more likely than the older version to acknowledge the significance of contextual forces such as social class. It also works with a much more open-ended and less formal notion of institutions, one which tends to define them as 'the formal or informal procedures, routines, norms and conventions embedded in the organizational structures of the polity or political economy'. See Hall and Taylor, 'Political Science and the Three New Institutionalisms', 938.

[11] As Immergut observes, 'Almost any construction of interests or contextual model will appear to be only explainable through history, until one has hit on a more general explanation': Immergut, 'The Theoretical Core of the New Institutionalism', 26.

factors.[12] Recognizing these potential hazards, the analysis that follows does not focus exclusively on the institutional setting or dynamic; it investigates other elements in the determination of childcare policy, notably the character of childcare as an issue and the pattern of demands and pressures it has given rise to, in their own right and without assuming in advance that these are essentially shaped by their institutional context.

None the less, to the extent that a historical institutionalist approach predominates in this study, this reflects a sense that the key to explaining Britain's particular record of childcare provision is likely to lie in the character of her political institutions and processes, and the policy legacy they embody. It is in this sphere above all that we may locate sources for the striking variations in the scale and forms of provision amongst countries of the developed world. This means looking at traditional assumptions about the role and scope of government, the general character of the policy-making process, and the way in which policy categories and priorities have been institutionalized.

But this institutionalist approach combines with a feminist perspective which is apparent first of all in the subject selected for analysis, the politics of childcare. Second, and to the extent that this is not explicit in most institutional accounts, the feminist perspective draws attention to the 'gendered' character of institutions, meaning that 'advantage and disadvantage, exploitation and control, action and emotion, meaning and identity, are patterned through and in terms of a distinction between male and female, masculine and feminine. Gender is not an addition to ongoing processes, conceived as gender neutral. Rather, it is an integral part of those processes'.[13]

In practice feminist explorations of specific institutions and notably of the state are at a fairly early stage. While early radical feminists

[12] Thus it is argued that historical institutionalism has been inadequately equipped to account either for the origins of institutions or for change. As Hall and Taylor note, many writers in this vein tend to divide history into periods of institutional continuity punctured by critical junctures which give rise to substantial institutional change: 'The principal problem here, of course, is to explain what precipitates such critical junctures, and, although historical institutionalists generally stress the impact of economic crises and military conflict, many do not have a well-developed response to this question'. See Hall and Taylor, 'Political Science and the Three New Institutionalisms', 942. Similarly, too great an emphasis upon the contingent and institutionally based process of political resolution could blind us to the extent of enduring, structural inequalities: 'while history is filled with examples of those that 'beat the odds', escaping from constraint and reforging their destinies, we nevertheless maintain an intuitive sense of the odds': Immergut, 'The Theoretical Core of the New Institutionalism', 28.

[13] Joan Acker, 'Hierarchies, Jobs, Bodies: A Theory of Gendered Organizations', *Gender and Society*, 4:2 (1990), 146.

importantly highlighted the 'patriarchal' nature of the state, its concep-
tualization was otherwise crude and over-general. Subsequently much
feminist energy was devoted to promoting a less monolithic, less reduc-
tionist but still quite general theory or understanding of the state. The
best distillation of this understanding probably remains that of R. W.
Connell.[14] He has coined the term 'gender regime' to describe the way
in which the state embodies a set of power relationships between men
and women, which is itself the precipitate of its earlier gender history.
The gender regime includes a gender hierarchy and a gender division
of labour.[15] Because of the way the state embodies gender it is motivated and able to 'do' gender or to regulate gender relations in the wider
society. Furthermore, in so doing it helps actually to reconstitute the
categories which are being regulated: 'Thus the state becomes involved
in the historical process generating and transforming the basic components of the gender order'.[16] This study draws, then, on Connell's
suggestive comments to consider the implications of the state's
'gender regime' for the process of making childcare policy.

   Within the confines of this 'gendered institutionalism' approach the
analysis focuses on a number of organizing elements or themes. Central
to the analysis are first, the institutional context of policy-making and
second, the character of childcare as an issue. These will be introduced
in turn.

THE NATIONAL POLICY-MAKING CONTEXT

Childcare politics takes place within the context of the national policy
process. How are we to conceptualize this context and in what ways
might it have shaped the making of childcare policy in Britain? In her
important pioneering analysis comparing policies towards working
women, including child daycare policies, in Britain and in Sweden, Mary
Ruggie[17] has emphasized the need to understand such policies in the
context of overall state–society relations. In Britain, she argues, these
relations are characterized by a 'liberal-welfare' approach in which state
intervention is hesitant, limited, and fragmentary. In contrast with the

---

[14] R. W. Connell, 'The State, Gender and Sexual Politics', *Theory and Society*, 19:5
(1990), 507–44.

[15] It also includes a 'structure of cathexis' or gender patterning of emotional
attachments.

[16] Connell, 'The State, Gender and Sexual Politics', 529.

[17] Mary Ruggie, *The State and Working Women: A Comparative Study of Britain and
Sweden* (Princeton, NJ: Princeton University Press, 1984).

'societal corporatist' approach in Sweden, this form of welfare state does not seek to transform social—even social class—relationships, only to mitigate their more pathological social consequences. Its liberal ideological disposition, emphasizing the distinction between public and private spheres, tends to inhibit state intervention in such 'private' realms as the market and the family, thereby allowing greater scope in particular for practices embodying 'traditional' conceptions of women's role. In sum, 'the reluctance of the British state to engage in day care provision, differently and further than it has, is linked to its adherence to liberal principles of state/society relations'.[18]

Ruggie's argument is a powerful one, and it is no object of the present book to minimize the value of this original insight. Her perception of the liberal assumptions of the British state is widely shared. It has more recently been reaffirmed and elaborated by David Marquand,[19] who writes about Britain's 'liberal' state tradition. He incidentally traces the origins of this tradition back to at least the nineteenth century: Britain has to an extent been a prisoner of its past. Its great economic achievement in becoming the first country to industrialize was due, at least in part, to its decisive break with the values of the 'Old Society'. That achievement in turn appeared to validate the new liberal values: 'To the British, it seemed almost self-evident that industrialism must be the child of individualism, that 'progress' could only come through setting individuals free to pursue their own interests to make what use they wished of their own property, without reference to society or interference from the state'.[20] The legacy of this particular history is that detailed interference in the private sphere, whether in the market, the realm of culture, or the family, has seemed to need special justification. Even though, in the era of the post-war welfare state, 'Keynesian social democrats' rejected classical market liberalism and the British state acquired a substantial public sector and capacity for public intervention, the underlying liberal assumption of the morally sovereign individual retained its hold, inhibiting the emergence of a 'philosophy of public intervention or what might be called the public realm'.[21]

To an extent, these observations about the character of Britain's state tradition are supported and complemented by characterizations of a distinctive national policy style. The concept of 'national policy style' was developed precisely in the context of trying to explain why, contrary to the expectations of convergence theorists, economic growth did not

---

[18] Ibid. 183.
[19] David Marquand, *The Unprincipled Society* (London: Jonathan Cape, 1988).
[20] Ibid. 8.   [21] Ibid. 11.

automatically or evenly erode policy differences—and childcare would be an excellent example—across nations.[22] The suggestion is that in different national contexts policy-makers 'develop characteristic and durable methods for dealing with public issues'.[23] Such styles reflect state traditions in that they incorporate long-standing assumptions about the appropriate scope of policy intervention, who should be involved in making policy, and so on. Thus Jordan and Richardson,[24] though careful to qualify their generalization by acknowledging the extent to which in practice styles have varied in different times and policy sectors, suggest that in Britain there has been a dominant or favoured approach to policy-making. This has tended to be reactive rather than proactive and has sought policy change through consensus. Among the institutional mechanisms serving to reproduce this style, they identify the highly departmental nature of British government and the corresponding sectoralization of policy-making, combined with an emphasis on consultation and even bargaining with key affected interests. Or in Jack Hayward's words:

Firstly, there are no explicit, over-riding medium or long-term objectives. Secondly, unplanned decision-making is incremental. Thirdly, hum-drum or unplanned decisions are arrived at by a continuous process of mutual adjustment.[25]

It must be acknowledged that these comments predate the full impact of 'Thatcherism'. But leaving aside questions of the degree or form of their pertinence to the more recent period, their characterization of long-standing features of British policy-making is highly relevant for our analysis.

While the argument about a liberal or non-interventionist state tradition is a valuable starting point for explaining British childcare policy, there are a number of ways in which it needs to be qualified or supplemented. First, of course, and as will be argued more fully in Chapter 6, while an interventionist tradition may be a necessary or highly propitious condition for generous public childcare provision, it is not sufficient.

---

[22] See Jeremy Richardson (ed.), *Policy Styles in Western Europe* (London: Allen & Unwin, 1982); Gary P. Freeman, 'National Styles and Policy Sectors: Explaining Structured Variation', *Journal of Public Policy*, 5:4 (1985), 467–96.

[23] Freeman, 'National Styles and Policy Sectors', 467.

[24] Grant Jordan and Jeremy Richardson, 'The British Policy Style or the Logic of Negotiation?', in Richardson (ed.), *Policy Styles in Western Europe*.

[25] Jack Hayward, 'National Aptitudes for Planning in Britain, France and Italy', *Government and Opposition*, 14: 1 (1979), 397–410, cited in Jordan and Richardson, 'The British Policy Style', 81.

More fundamentally, there are problems with the blanket label 'liberal' to describe the British state, both in what it seems to include and omit, and in the degree of consistency it implies over time and across policy areas. 'Liberal' is in any case a term with hugely variant connotations, although the literature makes fairly clear what is supposed to be distinctive about a 'liberal' state tradition. Clearly it is not to be equated simply with the values of the Liberal Party, although both Beveridge and Keynes, whose welfare or social liberalism contributed powerfully to the shaping of the post-war welfare state, were Liberal Party members.

These semantic considerations aside, the difficulty of pinning down Britain's liberalness has also been apparent in attempts to produce a comparative typology of welfare states. One of the most influential of the more recent attempts, by Esping-Anderson,[26] distinguished three broad categories of welfare state—social democratic, corporatist, and liberal. Focusing primarily on social security arrangements, the central criterion adopted for allocating countries to one category or another was the extent to which citizens' status or social rights were 'decommodified' or independent of market forces. But Britain was not easy to classify. While by the 1980s it fell into the third camp, though still according to Esping-Anderson one of the more generous countries in this category, in the early post-war period it was in many ways the paradigm social democratic welfare state.

But even if we accept the broad label 'liberal', this has to be taken in conjunction with another, seemingly rather contradictory feature of the British state. In the category of liberal states, Britain is unusually centralized. Whereas the United States, Canada, and Australia are federal systems in which state or provincial governments constitute significant political arenas in their own right, Britain is unitary. Local authorities' scope for independent policy-making has traditionally been highly constrained but has shrunk still further over the last two decades. Associated with this have been the absence of a policy-making role for the judiciary, attachment to the notion of an unpoliticized civil service loyally serving the party in power, and above all the strength of the two-party system and party government. To the extent that we might think of liberal political systems as plural, with many points of access and opportunities to create a 'market of ideas', this has clearly only been true in a very limited sense in Britain.

---

[26] Gøsta Esping-Andersen, *The Three Worlds of Welfare Capitalism* (Cambridge: Polity Press, 1990). As is discussed further in Ch. 6, his typology has been extensively criticized by feminist theorists for its neglect of gender issues.

Related in some ways to the centralization of government in Britain, but not simply explained by it, has been the paradox of the *capacity* of government. While liberal norms may have been deeply absorbed and manifest in many policy areas, there has been all along the potential for strong government. Patrick Dunleavy has referred to this as 'ungrounded statism'. Despite the absence of a 'philosophy of public intervention', as Marquand would have it, the method of government since the last war, and at least until the deliberate moves to roll this back in the 1980s, was marked by statism in the sense of 'a relatively heavy institutionalization of governmental machinery for implementing social and economic policies . . . and a relatively low reliance upon either non-governmental intermediary bodies . . . or on transfers as mechanisms for delivering public policies'.[27] One of the reasons Dunleavy adduces is Britain's experience during World War II of 'a system of state direction in social life more extensive than that in any other combatant European country except Russia'. This not only provided the opportunity for public sector growth; it created a strong and enduring public acceptance of governmental expansion.[28]

But not only has government been centralized, it has tended to dominate the policy process and demonstrated a surprising propensity and capacity for direct intervention given its liberal ethos: it is clear that its liberalness has varied from one policy area or issue to another. This is recognized by Ruggie herself, when she argues that the liberal approach has been 'particularly strong' in the case of childcare. This raises the obvious question of *why*, or according to what principle, the application of liberal tenets varies in this way.

To summarize then, childcare policy has been determined within a broadly liberal national policy context, in which the tendency has been for relatively discrete policy areas to become institutionalized over time and for policy to develop incrementally and reactively. But at the same time the national policy process has been relatively centralized and exclusive in the sense that it has been concentrated in central government and party institutions. Moreover in practice the 'liberalness' of policy has varied remarkably, pointing to the influence upon policy-makers of other predispositions, including gender interests and assumptions.

[27] Patrick Dunleavy, 'The United Kingdom: Paradoxes of an Ungrounded Statism', in Francis G. Castles (ed.), *The Comparative History of Public Policy* (Cambridge: Polity, 1989), 242–3.

[28] Ibid. 278. The other main reason Dunleavy suggests is the weakness of industrial capital, which might otherwise have been expected to play more of a social entrepreneurial role.

CHILDCARE AS AN ISSUE

The second analytic theme is the issue of childcare itself. Of course issues, as issues, do not exist outside a policy context. The process through which they are defined and brought onto the public agenda is itself highly political and dominated by powerful social and particularly institutional forces. Carol Bacchi has recently re-emphasized, through an examination of problem-defining in a number of 'women's issue' areas, the need to understand policies not as solutions or responses to a given issue but as themselves 'constituting competing interpretations or representations of political issues'.[29] Though I shall argue below that potential issues are not totally open-ended, but contain aspects within them of what could be called contingent fixity, this plasticity is a major factor to contend with. So while I may favour a particular account of what the issue of childcare is or should be, in practice in Britain it has been identified and articulated within a motley array of policy contexts and debates: nursery education, socially inadequate mothers, wartime labour shortages, the poverty debate, juvenile delinquency, 'home alone' and 'latchkey' children, women's right to work, equal employment opportunities, the 'demographic timebomb', and lone mothers, to name the most obvious. In other countries the list could be extended.

A primary motive for writing this book has been my perception as a feminist that the issue of childcare, in contemporary society at least, has the utmost relevance to the possibility of meaningful equality between women and men (a theme taken up in later chapters). It is crucially located at the intersection of women's public and private lives and of their simultaneous claims for equality of treatment and for accommodation of gender difference.[30] Sadly it is not one that the feminist movement has taken up wholeheartedly or vigorously. Still less has such an understanding of the issue of childcare become part of dominant policy discourse in this country.

Rather, to the extent that childcare has emerged as an explicit political issue, this has been in a number of fragmentary policy contexts, most of which have not been informed by any kind of feminist agenda.

---

[29] Carol Lee Bacchi, *Women, Policy and Politics: The Construction of Policy Problems* (London: Sage, 1999), 2.

[30] Bryson suggests that there is growing social acceptance of feminist demands based on equal rights arguments but that the possible policy gains are being exhausted. The need now is to tackle a more difficult set of questions about how to deal with female difference, exemplified in the issue of childcare. See Valerie Bryson, 'Feminism and Common Sense', paper presented to the ESRC-sponsored seminar on 'Feminism: Theory and Practice', University of Bath, 1996.

Describing those contexts will be the task of later chapters and certainly at times they will appear to have very little connection with one another. However, there are certain features of childcare as a nexus of possible issues and interests—confining ourselves for the moment to the British policy process—that arguably do tend to shape or at least to constrain the way in which it has been politically articulated.

The first of these is that it is about *children*. 'Children' or 'childhood' are not themselves unproblematic terms: historians debate when and how the concept of a distinct phase of 'childhood' emerged. But increasingly the notion has been incorporated and naturalized and with it the assumption that children require care, education, and protection. The issue of childcare raises or intermeshes with questions about society and the state's interest in children. While researching this book, it was suggested to me by one 'advocate' of children's interests that the British don't really like children, that indeed 'the whole national culture is anti-children'.[31] This is a sweeping remark and perhaps not meant to be taken very seriously but certainly a recognized public interest in children, as themselves or as the next generation, is not inevitable and in Britain has developed only gradually. In time, however, it has extended to a range of concerns, above all questions of health and education, but also broader notions of child development, child protection, and even children's 'rights'.[32] In this context, the 1989 Children Act, which does cover aspects of the regulation of private daycare provision for children, was widely recognized as an important landmark, both practically and symbolically, in 'bringing together both the private law affecting the relationship between parents or other carers and children and the public law concerned with their welfare and protection, for the first time in one statute'.[33]

Secondly, to the extent that childcare initially became a public issue, this was when 'private' family-based childcare arrangements amongst the working class appeared to be breaking down, or their shortcomings

[31] Tizard *et al.* appear to offer some support for this view when they point out how late government was in providing protective legislation and in setting up the NSPCC (National Society for Prevention of Cruelty to Children). See Jack Tizard, Peter Moss, and Jane Perry, *All Our Children* (London: Temple Smith, 1976). Similarly Gathorne-Hardy cites traditions of sending children out for apprenticeships and fostering, and more recently of (boarding) prep schools; the latter, he says, have no continental equivalent. See Jonathan Gathorne-Hardy, *The Rise and Fall of the British Nanny* (London: Hodder and Stoughton, 1972).

[32] See for example Bob Franklin (ed.), *The Rights of Children* (Oxford: Basil Blackwell, 1986).

[33] Gillian Douglas, 'Family Law under the Thatcher Government', *Journal of Law and Society*, 17:4 (1990), 412. See also Nigel Parton, *Governing the Family* (London: Macmillan, 1991).

were becoming more visible, with increasing industrialization and urbanization. As Blackstone writes, 'the working-class home had never been a suitable environment for the socialization of young children, by today's standards, whether the parents were involved in agriculture, domestic industry or both . . . But it is true that the possibilities of parental supervision of children were greater prior to the large-scale employment of both men and women away from their homes'.[34] The issue of childcare has raised questions about the manner and extent of parental responsibility for children and thus has inevitably become embroiled in more fundamental assumptions and arguments around *the nature and role of the family*. Partly this is again about the responsibilities respectively of the family and of the state. But that discussion has itself in practice, and with only recent and partial exceptions, tended to pivot on the further vital question of the respective roles of father and mother.

In Britain childcare policy has been determined in the context of a powerful 'ideology of motherhood',[35] or maternalism, which still exercises considerable informal influence. As will appear in this study, this has taken different forms at different times. It acquired a new prominence at the turn of the century, in the context of growing imperial rivalries and concerns about the fitness of British soldiers.[36] For a long time thereafter arguments about the need for mothers to stay at home focused on children's physical health. Only during the 1950s did the warnings of child psychologist John Bowlby, and others, of the psychological harm caused by 'maternal deprivation' become widely influential. As this orthodoxy was increasingly challenged, Brannen and Moss suggest that the rationale shifted to an emphasis instead on 'mothers as unfolders of their children's *cognitive* capacities' (my italics), through which maternal ambition is 'goaded (by a variety of experts and increasingly a 'child development' industry of manfacturers, retailers and media) to have the best developed child'.[37]

But in addition to raising questions about society or the state's interest in children and about gender roles and relations within the family, childcare has a further element of 'contingent fixity' as a policy issue. Childcare, or the kind of good-quality, affordable, publicly provided or

[34] Tessa Blackstone, *A Fair Start?* (London: Allen Lane, 1971), 16.

[35] The expression is coined in Jane Lewis, *The Politics of Motherhood* (London: Croom-Helm, 1990).

[36] Anna Davin, 'Imperialism and Motherhood', *History Workshop Journal*, 5 (1978), 9–65.

[37] Julia Brannen and Peter Moss, *Managing Mothers* (London: Hyman Unwin, 1991), 92.

subsidized childcare that many feminists and others would see as not only desirable but an essential component of a national childcare policy, costs money. To this extent, childcare policy is or should be what Theodore Lowi[38] has termed 'redistributive'.

In Lowi's original taxonomy of policy types, understood as forms of coercion open to government, redistributive issues were to do with redistribution, through taxation and government expenditure, between major status groups, notably social classes, and more generally between 'haves' and 'have-nots'. They had a 'zero-sum' character. As such, redistributive policies were distinguished from distributive policies which involve public payouts for singular recipients, such as specific projects or communities. They also differed from regulatory policies, which are about regulating what individuals or collective actors can do with their own resources. Writing in the context of American politics in the 1960s, Lowi saw redistributive politics as taking place, if at all, within its own distinctive policy arena, at the central or 'systems' level of decision-making and typically through a process of negotiation in which the main protagonists were the 'peak' interest organizations of business and labour, together with the political parties to which they were most closely allied.

Lowi's typology has been widely taken up, and inevitably criticized, and he has amended it over time.[39] However, for our purposes his typology is highly relevant. The issue of childcare clearly has regulatory dimensions, as in questions about local authority regulation of childminders and private nurseries. But most significantly, the implication of Lowi's analysis is that if progress is to be made on childcare as a redistributory issue, it will need to be taken up by the big producer interests. However, this assumes that the redistribution involved will be broadly from a middle or capitalist class to a lower or working class. In the case of childcare, although the resources are at one level being redistributed from the middle class to the lower class, it can also be seen, given the

[38] Theodore J. Lowi, 'American Business, Public Policy, Case-studies, and Political Theory', *World Politics*, 16:4 (1964), 677–715.

[39] Lowi has increasingly tended to equate redistributive policy with macroeconomic policy as a whole, with the subcategory of 'welfare' tending to come closer to the old meaning. He also added a fourth kind of 'constituent' policy, to refer to policies that constituted organizational practices and came to refer to 'promotional' rather than distributive policies. See for instance Theodore J. Lowi and Benjamin Ginsberg, *American Government: Freedom and Power* (New York: W. W. Norton, 1996), especially Chs. 15 and 16. Applications and criticisms of Lowi's model are well discussed in Robert J. Spitzer, 'Promoting Policy Theory: Revising the Arenas of Power', *Policy Studies Journal*, 15:4 (1987), 675–89. Spitzer focuses in particular on the difficulty of allocating specific policies to just one of Lowi's policy types and recommends instead that they be thought of as poles or ideal types with actual policies combining elements of two or more.

present domestic division of labour, as entailing a redistribution between men and women. The question then is how far the 'male-dominated' producer organizations have been willing to pick it up, and whether, failing this, the state itself will or should make the redistributory case.

ORGANIZATION OF THE BOOK

While the interaction of national policy-making context and the dimensions of childcare as an issue have crucially shaped the contours of the childcare policy process, they have not wholly determined its outcome. Other contributory themes are explored in this study, including the nature of demand for childcare, the childcare lobby and the part played within it by organized feminism, and the question of timing. The actual structure of the book reflects the general approach adopted.

The following chapter sets out the historical origins of childcare policy, tracing the story from the early nineteenth century up to the aftermath of the Second World War. It shows how, notwithstanding the dramatic episode of the 'war nurseries', policy reflecting a particular set of assumptions about childcare as primarily a residual, welfare function, distinct from nursery education, had become embodied in institutional arrangements and the policy process by the 1950s.

Chapters 3 and 4 likewise follow a broadly chronological narrative. In Chapter 3, we see how, under the joint stimulus of the growing numbers of mothers in paid employment and the 'rediscovery of poverty', a childcare lobby was beginning to coalesce by the 1970s and challenge prevailing policy inertia but its impact was cut short by retrenchment policies from the middle of the decade. Under Conservative rule, as Chapter 4 relates, government embarked on a more aggressive strategy of 'welfare state restructuring'. While support for childcare was growing within the trade unions and Labour Party, under Mrs Thatcher childcare policy languished, apart from the flurry of activity prompted by the 'demographic timebomb'. However, under Major there was a renewed interest in nursery education, resulting in the much-criticized nursery voucher scheme, and there were also the beginnings of a reframing of child daycare policy into a more positive dimension of welfare restructuring.

Although it is important to focus on policy-makers in order to demonstrate the institutional and policy constraints within which childcare issues were resolved, we need to consider separately the kind of pressure that policy-makers have been under to modify their approach to childcare. A recurring feature of childcare politics in Britain has been the weakness of the childcare lobby. Chapter 5 focuses directly on two related aspects of this weakness, the difficult question of the demand for childcare and the reasons for limited direct feminist involvement.

In Chapter 6, we turn from an exclusively British focus to a comparison of childcare policy across a range of countries in Europe and the Old Commonwealth. Rather than seeking to provide a comprehensive account of policy variations, the analysis is designed to shed further light on the significance of the national policy context and the potential role for other variables, including feminist intervention. The concluding chapter attempts to draw together the different strands in the overall argument, which then provides a vantage point from which to review and assess the policy changes introduced under the New Labour government from 1997.

2

The Institutional Roots of Childcare Politics

The origins of contemporary childcare policy in Britain lie in the nineteenth century. Social and political change, ensuing from the cumulative processes of industrialization and urbanization, combined with the imperatives of British policy as an imperial power to pose in stark and visible terms the issue of the care and education of young children. The institutional arrangements that emerged, certainly as they were crystallized in the aftermath of the First World War, though in some ways provisional, embodied central assumptions about responsibility for childcare, and particularly about the respective roles of mothers and the state, with significant and lasting consequences. At the same time a new educational doctrine, based on the child's own developmental needs, was beginning to gain adherents and would play a growing though not yet decisive part in the future determination of childcare policy.

The combination of national childcare policies and institutional arrangements installed by the 1920s—the childcare 'regime'—was not without its critics. It might seem to have come under serious pressure, especially during the Second World War. Yet the most striking feature of the childcare arrangements improvised during the war years is the speed with which they were dismantled afterwards and the lack of opposition to their removal. By the 1950s childcare was completely marginal to the public political agenda; public provision was minimal and policy was largely uncontested. It appeared to have become a non-issue again.

The primary function of this chapter is not to provide an exhaustive historical account. Some aspects of the story have already been most effectively explored,[1] while others would require extensive new research to do them justice. The aim is rather to show the extent to which a certain pattern and view of childcare provision, which has

---

[1] See in particular Tessa Blackstone, *A Fair Start* (London: Allen & Unwin, 1971); Sheila Ferguson and Hilda Fitzgerald, *Studies in the Social Services*, History of the Second World War: Civil Series (London: HMSO and Longmans, Green and Co., 1954), ch. 6 ('Day Nurseries'); Denise Riley, *War in the Nursery* (London: Virago, 1983); and Penny Summerfield, *Women Workers in the Second World War* (London: Croom-Helm, 1984).

had long-lasting consequences for British childcare policy, was institutionalized by the 1950s.

ORIGINS OF CHILDCARE POLICY

Although from a feminist standpoint it might be argued that childcare has always been, or should have been, a public issue, and although there is no suggestion that prior to industrialization the quality of childcare was all it should be from the child's point of view, it was the changes brought with industrialization and increasing urbanization that perhaps aggravated such shortcomings and certainly rendered them more visible. In this respect, the issue of childcare is similar to a series of other perceived 'social problems' emerging in the aftermath of industrialization. A related point needs to be stressed: the initial focus of concern was *working-class* children. The prospect of increasing numbers of children left unsupervised to roam the streets raised fears both for their safety and moral development and for social order and crime levels.

Even then such fears were in conflict with a long-established tendency to view children not only as the responsibility but the property of their parents. It was widely held amongst the 'governing classes' that 'to undermine parental responsibility was to undermine family stability and thus the stability of society'. Thus the great social reformer Lord Shaftesbury himself, even while he urged the need to curb the worst excesses of factory employment of the very young, opposed all proposals for compulsory education, on the grounds that this would be a direct infringement of the parents' (that is, the father's) right to bring up a child as they saw fit.[2]

Accordingly, actual initiatives to improve childcare provision emerged only very slowly and piecemeal. For a long time, to the extent that there was any institutionalized or collective form of childcare available, this did not mean daycare or care for the youngest children under 3 years of age. Rather it was provided by the charitable infant schools, which meant accommodating 3- to 5-year-olds in schools catering primarily for older children.

By the early nineteenth century some schools already catered for working-class children as young as 3 years old: Blackstone[3] lists charity

[2] See Ivy Pinchbeck and Margaret Hewitt, *Children in English Society*, vol. ii (London: Routledge and Kegan Paul, 1973), 357–8.
[3] Blackstone, *A Fair Start*, 18.

schools, schools of industry, 'dame schools', and common day schools. However, their quality generally left much to be desired. From the 1820s there began to emerge a new kind of infant school and the process of its development in many ways exemplifies the wider process of social reform at this time. The 1819 Factory Act, which outlawed employment in factories of children under 9 years of age and was therefore expected to increase the numbers of young children left untended, added to the growing concern about childcare provision. That is, in keeping with the 'administrative momentum' model,[4] the original reform, outlawing the use of child labour, contributed to the pressure for further educational reform.

Again, to illustrate another recurrent pattern of the reform process, it was 'philanthropists', in the expanding voluntary sector, who responded to begin with, bringing government intervention in their train. Inspired in part by Robert Owen's pioneering infant school established in 1816 at his factory at New Lanark, a number of specifically infant schools were established, initially in the capital, under the auspices of the London Infant School Society. By 1834 there were 150 of these infant schools throughout in England, and in practice most took in children aged 3–5 as well as children somewhat older.

The motives impelling the benefactors of these schools typically blended compassion with prudence. They were well expressed in Samuel Wilderspoon's influential treatise *On the Importance of Educating the Infant Children of the Poor*.[5] He wanted to rescue children by taking them 'at an early stage out of the reach of contamination on the streets, and removing them from the no less baneful influence of evil example at home', but at the same time he wanted to protect society from the dangers of juvenile delinquency.[6] But there was also at this stage some desire, whilst not necessarily uppermost, to make life easier for working

[4] For the notion of 'administrative momentum' see O.O.G.M. MacDonaugh, 'The Nineteenth Century Revolution in Government: A Reappraisal', *Historical Journal*, 1 (1958), cited in Derek Fraser, *The Evolution of the British Welfare State*, 2nd edn. (London: Macmillan, 1984), 106–7.

[5] He was appointed head of one of the first London infant schools and subsequently became superintendent of the Society.

[6] Cited in Blackstone, *A Fair Start*, 14. See also Margaret Hewitt, *Wives and Mothers in Victorian Industry* (London: Rockliff, 1958), ch. 11. Wilderspoon anticipates the broader 'social control' argument for educating working-class children, expressed by Leonard Horner in 1837, who maintained that it was 'loudly called for as a matter of policy, to prevent a multitude of immoral and vicious beings, the offsprings of ignorance, from growing up around us, to be a pest and nuisance to society': Leonard Horner, writing to N. W. Senior, 23 May 1837, in N. W. Senior, *Letters on the Factory Act* (1837), cited in Derek Fraser, *The Evolution of the British Welfare State*, 2nd edn. (London: Macmillan, 1984).

mothers.[7] Without such provision for their children, their anxieties would otherwise make parents 'unhappy and unfit for work'.[8] In this sentiment the benefactors to an extent reflected wider society; the question of the employment of mothers of young children had not yet crystallized into the widespread public concern and increasing disapproval to be found later in the century. There were still reformers like Mr Fletcher, who in his report in 1845 to the British and Foreign School Society opined that the working woman 'very properly seeks a nursery for her children'.[9]

While the infant schools constituted some kind of public response to the needs of children aged 3 and over, there was almost no provision for the very youngest children. Given that there was no system of paid maternal leave or certainty of re-employment, it was common for women to return to work ten or twelve days after giving birth. When not left with an adult relative, the baby might be placed in the charge of a child little more than an infant herself or an elderly 'day nurse'. Often these carers looked after several children at the same time, and fed them a diet of bread-and-water 'pap'. Children in their first two years, while scarcely a menace to society, were at the greatest risk of all. Yet the first day nursery was not set up until 1850.

The inspiration for this nursery, which was opened in Marylebone by a group of philanthropic women, was probably the charitably subsidized crèches initiated by Marbeau in Paris.[10] It was designed 'for the purpose of receiving the children of the married industrious poor during the working hours of the day' and accepted children aged between one month and three years. This first day nursery and another London-based nursery, in Kensington, were unusual in recognizing from the outset that they could not expect to be financially self-supporting because the mothers they were helping were too poor.

More typical, certainly in the industrial centres, was a day nursery opened in December of the same year, in Ancoats, Manchester. Though

[7] We have no reliable figures for the numbers of mothers of young children employed outside the home during the 19th century, and indeed official statistics only began to distinguish between married and unmarried women workers from the time of the 1851 census, when 24% of married women were reported to be gainfully employed. The proportion of mothers in paid work would have been smaller but it seems likely that their numbers grew overall during the first half of the century, especially in the textile and potteries regions. See Jack Tizard, Peter Moss, and Jane Perry, *All Our Children* (London: Temple Smith, 1976), 38–9.

[8] Cited in Blackstone, *A Fair Start*, 15.   [9] Ibid. 22.

[10] The first was opened in Chaillot in 1844. By 1867 there were 18 crèches in Paris, 10 in the *banlieues*, and another 400 in the provinces. This information is based on an anonymous pamphlet, *Public Nurseries*, published in 1851 and cited in Hewitt, *Wives and Mothers*, 186–7.

run on lines that again showed the influence of the Marbeau model, a fundamental principle was that it should be self-supporting. By 1854, having failed in this objective, it was closed and its failure for a time seemed to discourage imitators. From the 1870s a number of further nurseries opened in Manchester, Salford, Staffordshire, Glasgow, and Leicester, mostly charitably endowed and making only a nominal charge. By 1900 the London School Board also ran four day nurseries with no charge at all. Still, by 1906 there were only 30 such nurseries all told.

It was the charitable infant schools, therefore, that constituted the possible institutional basis for an extended and publicly administered system of under-fives provision. In fact their continuing expansion provided a foundation for the universal system of elementary education adopted under the 1870 Education Act. That legislation was a landmark development, signifying not only government's recognition of the need for universal elementary education but its acceptance that the state would need to play a major role in its provision. Whilst the motivation behind the Act and its timing have been much debated,[11] the traditional emphasis in liberal thinking on the role of education in developing the moral and reasoning capacity of the individual helped to legitimize state intervention in this field. Although we have noted Lord Shaftesbury's earlier misgivings, this was one area where a perceived public interest was eventually allowed to interfere both with the private and voluntary sectors of provision and with parents' autonomy in matters regarding their children.

The Act set up local School Boards to provide additional schools where they were needed. Attendance was not made compulsory until 1880. The starting age was specified as 5 but in fact the numbers of 3- to 5-year-olds attending infant schools continued to rise, reaching a peak in 1900, by which time they represented 43.1 per cent of that age group. On the other hand numbers of *under*-threes declined and ceased altogether after the 1902 Education Act specified that grants would no longer be available for children in this category.

But while numbers of 3- to 5-year-olds in attendance were growing, so too was pressure for their removal. A Consultative Committee set

---

[11] Compulsory education would provide a better-trained workforce in the face of growing international economic competition. There was also the political argument, in the wake of the 1867 Reform Act, of the need 'to compel our future masters to learn their letters' (Robert Lowe, cited in Fraser, *The Evolution of the British Welfare State*, 86). Finally there was the role of 'administrative momentum' already referred to. The government established a Committee of the Privy Council in 1839 to oversee the expanding voluntary education sector and this in turn established the first corps of school inspectors, who were to become a powerful constituency for reform.

up by the Board of Education in 1907 was directed 'to consider the desirability on educational and other grounds, of discouraging the attendance at school of children under 5 years'. The Board had already, in 1905, allowed local education authorities discretionary powers to refuse admission to under-fives. The Consultative Committee now argued that ideally all 3- to 5-year-olds were best cared for at home with their mother. For those children whose homes did *not* provide the right kind of environment, they recommended publicly provided and separate nursery schools, incorporating ideas of the new kindergarten movement. But since the Board of Education accepted the first part of the Committee's recommendations but did not feel able to provide additional funds for such nursery schools, the overall effect of the new policy was a sharp fall in the numbers of children under 5 attending school.

For Tizard *et al.* this represents a vital missed chance in the history of childcare: 'The opportunity in the 1900s to build on the increasingly well-established pattern of early schooling and combine this with the fund of knowledge and ideas on nursery schooling then becoming available, was wasted'.[12] Instead the government took the route indicated by the Consultative Committee: positively to discourage attendance by the children of 'better parents' under 5 years of age. One can contrast this outcome in particular with experience in France. There, as will be further discussed in Chapter 6, from the 1860s criticisms had been growing of the existing framework of 'maternelles' but rather than abandon them the official decision was to refashion them into 'an entirely new institution'.[13]

In seeking to understand why this route was taken in Britain we must look to the complex and shifting pattern of public and official attitudes to children on the one hand and to women's roles and the scope of state intervention on the other. In particular, attitudes towards children had been gradually changing. There is continuing debate as to how far our very concept of a distinct period of 'childhood' has been the product of a certain historical conjuncture.[14] However, the concept of childhood was firmly established by the nineteenth century. More importantly, there was a growing tendency, influenced both by romanticism and by evangelical thinking, to emphasize children's essential innocence and

[12] Tizard *et al.*, *All Our Children*, 66.

[13] See Alain Norvez, *De la naissance a l'école*, INED, Travaux et Documents, Cahier No. 126 (Paris: PUF, 1990).

[14] This was the position adopted in Philippe Ariès' classic thesis, *Centuries of Childhood* (London and Harmondsworth: Penguin, 1986). For a summary of some of the ensuing debate see Diana Gittins, *The Child in Question* (London: Macmillan, 1998).

vulnerability. Although contradictory notions of the socially disruptive and corrupting effects of delinquent children persisted, there was also an increasing feeling that children could and should be rescued from situations of physical degradation and moral depravity. Sometimes children were themselves perceived as the means of social regeneration; that is, there was a sense almost that children could rescue society.[15]

The eighteenth century had been largely characterized by the extraordinary harshness, from a twentieth-century viewpoint, of both parental and state approaches to children. A major barrier to increased protection for children, as already noted, was the continuing primacy, enshrined in law, of the father's authority over his family. The preceding chapter noted the claim sometimes made that the British have been particularly slow and reluctant to concern themselves with children's needs. Only very gradually during the nineteenth century did the state extend protection for the child. The campaign for prevention of cruelty to children actually originated as an extension to an appeal for a dogs' home, at a meeting of the Society for Prevention of Cruelty to Animals! It culminated, however, in the Act for the Prevention of Cruelty to, and Better Protection of, Children in 1889.[16]

As part of this growing public solicitude for children there was an increased focus on their physical health. Fears of the adverse effects of mothers' employment on the health of very young children had been mounting from at least the 1840s. The high rates of infant mortality amongst the children of working mothers was a cause of particular concern. It was commented upon during the debate on the 1847 Factory Bill and in the Registrar-General's introduction to the 1851 census; it

[15] See Carolyn Steedman, *Childhood, Culture and Class in Britain: Margaret McMillan 1860–1931* (London: Virago, 1990), ch. 3, 'Childhood'. It has been argued by many that a society's conception of childhood tends to be deeply bound up with its wider self-identity and sense of its own future. For a useful survey of the shifts in the social construction of childhood see Harry Hendrick, 'Constructions and Reconstructions of British Childhood: An Interpretative Survey, 1800 to the Present', in Alison James and Alan Prout (eds.), *Constructing and Reconstructing Childhood: Contemporary Issues in the Sociological Study of Childhood* (London: Falmer Press, 1997). In his conclusion he suggests that changing understandings of childhood have shared adults' 'intention to identify the existence of "childhood"; to define the desirable state of "childhood"; to incorporate the concept into a larger philosophy concerning the meaning of life; and to control "childhood", whatever its nature' (59).

[16] See Pinchbeck and Hewitt, *Children in English Society*, vol. ii. They observe 'That societies to protect animals from cruelty were established before societies to protect children is one of the better known, bizarre features of English social history. Less well known, perhaps, is that Parliament itself intervened to protect animals from abuse more than three-quarters of a century before it thought it proper to extend statutory protection to the young child' (622).

exercised both factory inspectors and doctors.[17] As we have seen, one manifestation of this concern was the creation of a limited number of charitable day nurseries. The medical profession in particular urged the need for state intervention: Hewitt for instance quotes the *Public Health Magazine* demanding that 'the Government should countenance and control day nurseries in factory districts'.[18] But this suggestion that the state itself should take legislative action was largely resisted.

In 1872 an especially lurid 'baby-farming' scandal led to the first infant life protection legislation. Although its focus was baby-farming or an arrangement in which a woman was paid to care continuously for children who were not her own, it was clear that many of the medical actors involved in the surrounding debate would have liked to extend the scope of the Act to daily childcare and specifically to require the registration and supervision of those nursing children. The Select Committee in question, however, insisted that 'innocent' childcare arrangements should remain the private responsibility of parents: 'It is not against the licensing of women as nurses that we protest . . . it is to the compulsion to be put upon parents to employ none but those holding such licences that we object'.[19]

The 1870 and 1876 Education Acts were also instrumental in increasing awareness and concern about the state of health of working-class children: 'Now, for the first time, could be seen, en masse, the results of the urbanisation of England expressed in terms of child health, physical and mental'.[20] By the late nineteenth century, such child health anxieties were being reinforced by more nationalist—or imperialist—calculations. On the one hand, censuses from 1881 showed that the birth rate was falling; on the other, high levels of infant mortality persisted, raising fears for population levels if nutrition and health provision for

---

[17] The link between mother's employment and infant mortality was explored first in connection with women textile workers in Lancashire, but then more widely. Hewitt, who examines available evidence carefully and emphasizes the many difficulties of interpreting it, none the less concludes that, whatever inferences one might draw, the case for an association between mothers' employment and infant mortality was compelling. See *Wives and Mothers*, ch. 8. Some of the later evidence is further reviewed in Carol Dyhouse, 'Working-class Mothers and Infant Mortality in England, 1895–1914', *Journal of Social History*, 12: 2 (1978), 248–67.

[18] Hewitt, *Wives and Mothers*, 169.

[19] Cited in Hewitt, *Wives and Mothers*, 172. See also Margaret L. Arnot, 'Infant Death, Child Care and the State: The Baby-farming Scandal and the First Infant Life Protection Legislation of 1872', *Continuity and Change*, 9: 2 (1994), 271–311. Arnot emphasizes the extent to which these attempts to draw attention to the issue of infant mortality were bound up with medical practitioners' drive to establish themselves as a profession.

[20] Pinchbeck and Hewitt, *Children in English Society*, ii. 632.

this vulnerable group were not improved. In addition recruitment during the Boer Wars (1880–1 and especially 1898–1900) revealed the often shockingly poor physical condition of the volunteers.

But this growing preoccupation with child health must be understood in the context of the changing public conception of the role of women, for which of course it provided apparent confirmation. During the eighteenth century, industrial expansion was associated with a gradual reduction in the range of economic activities centred in the home. The wives of the new industrial middle class in particular found themselves increasingly underemployed but simultaneously constrained from seeking work outside the home by an insidious and influential 'ideology of domesticity'. The origins of this ideology, or inflexion of traditional patriarchal thinking, are complex, reflecting both the social aspirations and the insecurities of this emerging social class. The wife was to be the 'angel in the house', providing a haven of safety and purity, whilst at the same time signifying in her decorative idleness her husband's social and economic achievement. According to Hall, 'There is plenty of evidence to suggest that by the 1830s and 1840s the definition of women as primarily relating to home and family was well established',[21] and, however much it was contradicted by the reality of working-class women's continuing employment in factories, as servants, and the like, its influence was extending into the poorer sections of society. Increasingly by the mid-century this found expression in public and official statements disapproving women's and especially married women's employment outside the home, through which, in the words of one prominent public figure, 'You are poisoning the very sources of order and happiness and virtue; . . . you are annulling, as it were, the institutions of domestic life decreed by Providence himself . . . the mainstay of peace and virtue and therein of national security'.[22]

Such sentiments not only persisted but, according to Davin, with the growth of imperialistic ambitions towards the end of the century, began to be articulated in a subtly different way which gave additional emphasis to women's mothering role. Fed by the concerns we have noted about population levels and the physical condition of the armed forces, there was a shift in the way that women's identification with the domestic sphere was rationalized: increasingly it 'was her function as mother that was being most stressed, rather than her function as wife'.[23] A powerful

---

[21] On the origins of this ideology, see Catherine Hall, *White, Male and Middle-class: Explorations in Feminism and History* (Cambridge: Polity, 1990), 75.

[22] Lord Ashley, 7th Earl of Shaftesbury, cited in Hewitt, *Wives and Mothers*, 49.

[23] Anna Davin, 'Imperialism and Motherhood', *History Workshop Journal*, 5 (1978), 13.

'ideology of motherhood' was emerging, in which giving birth and raising children in the proper manner came to be seen as almost a 'national duty'.

When the Inter-departmental Committee on Physical Deterioration reported in 1904, it devoted considerable attention to the welfare of young children, as bearers of the nation's future. In this context, it reiterated what had by then become largely received wisdom, that there was 'no doubt that the employment of mothers in factories is attended by evil consequences to themselves and their children'.[24] Thus it was clear that the increasing interest in the health of small children would not be associated with any attempt to provide greater state assistance to working mothers in providing care for their children.

But changing attitudes to children were also apparent in approaches to infant education. By the turn of the century, official thinking about education for the under-fives was dominated by the child health perspective outlined above. Yet there were also developments occurring in the philosophy of infant education which had their consequences for the route taken. When the first infant schools were established, the assumption prevailed that there was no need to treat the youngest children differently from their older siblings. Blackstone cites one of the early founders, Lord Brougham: 'Whoever knows the habits of children at an earlier age than six or seven . . . is well aware of their capacity to receive instruction long before the age of six'.[25] At the same time the underlying ethos of infant education still tended to be informed by a Calvinist view of the child, however young, as innately sinful and disobedient. Accordingly education was generally rigid and formal, with much learning by rote, and firm discipline imposed to bring under control their 'unruly passions'.

But as the century progressed, both reflecting and contributing to the overall change in views of childhood and children, an alternative, more child-centred educational philosophy began to emerge. This drew its original inspiration in particular from Jean-Jacques Rousseau's *Émile* (1762), which argued that rather than repressing innate qualities, education should help the child (more precisely the male child) to develop naturally, learning through experience rather than more formalized instruction. Rousseau's ideas influenced Friedrich Froebel, founder of the German kindergarten movement. As early as 1826 he set out his comprehensive theory of pre-school education, emphasizing the importance of the child as an individual, of self-discipline as opposed to exter-

---

[24] Cited in Tizard *et al.*, *All Our Children*, 41.   [25] Blackstone, *A Fair Start*, 20.

nal constraint, and of play. Arguing that providing the right kind of early
education could not solely be a mother's responsibility, he established
the first kindergarten in 1837.

In Germany Froebel's ideas were seen as quite subversive and following the collapse of the 1848 Revolution the kindergarten was forced
to close. But with the emigration of many liberal-minded Germans to
England the idea of the kindergarten was received in this country. Two
of Froebel's followers set up the first kindergarten in 1851. Several more
opened in succeeding decades. For the most part these catered for children of middle class families; only two made no charge for working-class
children. The Froebel Society, founded in 1874, also helped train young
women as kindergarten teachers. At the time this was, as Blackstone
insists, primarily a movement of the middle class for the middle class. It
had only a limited direct impact in the form of provision for working-
class children. The London School Board in particular showed interest
in kindergarten teaching but made little headway in implementing its
techniques within its elementary schools.

The experience and example of the kindergarten movement in the
longer run contributed to the cause of nursery education. Paradoxically
perhaps, it now fuelled criticism of existing infant schools, and especially
of their suitability for very young children, voiced by the new and
growing profession of school inspectors. These perceptions, and the professional interests developing around them, then helped to shape the
terms in which the issue of education for 3- to 5-year-olds was framed
at the turn of the century. As noted, despite some increased awareness
of Froebel's ideas, actual conditions and modes of instruction in the
infant 'baby classes' had changed little. One school inspector commented, 'The discipline expected is military rather than maternal'. In
1905 an influential *Report on Children under Five Years of Age in Public
Elementary Schools* was published, significantly perhaps authored by
women Inspectors of the Board of Education. They were in agreement
that 'children between the ages of three and five get practically no intellectual advantage from school instruction. . . . teaching in many infant
schools seems to dull rather than awaken the little power of imagina-
tion and independent observation which these children possess'. The
report recommended 'a new form of school' for children under 5, in
which formal instruction would be replaced by 'more play, more sleep,
more free conversation, story telling and observation'. But the report
also recommended that these new schools should be provided for poor
children only: 'The better parents should be discouraged from sending
children before five' altogether. As we have seen, this report was closely

echoed both by the 1907 Consultative Committee and the Board of Education.

It may be asked why working mothers' childcare needs were not championed more forcefully by feminists, or women trade unionists. The issue of childcare was scarcely addressed by 'first-wave' feminism as it emerged from the 1850s. Only within 'socialist feminism', manifest more in the arguments of some male socialist thinkers than as actual move-ment activism, was there recognition that childcare could be problem-atic for women. The communitarian thinking of Robert Owens and of those influenced by the French socialist Charles Fourier envisaged col-lective child care arrangements. Marx and Engels likewise, if most sketchily, anticipated the communalization of domestic services in a socialist society. But such ideas were scarcely taken up by the main-stream feminist movement.

For one thing, it was predominantly a movement of upper- and upper-middle-class women. To the extent that the equal rights agenda focused on women's rights to paid employment and fuller participation in public life, childcare did not present itself as an obvious obstacle, since there were always domestic servants to see to it. In particular there were 'nannies', specialized in caring for young children and dominating life in the nursery. In his detailed study on the subject, Gathorne-Hardy[26] estimates that at their high point, around the mid-1890s, the number of nannies totalled 250–500,000. But in any case most feminists did not dispute the principle that mothers should stay at home to look after their children.[27] In fact the issue of motherhood was interrelated in rather different ways with their central concerns. Particularly as the suf-frage movement took its more socially conservative turn, from the 1860s, to gain respectability and to help legitimate the demand for the vote, there was frequently a tendency to emphasize women's maternal role and virtues. At the same time there was a more particu-lar struggle going on in which women were precisely seeking to assert

[26] Jonathan Gathorne-Hardy, *The Rise and Fall of the British Nanny* (London: Hodder and Stoughton, 1972), 184.

[27] There were exceptions of course. Thus Hewitt cites a 'Memorial' published by the National Society for Women's Suffrage opposing proposals in the Infant Life Protection Bill to enforce the registration of day nurses because this could interfere with the infor-mal arrangements frequently encountered in manufacturing districts which enabled some mothers to go out to work and others, who minded their babies, 'to earn honestly a few pence': *Wives and Mothers*, 171. In the years immediately before the First World War, arguments in favour of state support for child daycare were put forward in the feminist journals *Freewoman* and *Common Cause*, cited in Susan Pedersen, *Family, Dependence and the Origins of the Welfare State: Britain and France, 1914–1945* (Cambridge: Cambridge University Press, 1993), 46.

their rights as mothers over the claims of their husbands. As Carol Smart writes:

Starting with proto-feminist campaigns over the custody of children on separation or divorce (for upper-class women . . .) and campaigns over wife torture that involved allowing poor women to leave their husbands and to take their children under 7 years of age with them . . . , feminists forced onto the public agenda the beginnings of an appreciation of the work of caring and the importance of mother-love for the welfare of children. These feminists were actively engaged in the social construction of motherhood as a recognized institution.[28]

For all these reasons, feminists were in general unlikely to prioritize child daycare in their campaigns.

Naturally the emerging, heavily male-dominated trade unions were unsympathetic to the working mother's cause. They supported protective legislation that excluded women workers from mining and industrial occupations, and most of the time rejected demands for equal pay for women in favour of putting forward claims for a 'family wage' to be made to the father as bread-winner. In 1877, three years after it was founded, the Trades Union Congress (TUC) declared that it was 'the duty of men and husbands to bring about a condition of things where their wives should be in their proper sphere at home instead of being dragged into competition of livelihood with the great and strong men of the world'.[29]

Women workers' rates of union membership were low and they exerted little influence within the trade union movement. But they also did little conspicuously to promote the childcare issue. This was true even of the Women's Trade Union League, set up by Emma Paterson in 1874, to encourage women workers to organize separately. Paterson, an equal rights feminist, concentrated her energies in the fight against protective legislation. Her successor, Lady Dilke, simply accepted that married women should not go out to work,[30] whilst Gertrude Tuckwell, a later President of the WTU, advocated 'the gradual extension of labour protection to the point where mothers will be prohibited from working until their children have reached an age where they can care for themselves'.[31]

[28] Carol Smart, 'Deconstructing Motherhood', in Elizabeth Bortolaia Silva (ed.), *Good Enough Mothering?* (London: Routledge, 1996), 44.
[29] Cited in Marion Shaw, 'The 53rd TUC Women's Congress', in Joy Holland (ed.), *Feminist Action 1* (London: Battle Axe, 1984), 60.
[30] See Olive Banks, *Faces of Feminism* (London: Martin Robertson, 1980).
[31] Cited in Jane Lewis, 'Models of Equality for Women: The Case of State Support for Children in Twentieth-century Britain', in Gisela Bock and Pat Thane (eds.), *Maternity and Gender Politics: Women and the Rise of the European Welfare States, 1880s–1950s*

In sum, if the decision actively to discourage attendance of 3- to 5-year-olds, without in practice providing the means for an alternative form of nursery education, was a 'missed opportunity', at the time it was scarcely perceived as such. The view that mothers of young children should stay at home to look after them was so widespread as to amount almost to a consensus. And while individuals were beginning to be impressed by the arguments for nursery education it was not until the First World War that they began to constitute anything like a movement.

FROM THE FIRST WORLD WAR TO THE SECOND

The First World War (and still more the Second World War) seems to present a sharp contrast and discontinuity with the prevalent approach to childcare. During the First World War, over one and a half million new women workers entered the workforce to replace men conscripted from 1916 for military service. The number of women in trade unions trebled. Day nurseries were established for the children of women working in armaments factories, sponsored by the Ministry of Munitions and funded by the Board of Education.[32] By 1919 they numbered 174.

Sarah Boston stresses the extent to which the customary disapproval for working mothers was suspended. The *Daily Mail* applauded 'Mothers who Make Munitions' and welcomed the nurseries, declaring that 'at last the deplorable waste of the service of willing women workers, the mothers of young children, has been recognised'.[33] And yet it seems that for almost all concerned such provision was regarded as temporary, a response to a specific emergency. Thus in 1915 the TUC passed a resolution to ensure that women workers were replaced by more suitable male labour at the end of the war.[34] Mary McArthur, Secretary of the National Federation of Women Workers, the leading

(New York: Routledge, 1991). Of course there were local exceptions to this pattern, notably in the cotton industry, where the rate of unionization of women workers was particularly high. In Lancashire many women trade unionists contested the assumption that working mothers put their children at risk, arguing that existing family networks ensured adequate childcare. See J. Liddington and J. Norris, *One Hand Tied Behind Us: The Rise of the Women's Suffrage Movement* (London: Virago, 1978).

[32] This division of labour caused some difficulties. See Ferguson and Fitzgerald, *Studies in the Social Services*.

[33] Cited in Sarah Boston, *Women Workers and the Trade Union Movement* (London: Davis Poynter, 1980), 126.

[34] See Sheila Lewenhak, *Women and Trade Unions* (London: Ernest Benn Limited, 1977); also G. Braybon, *Women Workers in the First World War: The British Experience* (London: Croom-Helm, 1981).

woman trade unionist by this time and the only woman on the union movement's War Emergency Workers' National Committee, believed strongly that mothers of small children should not go out to work, if it could be avoided, and saw the provision of crèches during the war as a last resort.[35] In keeping with this assumption, the number of government-sponsored day nurseries declined steadily following the war and by 1938 there were only 104.

The war, however, gave a further modest boost to nursery education. Before the war, and as the effects of declining pre-school provision, consequent upon the recommendations of the 1907 Consultative Committee, became apparent, many philanthropists and social reformers increasingly looked to the voluntary nursery school to fill the gap. The assumptions and activities of the McMillan sisters, especially Margaret, were both typical of and central to this trend. Margaret McMillan was associated with the beginnings of the Labour Party and with the Froebel Society. Combining the two prevailing strands of thinking about the care and education of young children described above, she was impressed by progressive educational arguments but above all believed that nursery schools had a vital role to play in monitoring and promoting the *health* of children from poorer homes. The sisters opened their Deptford nursery school in 1911, which by the early 1920s, with London County Council assistance, was catering for over 200 children. Elsewhere, for instance in Manchester and Salford, voluntary schools were established on a much more modest scale.

Following her sister's death in 1917 Margaret continued to promote the cause of nursery education. She set up a training centre for nursery school teachers and was a tireless and inspiring public speaker, influencing such prominent figures as Sir Robert Morant at the Board of Education and George Bernard Shaw. As a result partly of Margaret McMillan's campaigning, but also of the greater visibility of family needs under conditions of war, the 1918 Education Act finally authorized local education authorities to provide or support the provision of nursery schools for children aged 2 to 5.[36] This represented an advance, although the powers were made optional only and it was clearly targeted at children from 'inadequate' homes. It was reaffirmed that in other cases the place of children under 5 should be at home with their mothers.

[35] J. Lewis, *The Politics of Motherhood* (London: Croom-Helm, 1980), 80.
[36] Steedman, however, warns against attributing to McMillan too great an impact on the development of official policy, pointing out that her insistence on a long school day and her preference for large schools were successfully resisted by teachers' unions and the Nursery School Association. See Steedman, *Childhood, Culture and Class*, ch. 9.

But in addition to these effects on the nature and scale of daycare and nursery education provision, the First World War proved a catalyst and accelerator for the process of government institutionalization around emerging social policy fields. Nursery education was now established firmly as the concern of the Board of Education. In the meantime, military recruitment for the war had exposed, even more fully than during the Boer War, the poor physical state of the population: one survey indicated that only one in three conscripts were fit to enlist.[37] This further strengthened the case of those arguing both for expanded maternity and infant welfare services and for a separate Ministry of Health. In 1918 the Maternity and Child Welfare Act, building on earlier measures, authorized local authorities to establish grant-aided antenatal and child welfare clinics. As part of this service, they were also empowered to set up day nurseries and give grants to voluntary nurseries. All these activities came under the auspices of the new Ministry of Health, established in 1919.

Prior to these changes, educational and health aspects of childcare were often difficult to distinguish. Both the case for excluding under-fives from infant education and the case made *for* nursery education, as we have seen, relied strongly on health considerations. The advice of health officers attached to the Board of Education carried much weight, while during the First World War it was the Board which ran the day nurseries for children of munitions workers (it also financed childcare classes for mothers[38]). Thus this new institutionalization contributed to what was in some ways a quite arbitrary fragmentation of childcare provision. There was an implicit rationale of course. Day nurseries emphasized health requirements, and catered in principle for children of all ages under 5 but only in exceptional circumstances. In practice this tended to restrict care provision to the children of women without husbands for whatever reason or from very poor homes, and was accordingly stigmatized. By contrast, it was intended that nursery education would ultimately cater for much larger numbers of older children and include a greater educational component. Tizard *et al.* observe that 'A distinction between a child's health and physical requirements and his [*sic*] educational and social needs had unfortunately been made . . . and these two aspects had become the interests of two quite separate sets of people—the medical and nursing professions and the educationalists'.[39] This professional distinction was not initially mirrored in departmental organization. In particular, medical interests continued to play

---

[37] Cited in Fraser, *Evolution of the British Welfare State*, 166.
[38] Ibid. 134.   [39] Tizard *et al.*, *All Our Children*, 69.

a significant role in the making of nursery education policy. However, the pattern of government institutionalization formalized in 1918 encouraged over time an alignment of professional and departmental boundaries.

This institutional division not only gave rise to distinct sets of professional interests, but was reflected in the formation of interest associations seeking to influence policy. On the one hand was the National Society of Day Nurseries, founded in 1906 and initially representing some thirty nurseries. On the other was the Nursery School Association, formed in 1923, with Margaret McMillan as its first President and as a response to the limitations of the 1918 Education Act. Its presiding committee, all of whom were women, included many teachers, especially those involved in nursery teacher training.[40] This composition tended to shape its objectives: whilst the primary aim was to promote public awareness and the provision of nursery education, a major concern was with the conditions of training and employment of nursery teachers.[41]

Between the wars child daycare languished both as a policy concern and in terms of concrete provision[42] but in the field of nursery education there was greater progress. Actual expansion of provision was modest. Local education authorities, coping with a range of new responsibilities, were slow to take up their new nursery education powers, while national policy imposed a kind of stop–go rhythm. Expansion was reined in following the 1922 Geddes Report,[43] resumed at a glacial pace under Labour from 1924, reined in again following the 1931 economic crisis, and then cautiously encouraged from 1936. By 1938 there were still only 118 nursery schools established or approved, although a further nearly 170,000 children under 5 were in some form of pre-school class.

But, thanks partly to Margaret McMillan's campaigning efforts, public support for nursery education was growing. It was increasingly championed within the Labour Party, especially in the women's sections. In the run-up to the 1929 General Election all parties acknowledged the issue.

---

[40] By 1939 it had 26 branches.   [41] Blackstone, *A Fair Start*, 42–5.

[42] As noted earlier, it is difficult to gauge the extent of the need for child daycare. Even if we base our assessment on the number of mothers actually going out to work, available information is limited. By 1911 an estimated 13–14% of mothers were in paid employment. Their numbers rose during the war but fell back in the immediate aftermath. The officially recorded increase in the rate of married women workers from 13% to 16% from 1921 to 1930 is likely to have been an underestimate, but mothers' employment rates would have been lower.

[43] The (Geddes) Select Committee on National Expenditure, reporting in a climate of national economic crisis, criticized 'the atmosphere of financial laxity in which questions regarding education are apt to be considered': cited in Blackstone, *A Fair Start*, 42.

In 1933 the Hadow Committee, set up originally to report on secondary education, issued part III of its report, on nursery education. Illustrating the extent to which the medical profession still influenced policy-making in this field, the Committee had been particularly impressed by the evidence of the Chief Medical Officer of the Board of Education, which stressed the beneficial effects of nursery education for the health of children from needy backgrounds. Although Blackstone is critical of the Committee's continuing resistance to the argument that provision of nursery education should be universal, available for children from all social backgrounds, Tizard *et al.* nevertheless see the Hadow Report as offering the cause of nursery education an 'enormous boost'.[44]

CHILDCARE IN THE SECOND WORLD WAR

While foreshadowed by experience in the First World War, expansion of publicly sponsored childcare provision in the Second World War was on an entirely different scale. From approximately 100 day nurseries and 118 nursery schools on the eve of the war, the figures leaped by 1944 to 1,450 full-time nurseries, 109 part-time nurseries, and 784 nursery classes. Then, following the war, the figures almost immediately began to drop away again. The unprecedented scale of expansion and then its unravelling, the coincidence of these developments with a major qualitative and quantitative upsurge in the British welfare state, and the fact that these events form the immediate background to the postwar period require us to pay them particular attention.

Wartime growth of childcare provision began in the context of evacuation schemes. The initial impact of war was disruptive for daycare and nursery education provision alike, affecting both areas to be evacuated and those designated as reception areas for children and mothers. The combination of reduced provision and the extreme strain for all concerned that was so frequently associated with the billeting of members from one family in the home of another soon threatened to provoke a flood of returnees to the evacuated regions. This prompted the Board of Education's rather hastily improvised Nursery Centre Scheme. The nursery centres, 'a rudimentary form of nursery school',[45] were conceived as temporary responses to an emergency situation. One official commented, 'The very fact that a nursery centre is neither a nursery school nor a day nursery would stamp them as a purely temporary

---

[44] Tizard *et al.*, *All Our Children*, 70.
[45] Ferguson and Fitzgerald, *Studies in the Social Services*, 180.

expedient to deal with war conditions and would make it easier to get rid of them after the war'.[46] Ideally they would be staffed by voluntary workers. The whole emphasis was on minimizing costs of provision. Even so, the Treasury, fearing this scheme could provide a lever for the champions of nursery school education, showed extreme reluctance to pay up.

But by the time it began to be implemented the scheme was largely overtaken. For the real impetus behind the expansion of childcare provision came from labour supply considerations. Although there was actually an increase in female unemployment at the outset of the war, it soon became clear that women would have to make up the labour shortfall. In January 1940, the Cabinet agreed, following an inter-departmental report on the labour implications of the war programme, that greater 'dilution' of the workforce would be needed, including more use of female labour, but the Minister of Labour, Ernest Brown, still held out against this view. Pressure from the British Federation of Business and Professional Women, and from a number of backbench women MPs, led by Lady Astor, together with the appointment of Ernest Bevin as Minister of Labour in the new Churchill government of May 1940, secured the beginnings of change, signalled in the Extended Employment of Women Agreement.[47] While young 'mobile' single women were inevitably the preferred target of the ensuing registration scheme, increasingly the category of eligible women was extended. And while for registration purposes the presumption remained that mothers of young children should be exempt, as the labour shortage became more acute, 'the MOL made explicit its expectation that they would work'.[48] By 1943, the percentage of employed women who were married had risen from 16 in 1931 to around 43. Of these an estimated one-third had children under 14.[49]

As the preceding paragraph shows, the Ministry of Labour's primary concern was recruitment. The first official circular on childcare was not issued until June 1941, although registration had begun in April. According to Summerfield, the Ministry's approach to childcare provision was reactive rather than proactive until Bevin's arrival. Bevin made clear to the Ministry of Health amongst other audiences his view that nursery

---

[46] Cited in Riley, *War in the Nursery*, 119.

[47] See Harold L. Smith, 'The Womanpower Problem in Britain during the Second World War', *Historical Journal*, 27: 4 (1984), 925–45.

[48] Summerfield, *Women Workers in the Second World War*, 51.

[49] There was no census in 1941 but Summerfield (ibid. 62) arrives at this figure using the 1944 Wartime Social Survey, *Women at Work*. Riley (*War in the Nursery*, 123) similarly estimates that a good third of the 2.5 million women employed in industry had children at school or under school age.

provision was a precondition for the effective recruitment of married women needed for the war effort. While Bevin's own sympathy with socialist visions of universal nursery provision may have marginally influenced his approach, it was largely determined by pragmatic estimations of what the war effort required in conjunction with the pressures of those representing the 'producer' interests concerned. 'Big industrialists', directly hit with labour shortages, constituted one considerable influence on policy but the Ministry of Labour was also sensitive to the views of organized labour. The TUC's insistence on adequate childcare provision in turn partly reflected the demands of organized women workers. Boston comments on a general radicalization of women's trade union conferences at this time while TUC Conferences held in 1941 and 1942 devoted more time than traditionally to concerns of women workers. In 1942 a conference held to discuss nursery facilities, sponsored by the Standing Joint Committee of Working Womens' Organisations, resolved that 'the care and supervision of young children who enter employment is a national responsibility'.[50] Although the Ministry of Labour was the prime mover, pressing forward nursery policy, not all its officials were as enthusiastic as their Minister. Summerfield records the strong reservations of Mary Smieton, who as Assistant Secretary in the Factory and Welfare Department played a significant role in the implementation of policy.

While the initiative within government was coming from the Ministry of Labour, inevitably the war nurseries policy required the collaboration of several departments. The Treasury was ultimately concerned with the funding of the initiative. The District Inspectors of the Board of Education were expected to advise local health departments administering the scheme to ensure that educational aspects were not neglected. Most problematic, however, was the necessary collaboration between the Ministries of Labour and of Health. Here Summerfield identifies a counterpart to Miss Smieton, Zoe Puxley, Assistant Secretary in Charge of Maternity and Child Welfare; the two worked closely together. We have already seen that the Ministry of Health had its own, distinctive approach to the question of childcare. Summerfield illustrates the clashing of these rival perspectives over four specific dimensions of nursery policy. The first concerned premises and staffing. The Ministry of Health (through Miss Puxley) urged the Ministry of Labour to leave decisions about the provision of childcare to its Maternity and Child Welfare Specialists. In Summerfield's words, these specialists were 'largely

[50] Boston, *Women Workers and the Trade Union Movement*, 196.

concerned with setting high standards but refusing the funds which would make them attainable'.[51]

A second vital area of conflict was in assessing mothers' demand for war nurseries. Under the administrative procedure adopted, first the Ministry of Labour's local representative declared a nursery was needed and then the local Medical Officer of Health conducted an inquiry to establish whether the Ministry of Health should support this claim and persuade the local council to provide the nursery. The Ministry of Health was all along anxious to play down the extent of need, declaring 'It is important in any reference in the National papers to make it clear that the urgency and the extensive scale of this work is localised and not in the country as a whole'.[52] Local health officials repeatedly questioned the evidence cited and the recommendations of Ministry of Labour representatives. Thirdly, accusations were levelled by the Ministry of Health in 1943 that inadequate use was being made of the nurseries. The Ministry of Labour queried these charges, maintaining that the figures cited were based on a six-day week, which reflected unrealistic assumptions about patterns of employment and family life.

The fourth issue was childminding. Noting with approval the increased recourse to childminders by mothers returning to industry in the West Riding, the Ministry of Health used this as an argument to play down the need for nurseries. In contrast, the Ministry of Labour presented the first official minding scheme as temporary only. With Miss Smieton's connivance, however, the second scheme, adopted in November 1941, depicted nurseries as the last resort, when all possibilities of alternative minding arrangements had been exhausted. While the Ministry of Labour as a whole went along with this, there was considerable internal opposition to the shift, partly reflecting the concerns of the trade unions. Bevin's Parliamentary Secretary, for instance, wrote that 'The TUC and our Factory and Welfare Board . . . are extremely reluctant to give any blessing to anything in the nature of "childminding"'.[53]

The new 'war nurseries' that emerged out of these exceptional circumstances were of two main kinds. By far the largest category consisted of the full-time war nurseries, catering solely for the children, aged 0–5, of mothers working full time. Though subsequently described by

---

[51] Summerfield, *Women Workers in the Second World War*, 70.

[52] Cited in Riley, *War in the Nursery*, 119.

[53] Summerfield, *Women Workers in the Second World War*, 91. The Women's Cooperative Guild and Labour Women's Advisory Councils also objected to the scheme.

the Parliamentary Secretary of the Ministry of Health as essentially
'hybrid' institutions, these were in fact primarily agencies of care, as
opposed to education, and by September 1944 numbered 1,450. The
second category, building to some extent on the Nursery Centre model,
were part-day nurseries, open during school hours, with a more educational orientation and catering for a rather wider range of children,
aged 2–5.

A difficult question to answer is how really useful and appreciated
the war nurseries were. As we have seen, this issue was disputed by the
Ministries of Labour and Health. There is some doubt as to whether the
nurseries did actually help to release urgently needed womanpower.[54]
But were they welcomed by wartime mothers? The more general problems in the way of assessing need or 'demand' for child-care provision
are discussed in Chapter 5 but a few comments are in order here. First,
attitudes to the war nurseries were bound up with attitudes to mobilization as a whole, which could be quite complex. Amongst mothers
accepting or actually welcoming the opportunity for paid employment,
reasons varied widely,[55] whilst others held paid work to be incompatible with home responsibilities. Further, amongst women who were
called up many disliked the specific work they were allocated.

But in addition to attitudes to paid work, women's appreciation
of the war nurseries was affected by the terms under which they operated. These were not necessarily the most convenient for working
mothers. Cost and accessibility were relevant considerations but still
more important were the hours that nurseries were open and the categories of women whose children were eligible to enrol. Certainly it was
the case that initially some nurseries had difficulty filling their allotted
places:

A tendency to 'wait and see what they're like' or the dislike of an early journey
with the baby; the fear that baby might 'pick something up', a spell of bad

---

[54] Ferguson and Fitzgerald note that 'there seems to have been very little careful analysis of possible achievements before the policy of expansion was accepted': *Studies in the
Social Services*, 204. Subsequently the Ministry of Labour tended to put an optimistic
construction on such global figures as were available. More elaborate evaluations by individual local authorities suggested that 'total net labour releases may have been low',
although Ferguson and Fitzgerald suggest that 'it may still be argued that the type of
labour released or the encouragement given to mothers to work, made the contribution
of the nurseries more important than numbers alone can show' (ibid. 207).

[55] As reported by Mass Observation, some women claimed that they would work if it
could be fitted in with their home responsibilities and especially childcare. Many women
needed to earn money, particularly in view of rising prices. Indeed 'Many mothers were
believed to have taken up war work or kept on with it because they themselves could
eat at canteens and their children could eat at nurseries, all without any surrender of
rations' (ibid. 211).

weather—all these made some of the nurseries get off to a slow start and encouraged working mothers to go on making their own arrangements.[56]

But in the longer run, 'too few nurseries and long waiting lists became the rule'.[57]

From the origins, politics, and implementation of the war-time childcare policy, we must now turn to its suspension. The war nurseries were wound up speedily at the end of the war. The Exchequer grant available for nurseries was halved, responsibility for them was devolved to local authorities, and buildings which had been requisitioned for the nurseries were returned.

In seeking to explain these developments, Riley takes issue with a feminist 'myth . . . that they were done away with because the government wanted women off the labour market and back to the home and that it called in Bowlby's work to justify this'.[58] While the reassertion of 'traditional' attitudes to working mothers undoubtedly played its part, the story is more complicated. As discussed more fully in the following chapter, Riley is right to argue that Bowlby's thesis of 'maternal deprivation' really came into its own in the 1950s, and was not deployed in policy debates at this stage. Reflecting the continuing prevalence of health considerations, the most sustained criticism of the nurseries came from practitioners of medicine and paediatrics, rather than psychology. Particularly influential was the Committee of the Medical Women's Federation, which concluded from two surveys of nursery children, carried out in 1944–5, that 'the outstanding fact is the constant and considerable increase of respiratory tract infection', although if anything their own evidence seemed to indicate a net improvement to children's health.[59]

Moreover, as we should expect, the different ministries involved did not share a single perspective. It was the Ministry of Health that most strongly advocated closure of the war nurseries. A circular issued in 1945 made clear its continuing determination to regard the nurseries as a temporary response to the exigencies of war and re-affirmed the opinion of the Ministers concerned that

under normal peacetime conditions, the right policy to pursue would be positively to discourage mothers of children under two from going out to work; to make provision for children between two and five by way of nursery schools and classes; and to regard day nurseries and daily guardians as supplements to meet the special needs . . . of children whose mothers are constrained by individual circumstances to go out to work or whose home conditions are

[56] Ibid. 185.   [57] Ibid. 186.
[58] Denise Riley, 'War in the Nursery', *Feminist Review*, 2 (1979), 82.   [59] Ibid. 111.

in themselves unsatisfactory from the health point of view, or whose mothers are incapable for some good reason of undertaking the full care of their children.[60]

However, a somewhat different message seemed to be coming from the Board of Education. Still more than during the First World War, during the Second the impact of wartime policies fostered public support for nursery education. It is held that the experience of evacuation, bringing people in the reception areas into close contact with inner-city children, was in itself a 'revelation', strengthening arguments for the benefits such education could bring. Although numbers of the more educationally oriented part-day nurseries were limited, one contemporary commentator reported that they 'are doing much to popularise the idea of a nursery stage in education and are opening the eyes of numerous parents to the high quality of the nursery school'.[61] This theme was incorporated into the 1943 education White Paper, which advocated provision of nursery schools 'wherever they are needed', which would be in all districts because 'even when children come from good homes, they can derive much benefit, both educational and physical, from attendance at nursery school'. As Blackstone observes, 'This was the first time that official recognition had been given to the notion of pre-school education for all rather than a special class of needy children'.[62] Subsequently the 1944 Education Act stipulated that local education authorities should 'have regard to the need for' nursery education. This incidentally led many to presume that the old war nurseries could become the basis for expanded nursery education provision.

Nor did those formulating labour policy desire or foresee any simple exclusion of women from the job market. Although it was anticipated that many women currently employed in industry would be 'surplus' to requirements after demobilization, this would to some extent be offset by an expansion in such traditional areas of women's work as nursing and the social services. A statement by the Chancellor of the Exchequer in 1943 suggests some of the contradictory pulls of employment policy:

the guiding principles will be to maintain employment at the highest possible level and yet to interfere as little as possible with the speedy restoration of

---

[60] Ministry of Health, Circular 221/45.

[61] H. Dent, *Education in Transition, 1939–1943* (1944), cited in Blackstone, *A Fair Start*, 63. Blackstone also notes that membership of the Nursery School Association expanded and the Council for Educational Advance championed the nursery education cause, while in 1942 the *Times* advocated 'full and proper provision for the pre-school child' (ibid.).   [62] Ibid. 64.

home life. But clearly no guarantee can be given that all women who wish immediately to leave their employment will be able to do so.[63]

Even so, there is little suggestion that those devising labour policy departed from the widespread assumption that whenever possible, mothers of young children should not work outside the home.

The contradictory messages and confusion surrounding the ending of the war nurseries help to explain the relatively muted political response to the policy. But there was also little overt remonstration from mothers themselves. Again it is difficult to gauge how far women, and specifically mothers, wanted to continue in paid employment after the war. Relevant surveys indicated a range of attitudes but tended to conclude that the overwhelming majority of women saw their future in terms of marriage and the family.[64] For whatever reason, as Riley observes, 'there seems to have been no sustained and systematic campaigning by mothers with children in the nurseries to keep them open'.[65]

A large deputation, including representatives of the National Council of Maternity and Child Welfare, the National Society of Children's Nurseries, Froebel teachers, nursery nurse training colleges, Barnardo's and services' children's homes, addressed the Ministries of Health and Education on the question of nursery provision. There were various local campaigns and protests voiced by a number of local authorities as well as a National Nursery Campaign led by members of the London Women's Parliament. But the cumulative effect was slight. And once more there was a significant silence from the ranks of feminists themselves.

The parliamentary debate, in February 1945, on the closure of the war nurseries is revealing in a number of ways. Setting a pattern that has persisted, it was only an adjournment debate and its timing on a Friday afternoon meant that very few members were present. Retention of the nurseries was urged in several quite impassioned speeches and almost no one directly opposed them. But the case was made on various, sometimes contradictory, grounds, which were as revealing in what they left out as in the considerations they adduced. One argument for the continuation of the nurseries emphasized their contribution to family stability in the context of poor housing conditions exacerbated

---

[63] Cited in Riley, 'War in the Nursery', 93.

[64] Both Mass Observation and the Wartime Social Survey collected information which, according to Summerfield, showed that large numbers of women wanted to continue with their wartime jobs, while others felt that their decisions would depend on conditions of work prevailing after the war: Summerfield, *Women Workers in the Second World War*, 189–90.

[65] Riley, 'War in the Nursery', 92.

by wartime bombing. Mr Cove drew on his personal experience of growing up in a large working-class family in the Rhondda Valley, where 'There was never any leisure for the working-class mother and never any hope of being free from the care of the children'.[66] It was further suggested that nursery provision would be necessary if couples were to be persuaded to have more children, in the context of growing population concerns. There was also some brief reference to the likely continuation, in the immediate postwar period, of the demand for women's labour. These arguments were as close as discussion got to considering women's needs.

Alternatively, a more child-health-centred argument was that the nurseries had been invaluable not only directly in improving the health of the children who attended them, but in educating working-class mothers in the proper way of looking after their children. Sir Percy Harris claimed that the nursery in Bethnal Green had 'revolutionised' the neighbourhood and 'changed the attitude of the ordinary East End mother'.[67]

But a different kind of concern was expressed by those who saw the war nurseries as representing the basis for a real expansion of nursery *education*. They wanted to ensure that, even as their wartime function ceased, premises and staff would be retained for use in the nursery education programme heralded in the 1944 Education Act. This illustrates what has been a continuing area of ambiguity that politicians have been able to exploit—the relationship between day nurseries and nursery education, between childcare and pre-school education. Mrs Tate, whose distaste for day nurseries was very evident, and who indeed somehow managed in her speech to link day nurseries with the provision of poisoned (that is, pasteurized) milk, declared that resource constraints meant that they had to choose between day nurseries and nursery education; they could not have both.

Miss Horsbrugh, for the government, exploited this area of confusion quite skilfully. She suggested that the war nurseries were designed to be 'neither the day nursery of the local authority before the war nor the nursery school, but hybrids' (this was not really true). Claiming that many nursery places for children aged 0 to 2 were not actually taken up, she conjured a seemingly ridiculous scenario: it would be 'quite stupid for one local authority to have a nursery for children from two to five and, as a sort of opposition, a nursery school'. She summarized the government's position with an almost Alice in Wonderland logic: the war nurseries were not closing down at a significant rate, there was no

---

[66] Hansard, vol. 408, 9 Mar. 1945, col. 2438.   [67] Ibid. col. 2430.

question of closing down nurseries while they were still being attended, although in many cases there was little demand for nursery places, and in any case the nurseries were funded by a war grant on the clear basis that they were for the children of mothers who were working.[68]

CONCLUSION

The institutional arrangements framing childcare policy in the 1950s were largely established by the 1920s. They built upon a functional distinction between child daycare and nursery education, although the need for both was primarily derived—as far as government was concerned—from health considerations. They also embodied basic and enduring assumptions about the respective roles of mothers and of the state in regard to childcare.

In one sense, what is striking is how little change there was over this period. Despite the expansion of day nursery provision in the First World War, and even more dramatically in the Second, there was each time a rapid reversion to the preceding scale of provision and almost no lasting increase in its acceptance as a peacetime service. The case of nursery education was in some ways different: its legitimacy as public policy made steady progress. By the late 1930s its value for working-class children was in principle accepted, and experience of the war nurseries helped to extend that legitimacy to provision for children of all social classes. Even so, in practice, and indicating at the very least how marginal was its position in the gamut of policy commitments, it was one of the first casualties of public expenditure retrenchment in the early 1920s and again in 1931.

But this period can also be seen as a time of lost opportunities. The first was at the very beginning of this century, when the decision was taken not to build on existing levels of school attendance by 3- to 5-year-olds. The second was after the Second World War. Admittedly the enormous expansion of nursery provision was presented all along as an emergency measure. But as Major Sir Derrick Gunston, Conservative MP for Thornbury, pointed out during the adjournment debate, 'many things during our history have been started for one purpose, and, because they have proved so valuable, have been developed for another purpose'.[69]

Finally, we have seen that these childcare policies took shape in the

---

[68] Ibid. cols. 2443–50.   [69] Ibid. col. 2431.

context of Britain's emerging welfare state. The welfare state developed gradually rather than springing up suddenly at the end of the Second World War, on the basis of an *ab initio* appraisal of social needs. Structures and policies of the post-war welfare state to an extent incorporated arrangements already in place from before the war, as in the case of childcare. None the less these various enactments together constituted a high-water mark in social intervention by Britain's 'liberal' state and undoubtedly reflected in part the political clout and priorities of organized labour. But, once the emergency of war was over, these priorities no longer included child daycare.

3

Post-war Policy and the
'Rediscovery of Poverty'

By the 1950s the issue of child daycare appeared to have returned in good measure to the status quo ante, that is to its position before the war. The level and fragmentation of public provision were back to pre-war rates, and such provision was justified in ways which often seemed to hark back to the earlier period, although they also took new forms. This chapter examines the challenge to this 'traditional' pattern that emerged in the 1960s and '70s. As in the previous chapter, while developments are analysed in broadly chronological fashion, the material is organized around a succession of central questions, which are aimed both at trying to answer why childcare policy was as it was and how we can most fruitfully think about these matters. We must begin by establishing the status of child daycare as an issue in the early post-war years.

CHILD DAYCARE IN THE FIFTIES

The expansion of child daycare provision during the Second World War was rapidly unscrambled in the years of peace. Daycare was once more compartmentalized into nursery education, overseen by the Ministry of Education, and child daycare under the auspices of the Ministry of Health. Following its 1945 circular advocating closure of most wartime day nurseries, the Ministry of Health did not produce another on this question until 1968, and even then largely reiterated the policy assumptions of the earlier circular. Already in 1946, large numbers of wartime day nurseries were transferred to local education authorities. From 1,300 in 1945 the number of day nurseries was down to 902 by the beginning of 1947. In 1951 the Ministry of Health's annual report reaffirmed that day nursery places should only be provided for 'children in special need on health or social grounds' and not because of 'the mother's desire to supplement the family income by going out to work'. In 1952 local authorities were permitted to levy a charge on nursery places closer to the actual cost of their provision and thereafter, though with local variation and account taken of people's ability to pay, charges rose, inevitably depressing effective demand for places. The number of publicly provided day nurseries fell steadily, to 477 by 1960 and an all-time low of 444 in the late sixties. By 1963 13 county councils (out of 48) and 13 county boroughs (out of 79) offered no daycare places at all.[1]

The 1945 Ministry of Health circular, while advocating closure of most wartime day nurseries, indicated that for children aged 2 to 5, nursery schools and classes should be made available. However, although as we have seen the requirement under the 1944 Education Act that local education authorities 'have regard to the need for' nursery education had represented some kind of enhanced official recognition of its potential importance, in practice its provision remained extremely limited, competing as it was with new claims on these authorities' constrained resources. In 1949 and 1951 Ministry of Education circulars, while not expressly indicating nursery education, emphasized the need for extreme economy in the administration of education as a whole. As a direct consequence, in Blackstone's view, four county councils decided to stop providing nursery education altogether while many other local education authorities made plans to cut back provision. 1952 marked the end of a period of modest expansion, both in nursery schools and in nursery classes. Further circulars in the mid-fifties imposed specific restrictions on admissions of children under 5 to primary schools and finally Circular 8 of May 1960 forbade any further expansion in the overall number of nursery education places. This circular was moreover noteworthy in encouraging what became a cumulative shift away from full-time to part-time modes of attendance, further weakening the contribution nursery education could make to an effective system of child daycare. The circular explicitly related this change to the question of daycare. It noted that a main purpose of the wartime nursery schools had been 'to release mothers of young children for work of national importance' but implied that this was in response to exceptional circumstances. Now the aim of nursery education should be to serve the needs of children themselves and 'normal children' from 'normal homes' might well be better suited by part-time than by full-time attendance, such a policy also enabling a larger number of children to attend.[2]

These policy developments were not strongly contested. This is especially true in regard to day nurseries. Although, as we have seen, there was some protest immediately following the realization that the pro-

---

[1] Jack Tizard, Peter Moss, and Jane Perry, *All Our Children* (London: Temple-Smith, 1976), 75.

[2] Tessa Blackstone, *A Fair Start: The Provision of Pre-school Education* (London: Allen Lane, 1971), 67–8.

gramme of public daycare provision introduced during the war was to be wound down, by the 1950s it scarcely survived as an overt political issue. In addition to the National Society of Children's Nurseries, one exception to the general pattern of indifference was the TUC's women's conference (known earlier as the conference of the Representatives of Unions Catering for Women Workers), which continued regularly to call for the expansion of day nurseries, as one of its 'hardy perennials', through the 1950s and '60s. But, as discussed further below, the women's conference is only an advisory body and its resolutions largely failed to move the TUC.[3] The terms in which this demand was made, moreover, soon began to shift to a narrower, more instrumental justification. Nor was there any noticeable feminist opposition; rather, so-called feminists such as Viola Klein tended to endorse prevalent views of the role of women.

Nursery education policy proved more contentious, although the situation was complicated by the government's recognition in principle of the virtues of extending public provision, even while such provision was constrained in practice. The Nursery Schools Association continued of course to promote the cause of nursery education but significantly its membership, which had more than doubled during the war, declined thereafter, falling from 9,000 in 1945 to around 5,000 by 1965.[4] Within the labour movement, belief in nursery education as a means of raising educational standards and of increasing social equality had been strengthened, as we saw, by the wartime experience. The TUC continued its support: its General Council regularly voiced its dissatisfaction, through letters and deputations, with the government's failure to expand nursery education.[5] 'Progressive' local education authorities, and most of all the London County Council, also put forward expansionary nursery education plans.[6]

NEED AND DEMAND FOR CHILD DAYCARE

One of the arguments used by the Ministry of Health to justify closure of the war nurseries at the end of the war was that there was no longer

---

[3] Sarah Boston, *Women Workers and the Trade Union Movement* (London: Davis Poynter, 1980), 255.

[4] Blackstone, *A Fair Start*, 74.

[5] See for instance Trades Union Congress, *1960 TUC Report*, 60, and *1961 TUC Report*, 181, where reference is made to a continuing argument between the General Council and the Ministry of Education over the latter's refusal to sanction the expansion of nursery education provision.

[6] Blackstone, *A Fair Start*, 65.

any 'real demand' for them.[7] If after the initial protestations, post-war childcare policy occasioned little protest or conflict, was this perhaps because it corresponded to actual daycare requirement—because, that is, there was no daycare problem? Chapter 5 considers further the difficulties of both defining and assessing mothers' or parents' need for child daycare. Here, however, we need to examine some of the key factors shaping policy-makers' perception, beginning with the pattern of women's employment.

During the war, it was widely assumed that the high female employment rates were and should be temporary, especially in the case of married women, most particularly mothers. Such an assumption informed Beveridge's report in 1942, which anticipated a post-war pattern of female employment similar to that of the 1930s.[8] However, the reality of women's post-war employment was rather different. Already by 1944 'government ministers were becoming increasingly confident that the main labour problem in the post-war years would be a shortage of workers, rather than a shortage of jobs'.[9] In 1947 an Economic Survey, commissioned by the Ministry of Labour, estimated that the prospective labour force would fall 'substantially short' of national requirements, especially in manufacturing industries such as textiles but also in service industries and in professions, notably teaching. It identified women as 'the only large reserve of labour left' and appealed 'to women who are in a position to do so to enter industry'.[10] By 1952, further concerned by expectations of a worsening dependency ratio as the population aged, the Ministry was pinpointing older married women as one group employers should turn to.

The assumption remained that mothers with dependent children should not be employed full-time.[11] At the same time we have noted Summerfield's argument that some policy-makers had been convinced by the war experience that it was possible for women to combine limited hours of paid work, whether on a part-time or shift basis, with marriage and motherhood. The 1947 Economic Survey encouraged employers to provide flexible working conditions 'to suit, so far as possible, the convenience of women with household responsibilities'.[12]

In practice, then, overall rates of women's employment and even of

[7] Cited by Denise Riley, *War in the Nursery* (London: Virago, 1983), 119.

[8] See J. Lewis, *Women in Britain since 1945* (Oxford: Blackwell, 1992), 71.

[9] Harold L. Smith, 'The Womanpower Problem in Britain during the Second World War', *Historical Journal*, 27:4 (1984), 939.

[10] Cited in E. Wilson, *Only Halfway to Paradise: Women in Postwar Britain 1945–1968* (London: Tavistock, 1980), 43.

[11] Lewis, *Women in Britain since 1945*, 71.   [12] Ibid. 72.

married women's employment were less affected by the ending of
war than might have been expected. From around 10 per cent in the
inter-war years, the employment rate for married women reached 50 per
cent at its highest point during the war, but although it fell again in the
late 1940s, it was already 26 per cent by 1951 and 35 per cent by 1961.[13]
But while the rates for mothers with dependent children are more
difficult to establish, they were certainly much lower. As late as 1961,
according to the 10 per cent Census sample, only 11.5 per cent of women
in this category were in paid employment.[14] In fact Lewis suggests that
already in 1951 a two-stage or bimodal pattern of women's employment
was beginning to be apparent, which emerged more clearly by 1961.
There were two peaks of economic activity, for the 20–24 age group
and for those aged 45–50, with a particularly sharp drop for those
in the 24–34 age range. That is, in these early post-war years, at least,
women tended to drop out of the labour market when they became
mothers and not resume employment until their children had finished
school.[15]

Also relevant is the growth of part-time jobs. Before the war, employment, certainly officially registered employment, 'almost invariably'
meant full-time employment,[16] although women probably undertook a
significant amount of informal part-time work, which went unrecorded.
The growth in part-time employment has been essentially a post-war
phenomenon. The 1951 Census indicated that 12 per cent of women
were working part-time[17] and after 1951 overall expansion of the female
labour force was almost entirely due to the expansion in the number of
part-time jobs, with the rate of women's full-time employment actually
though slowly declining.[18] To summarize this discussion of employment
patterns, they would not seem, at face value, to have been contributing
to an urgent need for child daycare, although it is more difficult to assess
how far the dearth of public childcare provision was actually preventing mothers of young children from seeking work, that is to what extent
it was a cause instead of an effect.

[13] Figures from Irene Breugel, 'Women's Employment, Legislation and the Labour
Market', in J. Lewis (ed.), *Women's Welfare: Women's Rights* (Beckenham: Croom-Helm,
1983), 134. However, the increase in the employment rate of married women must be
seen in the light of demographic changes, notably the fall in the average age of marriage
and the increase in the number of married women.

[14] Tizard *et al.*, *All Our Children*, 124.

[15] Lewis, *Women in Britain since 1945*, 74.

[16] Catherine Hakim, 'The Myth of Rising Female Employment', *Work, Employment
and Society*, 7:1 (1993), 101.

[17] But Lewis, *Women in Britain since 1945*, 72, suggests this is an underestimate.

[18] It fell from 6 million to approximately 5.7 million from 1951 to 1961, and then to
5.4 million by 1971.

One indirect indicator of the need for publicly provided child daycare is the use of private nurseries and childminders.[19] In the 1960s the incidence of such private provision soared. The absolute figures for the 1950s were much smaller but the trend was already relentlessly upwards. In fact, according to the 1948 Nurseries and Child Minders Regulation Act, which required their registration, the figures for both forms of provision rose steadily. In the 1950s the number of registered private nurseries nearly doubled, though this was from a low global figure of 326, while the number of officially registered childminders, though again starting from a low baseline, more than tripled by 1960.[20]

In interpreting this 'evidence', policy-makers, and their advisers, were influenced by continuing assumptions about the childcare responsibilities of young mothers, but these were refracted through more specific policy concerns and drew new inspiration and rationalization from developments in child psychology. Initially one relevant area of public concern was population. Fears of a declining birth rate had persisted through the war and contributed to predictions of a labour shortage. In 1945 a Royal Commission was established to examine the issue, although by the time it reported, in 1949, the post-war 'baby boom' had helped to reduce the sense of urgency.[21]

Fears about the birth rate were linked to, and to some extent overtaken by, renewed appreciation of the family as a social institution and, at the same time, fears for its viability. As Lewis notes, anxiety about the family has been a recurrent theme in both this and previous centuries. In the aftermath of the Second World War, there was widespread concern amongst professionals and politicians alike to 'rebuild' the family, which was paradoxically viewed both as the 'bedrock' of society and as weakened by the upheavals of war, and before that of the Depression, as symptomized in the rising rates of divorce and illegitimacy.[22] The family was needed above all to care for its members, and especially to care for and socialize children. And within the family the mother's role was inevitably pivotal.

---

[19] As pointed out by Jennifer Marchbank, 'Agenda-setting, Policy-making and the Marginalization of Women', unpubl. Ph.D. diss., University of Strathclyde, 1994.

[20] This greatly underestimates the actual numbers since although, under the Act, childminders were supposed to register with the local authority it is clear that the majority did not.

[21] Lewis, *Women in Britain since 1945*, 17. Its report incidentally identified feminism as a major contributory factor, one reason being that it had encouraged women to find fulfillment in paid work rather than in motherhood, although it also accepted, as a fact of life, that women would want to work outside the home.

[22] Ibid. 11.

This new familism did not lead to a more *active* family policy[23] that sought to increase forms of material support for family life. The 'liberal' strain in official thinking constrained a more interventionist approach, except in cases of family breakdown. Concern for the family need not have taken the form of opposition to day nurseries. Discussions of the needs of the family in the immediate post-war period, as anticipated in the 1945 adjournment debate,[24] clearly could lead to different conclusions about the family's *need* for daycare provision.

Here the sociology of the family, and liberal reticence about interfering in 'private' family relationships, converged with the new orthodoxies of child psychology. In the previous chapter, we touched on Riley's discussion of the influence of John Bowlby.[25] Riley is adamant that his ideas concerning 'maternal deprivation' did not play a significant role in the implicit decision to wind down the nurseries after the war. However, as they seeped into professional and public consciousness they acquired a tremendous hold, to the point where Riley claims, 'the general spirit of Bowlbyism in Britain in the mid-1950s would have made the question of provision of child care for working mothers almost unaskable'.[26]

Bowlby worked in the tradition of the Kleinian school of psychoanalysis, which emphasized the mother–child bond. His earlier research centred on innate aggression, and even when he turned to environmental factors, including separation from the mother, he was still prepared to argue in 1940 that:

Provided breaks are not too long, and continuity is preserved, there seems no evidence to suppose that the child who is always with his mother is any better off than the child who only sees her for a few hours a day, and not at all for odd holiday weeks.[27]

Bowlby's views about the damaging effects of prolonged separation from the mother were initially developed in reference to wartime experience of evacuation and to residential nurseries. However, in his advice to the World Health Organization's Committee on Maternal Care and Mental Health in 1951, which maintained that the decision in many countries to provide crèches and day nurseries to enable mothers to work 'has been taken in complete ignorance of the price to be paid in

---

[23] There are difficulties in defining what a family policy is, or should consist of. The term is used differently in different contexts. See the discussion in Lorraine Fox Harding, *Family, State and Social Policy* (London: Macmillan, 1996), ch. 6.

[24] See pp. 41–3 above.   [25] See p. 39 above.

[26] Denise Riley, *War in the Nursery* (London: Virago, 1983), 116. The following discussion draws on Riley's account.

[27] Cited in ibid. 94.

permanent damage to the emotional development of a future generation' and in *Childcare and the Growth of Love*, published in 1953, he
moved closer to the position with which he is associated and which
he subsequently helped to popularize. Bowlby was not alone in these
views—others, like D. W. Winnicott, took a similar position—but he was
the most influential.

His perspective was incorporated into the training of the growing
numbers of professionals concerned directly or tangentially with children. Following the war, local authority Children's Departments were
established under the 1948 Children Act, responsible for childcare in its
other sense, that is for children separated from their families. According to Frost and Stein, Bowlby's *Childcare and the Growth of Love*
'became the key work in the training of child care officers'. By the late
sixties this 'child care service' had developed considerably and 'possessed a strong professional identity, with a powerful group of workers
who would go on to form the core of the emerging unified social work
profession', many of whom ultimately became Directors of Social
Service Departments.[28] Outside the childcare service, trainee social
workers intending to work with children were also steeped in the works
of Bowlby and Winnicott.

Such ideas were absorbed into national policy-making. Childcare case
workers were strongly represented in the Home Office's Children's
Division.[29] Bowlby's thesis was regularly invoked in internal policy
deliberations in the Department of Health in the early sixties. In 1966
a draft Departmental review of effects of current day nursery policy
included a strong and lengthy endorsement of Bowlby's argument.[30]
Indeed, in interviews Ruggie conducted in 1977 and 1982 of officials
responsible for child daycare policy at the Department of Health
and Social Security, she still found that they continued 'either to be
influenced by Bowlby's work or to use it to justify limiting day care
provision'.[31]

We return to the question of the real dimensions of need in a later
chapter but at this point we can conclude that in the early post-war
period, there was no strong evidence of the need or demand for child
daycare from the indirect indicators of women's employment patterns

[28] N. Frost and M. Stein, *The Politics of Child Welfare* (London: Harvester Wheatsheaf,
1989), 37.
[29] Ibid.
[30] Departmental review of 'The Effects of Present Policy on Local Authority Day
Nurseries', Public Records Office (PRO) Ministry of Health (MH) 156 54.
[31] Mary Ruggie, *The State and Working Women: A Comparative Study of Britain and
Sweden* (Princeton, NJ: Princeton University Press, 1984), 206. She strongly suspected the
latter.

and trends in private daycare provision. In its absence, policy-makers were inclined to interpret the need for childcare in the light of specific policy concerns—first a declining birth rate, later the stability of the family—and still more of a continuing maternalist ideology, now rearticulated and legitimized through the Bowlby doctrine.

CHILDCARE AND THE POLICY PROCESS

In the 1960s came specific, if modest, pressures for change. But before these can be discussed, we need to step back for a moment to ask how the situation so far described can best be understood in terms of policy dynamics. What kind of a policy process determined the provision of child daycare? Building on the historical analysis of Chapter 2, we could argue, following Schattschneider, that certain understandings or premises of childcare policy had been 'organized into' the decision-making process, or institutionalized, while other possible approaches were organized out.[32] However, it was not the case that these alternatives were being clearly or forcefully enunciated. The situation came closer to Steven Lukes's 'third face' of power: in the 1950s, child daycare, or at least working mothers' need for child daycare, was largely a 'latent issue', one which would be implicit in a (more recent) feminist reading of women's situation but was not in general articulated at the time.[33]

Alternatively we can analyse the policy process in terms of more 'middle-range' theoretical categories, which help us to understand *how* policy was institutionalized in this way. As we have seen, to the extent that the issue of childcare was acknowledged and incorporated in national processes of public policy-making, this was primarily within two distinct contexts: the provision of day nurseries, under the auspices of the Ministry of Health and largely as a residual welfare function, and the provision of nursery education, under the auspices of the Ministry of Education. In each case responsibility was nominally devolved to individual local authorities at the same time as these were subject to considerable financial controls from the centre. This marginalization and fragmentation of childcare decision-making led Ruggie to observe that

it is difficult to say who decides on daycare, for while all other branches of government absolve themselves of responsibility and defer to the DHSS, the

---

[32] E. E. Schattschneider, *The Semi-sovereign People: A Realist's View of Democracy in America* (Holt, Rinehart and Winston, 1960).
[33] Steven Lukes, *Power: A Radical View* (London: Macmillan, 1974).

DHSS itself defers to traditional conceptions, local authorities and financial constraints.[34]

One way to analyse this matrix is in terms of 'policy communities'. The idea of the 'policy community' forms part of a larger body of theoretical work concerned with 'policy networks' that derives from the seminal work of Heclo in the 1970s and has since expanded exponentially, both in Britain and the United States.[35] Policy networks provide a way of conceptualizing the interactions between government and organized interests in different policy fields. Policy communities are generally seen as lying at one end of the policy network continuum and conceived to be relatively stable and exclusive communities of policy-makers, with few member groups; most of these communities are based on shared economic or professional interests and a high degree of interaction and consensus, and, although one group may dominate, the resources of each group are roughly equal. Jordan and Richardson have noted a 'natural tendency for the political system in Britain to encourage the formation of stable policy communities', partly as a consequence of the departmentalism of British government.[36]

The policy community model certainly has relevance for childcare policy-making in this period. However, childcare did not 'own' its own policy community; rather it was dispersed and marginalized within two others. It is possible, that is, to identify education and welfare/social services as constituting policy subsystems with many 'policy community' features, relatively integrated and stable. Local authority organizations and professional interests were incorporated in the policy process and their expertise and role in implementation gave them something more than a merely consultative role, although central government was plainly the dominant actor. Yet, within these policy networks, nursery education and local authority daycare, the constituent elements of childcare, were always the poor relations. The rationale for their provision was couched in terms of the dominant policy 'discourses' within these policy communities and their claims on resources perceived to be correspondingly marginal. Thus, for example, a policy review circulated internally in the Department of Health in the early sixties reiterated the constantly heard refrain of the admittedly high cost of establishing new

---

[34] Ruggie, *The State and Working Women*, 233.

[35] For a useful summary of the development of this analysis see D. Marsh and R. Rhodes, 'Policy Community and Issue Networks: Beyond Typology', in D. Marsh and R. Rhodes (eds.), *Policy Networks in British Government* (Oxford: Oxford University Press, 1992).

[36] G. Jordan and J. Richardson, *Government and Pressure Groups in Britain* (Oxford: Oxford University Press, 1987), 181.

local authority day nurseries and declared that such expenditure could not be contemplated at a time when local health services were being expanded to meet in particular the needs of the elderly and the mentally disordered.[37] Nursery education was always depicted as competing for resources with schools, whose needs were greater and more urgent. In turn, the professional groups directly associated with these sub-policy areas—nursery teachers and especially nursery nurses—were of relatively low status and their expertise was not highly valued.

Although, at this period, there was very little pressure coming from 'outside' the policy community or communities to produce more effective or extensive systems of child daycare, it must also be stressed that it is misleading to think simply in terms of policy-makers responding, or not having to respond, to their environment. To some extent the institutionalized process itself, for instance by separating issues of daycare and education for small children, by associating daycare with families or mothers which were in one way or another 'inadequate', and by not encouraging the systematic collection of information about daycare needs, contributed to the situation in which it became difficult to think differently about childcare provision, in which professional interests inhered in the prevalent arrangements, and in which the potential beneficiaries of change, mothers of young children, lacked the solidarity or empowering arguments to legitimize such a demand.

While policy network analysis is valuable in demonstrating mechanisms of continuity in policy-making, it is less so in explaining the origins and causes of change. Networks serve primarily to routinize the relationships involved in making policy. Especially when they tend towards the policy community type, they are resistant to change and so long as the policy in question remains of low salience for government they dominate policy-making and change is at most incremental.[38] Accordingly in order to explain change, we have to look outside such networks, as well as within.

Specifically, in order to understand childcare policy developments in the sixties and seventies, it is helpful to think in terms of an interaction between government initiatives, arising from the Departments' internal processes of self-reflection and reform, and pressures from beyond the policy communities in question. On the one hand, a range of associated social changes was transforming childcare into a 'social problem' which, given existing commitments to child welfare, it was difficult to ignore.

[37] PRO MH 156 51, '1962–64 Day Care and Day Nurseries (Developments since 1945. Statement of Present Situation)', p. 38.
[38] Marsh and Rhodes, 'Policy Community and Issue Networks: Beyond Typology', 262.

This perception was then incorporated into the process of reviewing and reorganizing national social service provision. On the other, and with potentially greater policy consequences, the emergence of the 'poverty lobby' and its coincidence with an official review of primary education gave a new impetus to arguments for nursery education.

CHILDCARE FOR WORKING MOTHERS: DEPARTMENTAL FIREFIGHTING

But before turning directly to the construction of child daycare as a social problem, it is illuminating to consider an episode revealed in Departmental papers recently made available at the Public Records Office, which shows that there *was*, briefly, the possibility of an alternative or third construction of the issue in terms of the needs of working mothers which, however, government departments and especially the Department of Health stoutly resisted. A main reason why childcare was to emerge as a social problem was the continuing growth in the numbers of mothers of young children taking up paid employment (although, as an illustration of the point just made about information decisions, nobody was quite sure how many working mothers there were, and what proportion of them were full- or part-time). On the basis of 10 per cent sample Census tables, this is estimated to have jumped from 11.5 per cent in 1961 to 18.7 per cent in 1971.[39] Probably the bulk of this was part-time; in the mid-sixties Plowden estimated on the basis of existing studies that 'at least five per cent of mothers with children between three and five work full-time'.[40]

Working or would-be working mothers did not actively demand more publicly provided or subsidized child daycare. For practical childcare assistance they resorted to friends, relatives, nannies and childminders, and private nurseries. In the 1960s the numbers both of registered childminders and of private nurseries soared. Waiting-list numbers grew: according to the DHSS, the number of children regarded as priority cases on waiting lists of local authority day nurseries in England and Wales in 1973 was 9,899.[41] Again, the real extent of working mother's childcare needs will be considered in Chapter 5. But the point being made here is that although the increase in the number of working

---

[39] Tizard *et al.*, *All Our Children*, 124.
[40] Central Advisory Council for Education (Plowden), *Children and their Primary Schools* (London: HMSO, 1967), 127.
[41] Figure cited in Tizard *et al.*, *All Our Children*, 101.

mothers underlay issues that came to be of public concern, the direct question of their need for child daycare still ultimately failed to present itself as a legitimate 'problem' requiring a policy response.

I say 'ultimately' advisedly, for there is newly available evidence that in the early sixties officials in the Department of Health responsible for daycare policy were increasingly aware, as they had not been before, of pressures, or potential pressures, on them to revise their policy in light of the needs of working mothers. Indeed, in many of the internal communications at this time there is almost a sense of 'firefighting'. In 1962 the first internal review of daycare policy since the 1945 Circular was mounted, largely in anticipation of the need to explain and defend it to outside groups and other Departments. Partly as a means of conciliating the unions, the new Conservative government seemed to be conceding the case for some economic planning, as symbolized in the setting up of the National Economic Development Corporation in 1961. Ensuing surveys pointed to married women as the chief remaining untapped labour force in the country. To the extent that an insufficiency of daycare facilities was seen to be restraining married women with children from taking up paid employment, the fear was that the Department of Health would be expected to come up with the answer. The review did incidentally accept there might be a case for some extra provision to cater for 'expanded priority classes', within the definition of priority laid down by the 1945 Circular, a judgement that was later incorporated in the Seebohm Report, as we shall see. But it was anxious to conclude simultaneously, if rather contradictorily, that working mothers' childcare needs did not really present a problem, since they could be adequately catered for through private arrangements, that mothers of children under two years of age should not be working, and that, *if* more local authority daycare provision for working mothers was needed, it was down to the Ministry of Labour to take the initiative.[42]

A revealing internal discussion took place at this point about whether the Department of Health, under the relevant Section 22 of the 1946 National Health Service Act, *could* legally expand day nurseries to cater for working mothers. The view was expressed that it would be easier for the Department if such a step was not within its powers. Upon being advised by their legal consultant that this would indeed be *intra vires*, since the Act required them to care for the child irrespective of why the child was not being looked after by its mother, the comment was made that they should not encourage such an interpretation of their

---

[42] DoH early draft of internal review of daycare, 'Day Care of Children under Five Years Old', 1962–3; see PRO MH 156 51.

powers.[43] This discussion illustrates the extent of officials' apprehension and their determination to resist any attempt to foist responsibility for working mothers' childcare needs on their Department.

Pressure continued as the Ministry of Labour—prompted both by an inquiry from the TUC General Secretary following a resolution of the TUC Women's Conference, and by the advice of its own newly established Manpower Research Unit—asked the Department of Health if further consideration could be given to the issue. It soon became clear, however, that the Ministry of Labour was not proposing to do anything itself. A report commissioned from its own 'Regional Controllers' was reassuring: the majority view was that the absence of childcare facilities had little effect on the availability of married women for employment.[44] Eventually the Ministry of Labour replied to the TUC that 'The provision of child-care facilities is of course a matter for the Ministry of Health and the Department of Education and Science', supplying an account of existing daycare provision almost entirely compiled by the other two Departments.[45] The issue briefly subsided, partly because when the 1961 Census figures finally emerged they indicated that fewer mothers of young children were in paid employment than had been suspected. A little later, as the Plowden Committee was established (see below), we find one Department of Health official contemplating as a possible solution that local education authorities should accept full responsibility for the care of children.[46]

What this all indicates is that already by the early 1960s the childcare needs of working mothers *were* beginning to be articulated and were perceived as a potential issue by policy-makers, who however generally sought ways of denying or deflecting it. That is, the childcare issue posed in terms of the needs of working mothers at this time provides a very good example of 'non-decision-making', the decision not to recognize an issue requiring decision. What it also incidentally illustrates all too well is the consequences of the fragmentation of the institutional matrix within which childcare issues were resolved. The main concern of all three Ministries involved—Health, Labour, and Education and Science—was to ensure that responsibility for such childcare provision should not devolve to them. Finally, we see here on a small and transi-

---

[43] Internal correspondence relating to daycare review, ca. 1963, PRO MH 156 51.

[44] Information from Regional Controllers of the Ministry of Labour, Apr. 1964, PRO MH 156 51.

[45] Letter to George Woodcock, General Secretary of the TUC, from the Ministry of Labour, *c.* 1962, PRO MH 156 51.

[46] Mr Mayston commenting on Miss Boys's draft of second policy review, 19 Jan. 1965, PRO MH 156 30.

tory scale what was much more apparent in the two world wars and would emerge again in the late 1980s, that the needs of working mothers have had the most chance of being taken seriously when linked to arguments about anticipated labour shortages.

CHILDCARE AS A SOCIAL PROBLEM

To return to childcare as a social problem, the social changes stimulating policy change, such as it was, in the field of child daycare and of nursery education were not, of course, discrete but interconnected. The 'rediscovery of poverty' influenced the policy process in both the education and welfare fields. At the present juncture, however, exposition will be clearer if the two policy fields are kept apart.

If there was continuing reluctance to acknowledge the needs of working mothers as a policy issue in itself, working mothers were still seen as one social trend amongst several together creating increased problems for the care of young children. That is, a somewhat heightened consciousness of child daycare as a potential issue was itself the result of a long-standing concern with child protection and welfare responding to changing social circumstances. This was especially clear in the case of childminding, which was increasingly a subject of concern. The 1948 Nurseries and Childminding Regulation Act had been prompted by the specific tragic case of children being burned to death whilst in the care of a childminder when an oil-heater overturned.[47] It required that anyone looking after someone else's pre-school child must register with the local authority if the child was not a relative and if a money transaction was involved. The system of registration was meant to enable local health departments to ensure minimum standards of childcare. However, even monitoring registered childminders was not necessarily easy for local authorities and it was widely accepted that unregistered childminders might account for at least as many children.

As a result of concerns expressed in particular by representatives of the Health Visitors' Association, the Department of Health consulted eleven Medical Officers of Health based in areas where childminding was concentrated as to their personal appraisal of the working of the 1948 Act. The replies were interesting and it is certainly the case that experiences were mixed. Nicest of all was the comment from the

---

[47] Angela Coulter, *Who Minds about the Minders?* (London: Low Pay Unit, 1979), citing R. I. Mawty, 'Childminding and Social Change', *Social Services Quarterly*, 48:(1974).

Blackburn MOH—'In cotton towns I think children are born to be minded'. However, several responses detailed cases of alarming neglect, overcrowding, and safety risk. The most extended and graphic came from Birmingham. The internal Departmental report on this inquiry concluded that five of the eleven had found the present legislation to be adequate, implying that six had not.[48] But in a memo from one health official to another, a few months on, the emphasis was on playing down the gravity of the findings, by depicting this as a problem largely confined to immigrant communities.[49] None the less the legislation was slightly strengthened in 1968, recommending that a childminder should not normally look after more than a total of three children under 5, including their own.

At the same time as working mothers were seeking child daycare, other aspects of social change, including increased geographic mobility, urban redevelopment, the social isolation associated with living in the new high-rise blocks, and greater car use, posed new problems for home-based mothers seeking to provide their children with adequate care and play opportunities. Alarmed at the implications of these 'modern times' for young children's social and emotional development, representatives of around thirty organizations met at the behest of the National Society of Children's Nurseries in October 1964 to consider joint action. The meeting set up a working party whose report, *0–5: A Report on the Care of Pre-school Children*, authored by Simon Yudkin, and constituted one of the earliest attempts outside government circles to collect and synthesize information relevant to this emerging issue.[50]

In time some of the more middle-class, home-based mothers did take steps to help themselves. The first playgroup movement had emerged in New Zealand, but a British playgroup movement was launched in 1960. By 1965 there were 500 such groups and by 1972 there were 15,266 in England alone.[51] Playgroups were subsequently criticized for catering predominantly for middle-class areas, although there were exceptions. From the standpoint of day-long childcare, too, the playgroups were decidedly a mixed blessing, since they typically offered half-day sessions and only for two or three days of the week. However, the playgroup movement helped to raise the profile of the childcare question by pointing to the needs of children that could not be met at home.

A third aspect of social change already beginning to emerge and to

---

[48] Internal Department report on childminding, PRO MH 156 87.

[49] Ibid. A second file on this broad question of childminding is closed for 100 years!

[50] Simon Yudkin, *0–5: A Report on the Care of Pre-school Children* (London: National Society of Children's Nurseries, 1967).

[51] Tizard *et al.*, *All Our Children*, 78.

be recognized by officialdom by the later sixties, though by no means with the urgency of more recent years, was the growth in single parenthood. The Committee appointed to review this question in 1969 noted in its report, five years later, that such families included over one million children. In addition to the long-standing organization, now known as the National Council for One Parent Families (NCOPF), two new self-help groups were established to serve this constituency, Gingerbread and Mothers in Action. For single parents, the great majority of whom were mothers, the problem of childcare was particularly acute; so, for example, a deputation from the NCOPF raised the issue of childcare with the Department of Health in 1965[52] while in 1968 Mothers in Action organized a letter-writing campaign to protest against the shortage of day nursery places.

These developments coincided with a reorganization of local government social service provision. The report of the Seebohm Committee in 1968 reflected to a considerable degree the victory and embodiment of a belief, developing since the early 1960s, in the importance of case-based social work, aimed at preventing the breakdown of families 'at risk'. The new social service departments it set up were meant to bring together the different sets of professionals involved in this work, whose numbers and 'clout' had been steadily growing, in order to provide 'an effective family service'.[53] In 1968 the Ministry of Health reiterated its long-established position that 'wherever possible the younger child should be at home with the mother ... because early and prolonged separation from the mother is detrimental to the child' and identified the following priority groups for publicly funded childcare: 'lone parents who have no option but to go out to work', and children whose mothers were ill or 'incapable of giving young children the care they need' or for whom 'day care might prevent the breakdown of the mother or the break-up of the family'.[54] And yet despite this commitment to shoring up the 'normal' family in which the mother looked after young children herself, Seebohm did call for some expansion in local authority daycare provision simply to supply these priority needs.

When the Finer Committee reported on one-parent families in 1974, it still stressed that most young children's 'social and emotional needs are best met if the periods they spend away from their mothers are

---

[52] PRO MH 156 30. At that time the NCOPF was known as the National Council for the Unmarried Mother and Her Child.

[53] Committee on Local Authority and Allied Social Services (Seerbohm), *Report of the Committee* (London: HMSO, 1968).

[54] MoH Circular 37/68, cited in Tizard *et al.*, *All Our Children*, 86–7.

short rather than long', ideally half a day rather than a full day.[55] But it also referred to more than sixty submissions it had received 'demonstrating an overwhelming desire among many lone parents and the organizations representing their interests for the expansion of day-nursery provision by local authorities'[56] and declared 'We have no doubt whatever that there is urgent need for considerable expansion' in such services.[57]

NURSERY EDUCATION, PLOWDEN, AND THE 'POVERTY LOBBY'

As already stressed, I do not mean to suggest that what I shall refer to as the 'poverty lobby' had no impact on the findings of Seebohm and Finer. On the contrary, the Finer Committee, in particular, was set up to investigate a section of society, lone-parent families, in which poverty was thought to be concentrated. The so-called 'rediscovery of poverty' has been well analysed by Banting.[58]

He argues that throughout the 1950s the dominant assumption was that the post-war welfare state had largely eradicated family poverty. The central figures in its 'rediscovery' were left-wing social scientists, led by Richard Titmuss, who was appointed Professor of Social Administration at the London School of Economics in 1950. In challenging the general complacency, they gathered relevant data and argued for a new and higher official poverty line. When it became clear that their informal links with the Labour Party were insufficient to secure action, they launched the Child Poverty Action Group (CPAG) in December 1965. Despite its limited resources, through its expertise and skilful use both of the media and of the emotional connotations of child poverty, CPAG succeeded in greatly raising consciousness of the issue both in the ruling Labour Party and in the Conservative opposition.

Banting is careful to stress the limitations of this conversion. Even within the Labour Party, 'While concern about poverty was widespread, . . . its intensity should not be overstated'.[59] McCarthy likewise points out how in the run-up to the 1964 General Election social reform gave way to economic growth and technological progress as party leadership

[55] Committee on One-Parent Families (Finer), *Report of the Committee* (London: HMSO, 1974), 466.

[56] Ibid. 454.   [57] Ibid. 462.

[58] K. Banting, *Poverty, Politics and Policy* (London: Macmillan, 1979).

[59] Ibid. 75.

priorities.[60] According to Banting, civil servants were more sceptical and trade unions endorsed measures to combat family poverty but did little more actively to promote them, while the general public's sympathy for the poor either was, or was certainly perceived to be, far from unqualified. The rediscovery of poverty nevertheless had implications for policies relating to children.

Under the terms of the 1944 Education Act, the Minister of Education was required periodically to set up a Central Advisory Council, whose members included professional educators and academics, to examine areas of policy. Such a council was appointed in 1963, with Lady Plowden as Chair, to consider primary education, which had not been the subject of a systematic review since 1931. Its deliberations were soon influenced by the new concern with poverty and more specifically by a succession of studies demonstrating that despite the educational reforms of 1944, working-class children continued to be disadvantaged within the educational system. Somewhat paradoxically, these discussions also reflected a shift in professional thinking away from an emphasis on inherited genetic differences towards a recognition of the impact of environmental factors: to quote Banting, 'The 1960s saw the high-water mark of the environmental perspective and of faith in the capacity of education to change society'.[61] David Donnison, a social scientist serving on the Plowden Committee, declared, 'Education is one of the most powerful agents in the field of human change'.[62] If education had failed working-class children, then it was also identified as the way to put things right. Within this perspective nursery education assumed a special importance. In addition, at this point, its advocates were able to cite the impact of America's 'Head Start' programme of pre-school education, launched on a massive scale as part of President Johnson's War on Poverty. Although later evaluations of Head Start were more critical, to begin with it appeared to meet with considerable success and impressed in particular another eminent social scientist on the Committee, Michael Young.

The Plowden Report noted the high degree of consensus amongst 'informed observers', including local authority and teachers' associations, that nursery education was in principle desirable. The Committee saw a general need in part as a consequence of the new constraints—smaller families, less contact with members of the 'extended' family, high-rise accommodation, mothers at work—produced by 'modern life'. The issue was not *whether* under-fives should be educated, 'because that

[60] Michael McCarthy, *The Politics of Welfare* (London: Croom-Helm, 1986), 38–40.
[61] Banting, *Poverty, Politics and Policy*, 114.   [62] Ibid. 115.

is happening anyway', but *how*. There were further, more specific arguments stemming from the special needs of children from 'deprived or inadequate home backgrounds'.

Plowden's recommendations were significant both for their positive endorsement of nursery education and for their conservative response to working mothers. Nursery education should be available for all children, aged 3 to 5, whose parents demanded it, though this should in general be part-time. A minority of around 15 per cent of children, with special needs, should however attend full time. In elaborating on the provision of full-time nursery places, the Committee worried whether this might tempt women away from their maternal responsibilities. Admittedly some mothers had no choice but to seek paid employment: 'But some mothers who are not obliged to work may work full-time, regardless of their children's welfare. *It is no business of the educational service to encourage these mothers to do so*' (italics mine).[63]

Plowden was significant too in the effort it made to think through the practical implications of its policy prescriptions. It recognized that changes would have to be implemented at a realistic pace, should not be at the expense of existing standards in primary schools, and in particular should not divert teachers away from the primary school sector. But it also reflected a growing acknowledgement of the need to integrate educational and care elements of under-fives provision. In this context, it made the quite innovatory suggestion that nursery centres, providing part-time nursery education, be combined with day nurseries in 'children's centres', thus facilitating an educational component in the provision for older day nursery children.

I have stressed that Plowden recognized the case for nursery education for all—or most—children. However, its policy impact, at least in the short run, was rather different. In keeping with the new emphasis on poverty, the Report as a whole had given 'absolute priority' to the concept of Educational Priority Areas (EPAs), in the most deprived urban locations, where educational resources should be concentrated. In the event, and especially following heightened concern about racial discrimination triggered by Enoch Powell's speeches in April 1968, the expansion of nursery education was largely restricted to the new EPAs. The implicit DES argument otherwise was that 'basic' educational needs, that is expanding school provision to cope with growing school numbers, took precedence.

Still, the intellectual arguments about the intrinsic value of nursery education were taking hold. The Campaign for Nursery Education,

[63] Central Advisory Council for Education (Plowden), *Children and their Primary Schools* (London: HMSO, 1967), i. 127.

founded in 1965, enjoyed significant public support. Middle-class parents, in particular, took up the cause. Both Blackstone and Tizard *et al.* comment on the importance of this middle-class pressure in getting some kind of steam behind the nursery education issue.[64] In the longer run, therefore, the (now Conservative) government appeared to accept the broader Plowden argument about universal nursery education. The DES White Paper, *The State of Nursery Education: A Framework for Expansion*, issued in 1972 while Mrs Thatcher was Minister, generally endorsed Plowden and announced a major initiative to expand nursery education to meet the requirements of all 3- and 4-year-olds by 1982.

To summarize this account of policy developments from the mid-sixties, there was then a growing recognition of the need to expand nursery education (albeit part-time education) on the one hand and child daycare provision (albeit still with its welfare connotation) on the other. There was moreover increasing acceptance of the necessity for greater integration of educational and care aspects, both at local level in terms of service delivery and in the national policy process. Following Plowden's suggestion, seven experimental 'combined nursery centres' were established with the help of Urban Aid grants, in 1973–4, and were carefully monitored and evaluated. Also, from 1971 a Consultative Group on Provision for Under-5s, including representatives of both the DES and DHSS, began to meet on a quarterly basis. In the wake of a report by the Central Policy Review Staff (CPRS), in 1975, on the need for improved co-ordination in the making of social policy generally, the CPRS was specifically commissioned to report on services for children of working mothers. The report was not produced until 1978, by which time, as we shall see, existing provision was being hit by policies of economic retrenchment. None the less it still recommended expansion of services and was particularly concerned to improve co-ordination centrally and locally. At national level, it proposed a joint unit, under a Minister of State attached both to the DES and DHSS, to oversee policies and expenditure for young children.[65]

BEGINNINGS OF AN UNDER-FIVES LOBBY?

Originating in the 1960s and strengthening in the 1970s, what could be described as an embryonic under-fives lobby was forming. It was diverse,

---

[64] Blackstone, *A Fair Start*, 150; Tizard *et al.*, *All Our Children*, 59.
[65] Central Policy Review Staff, *Services for Young Children with Working Mothers* (London: HMSO, 1978).

organizationally fragmented, and lacking in political clout, but still it represented a further stage in the development of British childcare politics. The modest policy changes related above may well have indirectly contributed to its emergence, to the extent that they focused official and professional attention, helped to expose and publicize what were seen as the underlying problems and issues, and stimulated the commissioning of new research. Thus David, noting the spate of research publications during the late seventies, described the study of childcare as a 'major growth industry in social policy'. This included six volumes produced by the Oxford Pre-school Research Group, established in the early seventies under the joint sponsorship of the DES and the Social Science Research Council.[66]

But once again these more 'top-down' policy shifts interacted with the effects of wider social change. Amongst these were the continuing growth in mothers' paid employment—the percentage of children aged 0–4 with working mothers rose from 16 per cent in 1971 to an estimated 24 per cent by 1976[67]—and the impact of the so-called 'new' social movements, in particular of a revitalized and radicalized feminist movement.

From the early seventies, a small but articulate group of academics and researchers began to advocate a more 'holistic' approach to childcare. We have already noted the expansion, especially following the 1948 Children Act, of the child-centred professions, and at the same time the powerful influence exercised over them by the 'maternal deprivation' thesis. Increasingly, however, this thesis was challenged by new psychological research findings, which at the least made it easier to adopt a more agnostic stand on the question, even if, as we have seen, this took some time to filter through to policy-making circles.[68] One of the new childcare advocates was Jack Tizard, who took the criticisms of Bowlby's arguments on board, accepted also that many women would either want, or have, to go out to work, and concentrated on devising the best form of under-fives provision. Tizard's earlier work had concerned residential care and mentally subnormal children. Under the influence of the libertarian ideas that had become popular in student circles in the sixties, he was highly critical of 'institutions' and advocated community-based, integrated, early-years services. He was instrumental in obtaining funding from the Department of Health to set up the Thomas Coram

[66] Miriam David, 'Day Care Policies and Parenting', *Journal of Social Policy*, 11:1 (1982), 81.

[67] See CPRS, *Services for Young Children with Working Mothers*, 40.

[68] This reappraisal is summarized in Michael Rutter, *Maternal Deprivation Reassessed* (London: Penguin Books, 1972).

Unit in 1974, and under its auspices established two 'model' centres. His wife describes him as a 'visionary': 'He fought for the principle that these Centres, like schools, should be open to all in the neighbourhood and free of charge'.[69] Tizard in turn influenced the thinking of people around him, a number of whom continued to champion the childcare cause after his death and from different institutional bases, for instance Peter Moss.[70]

In the late sixties and seventies voluntary organizations concerned in one way or another with young children multiplied. The Voluntary Organization Liaison Council for Under Fives (VOLCUF), an umbrella group for over thirty such organizations, was established in 1975–6, largely on the initiative of Lady Plowden, whose experience as the Chair of the Plowden Committee had convinced her of the importance of this field. Its affiliates ranged from old charities like the Salvation Army and the NSPCC to new groups like MIND; more squarely within the child-care domain, they included the National Children's Bureau (NCB), set up in 1963 'to identify and promote the interests of all children and young people', and the National Campaign for Nursery Education, as well as organizations concerned with childminders and the Pre-school Playgroups Association. The diversity of its membership inevitably meant a motley collection of competing interests and perspectives. What the different groups were able to unite around was the need for a *national policy* for under-fives, and for much more effective co-ordination of existing service provision.

Demand for fuller integration of under-fives services was also coming from some of the local authorities through their collective associations. In 1976 the Association of County Councils (ACC) and the Association of Municipal Authorities (AMA) formed a joint working party on under-fives provision, noting that this was partly in response to requests from individual local departments. Reporting in 1977, this working party, which incidentally drew extensively on advice from VOLCUF, criticized government for the inadequacy of its information on costs and other aspects of under-fives provision but above all inveighed against the 'failure of the DES and DHSS hitherto to work together in the interests of young children'. It strongly implied that the inter-ministerial Consultative Committee, referred to above, had been ineffective, and pointed to a lack of co-ordination, including separate and inconsistent capital programming.[71]

---

[69] As described by his wife, Barbara Tizard, 'Introduction', in P. Moss and E. Melhuish (eds.), *Current Issues in Day Care for Young Children* (London: HMSO, 1991), 3.

[70] Subsequently Senior Research Officer at the Thomas Coram Research Institute.

[71] Association of County Councils and Association of Metropolitan Authorities, *Under Fives* (London: Oyez Press, 1977), 11.

While these various organizations shared a common concern with
under-fives provision, they were by no means in agreement as to either
its primary rationale—why it was needed—or the form it should take.
Tizard and his colleagues took seriously the needs of working mothers;
within VOLCUF, however, no such consensus prevailed. One of the
most outspoken opponents of such a view was Mia Kellmer Pringle, the
Director of the NCB. She claimed to be speaking only for herself—but
the fact that she was the sole NCB representative made that claim somewhat disingenuous—when at the Sunningdale conference, discussed
below, she argued against full-time daycare. She declared that 'the care
of young children is too important and too arduous to be considered a
part-time occupation'. For Pringle, the answer was to provide mothers
with the right kind of recognition and financial support. Once this was
available,

then to bring children into the world without one parent being willing to
devote at least three years to their fulltime care, should come to be regarded
as selfish indulgence. After all, women themselves now have the choice to
remain childless or to have a career interrupted by a few years . . . Just as
for too long children have been used as pawns by parents fighting for their
custody in divorce proceedings, so there is a danger now that children are being
made pawns in the quest for economic prosperity and in the battle for women's
liberation.[72]

Partly related to differing attitudes to working mothers, there were
different evaluations of the usefulness of playgroups. For those who
remained at best ambivalent about mothers of young children going out
to work and whose main concern was for child development and helping
mothers to care for their children themselves, playgroups could be
ascribed a central role, whereas for Jack Tizard and his colleagues their
contribution to the need for daycare could only be marginal. Another
area of disagreement was childminding. The research of Yudkin (mentioned above) and others had highlighted deficiencies in the existing,
only minimally regulated system of childminding. Although there was
increasing recognition that childminders were often paid only a pittance,
for a time the tendency was to blame childminders for the inadequacy
of their childcare provision. Subsequently an alternative view, more
sympathetic to the situation of childminders, began to emerge with the
publication of a study of childminding in ethnic minority communities[73]

---

[72] Mia Kellmer Pringle, 'A Policy for Young Children', in DHSS and DES, *Low Cost Day Provision for the Under Fives* (London: DHSS, 1976), 28.
[73] Community Relations Council, *Who Minds? A Study of Working Mothers and Child-minding in Ethnic Minority Communities* (London: Community Relations Council, 1975).

and as NUPE, the public employees' union, took up the childminders' cause. The National Childminding Association, established in 1977, pledged both to promote daycare facilities and to 'encourage the recognition of childminding as a positive part of the provision'.[74]

If the needs of working mothers figured only patchily in arguments deployed by the groups cited so far, they were of course much more categorically central to the revitalized feminist movement. The Women's Liberation Movement was gathering momentum from the late 1960s and from the start identified childcare as, in principle, a central issue: one of the four Movement 'demands' formulated at its first Conference at Oxford in 1970 was for '24 hours childcare'. Early socialist feminist journals took up the question of childcare and feminists were involved in a number of local childcare initiatives, especially in London, where they combined to form the London Nursery Campaign. Socialist feminists also helped to promote the Working Women's Charter, which included the demand for childcare, within the trade unions. But for reasons that are explored more fully in Chapter 5, a significant and direct feminist input into national childcare policy-making was slow to materialize. The first explicitly feminist national organization, the National Childcare Campaign (NCC), was not founded until 1980.

That is not to say that the resurgence of feminist politics had no impact. Apart from the specific initiatives mentioned, feminism was firstly of great relevance in a more diffuse and ambient sense. 'Women's Liberation' did not develop in a vacuum. As is well known, it grew out of the student radicalism of the sixties and was part of a fairly comprehensive critique of conventional social and political understandings. This critique, which fed into the 'new social movements' and a range of single-issue campaigns, was soon also setting trends in the media, in academia, and professions like social work and teaching. By the early seventies the notion of sex equality and a more critical attitude to power relations within the family were seeping into public consciousness, raising expectations and helping to legitimate further demands.

Feminist pressures also contributed, though they were not necessarily the decisive factor, to the equal opportunities legislation enacted in 1970 and 1975. This was focused on equal pay and sex discrimination within employment and did not directly address the question of childcare. However, it helped to set in motion a drive to make equal opportunities more meaningful, or what Cockburn[75] has described as the

---

[74] Cited in Coulter, *Who Minds about the Minders?*.
[75] Cynthia Cockburn, 'Equal Opportunities: The Short and Long Agenda', *Industrial Relations Journal* (1989), 213–25.

expansion from a short-term to a long-term equal opportunities agenda.
In it the importance of childcare was recognized, through creating the
sustaining institutional infrastructure, notably the Equal Opportunities
Commission (EOC), set up in 1975, and through providing the context
in which feminist trade unionists, lawyers, and others acquired experience of trying to make equal opportunities work. Already in 1978 the
EOC commissioned three 'background papers' and was arguing for full-
time daycare, provided in a flexible range of forms and at reasonable
cost to assist working mothers, noting that 'The Commission's concern
with day care arises out of its recognition that although recent legislation designed to eliminate discrimination against women in education and employment is an important first step towards equality,
legislation needs to be accompanied by complementary changes in
social policy'.[76]

DAYCARE AND THE UNIONS

The impact of feminism also played a considerable part in the gradual
shift of trade union attitudes. The trade unions, or at least the TUC, were
as instrumental as the women's movement, if not more so, in securing
the equal opportunities legislation and in the seventies this body,
together with a number of important member organizations, finally
came round to supporting the demand for substantially expanded and
improved child daycare provision.

   As we have seen there was little trade union support on this question
through the fifties. A TUC Resolution in 1947 had urged increased day
nursery provision for priority cases, including widowed mothers, unmarried mothers, and deserted wives, '*while welcoming the Minister of
Labour's statement that mothers of young children should not be encouraged to go into industry*' (my italics).[77] To this argument against expanding public childcare provision for working mothers were added, in 1953,
references to the prohibitive cost—'the economics of day nurseries have
gone completely haywire'—and the observation that it was 'unfair to
ask the one-wage family [for which it is surely reasonable to read 'the
male breadwinner family'] to subsidise a two-wage family'.[78] This
approach persisted into the sixties.

   In seeking to explain the prevalence of these views, one obvious

[76] EOC, *I Want to Work . . . but What about the Kids?* (Manchester: EOC, 1978), 5.
[77] Trades Union Congress, *1947 TUC Report*, 105.
[78] Trades Union Congress, *1953 TUC Report*, 370–1.

consideration is the predominance of men in the trade unions. Although during the 1960s women were the single largest source of new trade union membership, they remained drastically underrepresented in leadership positions. Indeed as late as 1983, of 1,600 permanent trade union officials, only 90 were women.[79] Women tended to be concentrated in certain unions and almost absent from others, but even where they constituted a majority of union membership this was by no means reflected in leadership composition. In 1980 there was still only one female General Secretary of an affiliated TUC union, and that was in the Health Visitors' Association, with 99 per cent female membership.[80]

However, this is not simply a matter of women's underrepresentation. As noted earlier, while the advisory TUC Women's Conference regularly demanded expanded day nursery provision, the terms in which it did so began to shift soon after the war ended. Whereas initially there was an emphasis on the value of nurseries both to enable women workers to remain in industrial employment and as a community service to help all mothers, by 1948 day nurseries were justified more exclusively in terms of the current government drive to recruit more married workers to specific sectors of industry. As Riley notes, there was a growing tendency to restrict the argument for nurseries to 'adjuncts of production',[81] meaning that where no real 'need' for women's labour could be demonstrated the case for nurseries was dispensed with. Strikingly, on the few occasions when the issue was debated by the TUC, participants on both sides of the debate were mostly women. Though this suggests in part a kind of manipulative disdain on the part of the male leadership—these were women's issues and it would also look better if women themselves voiced the official line—it also shows that many women trade unionists accepted the official view themselves. Individual organizations like the Women's Public Health Officers' Association and the Health Visitors' Association, on the other hand, though intensely concerned for the needs of pre-school children, were especially reluctant to condone their mothers going out to work.

In accounting for British trade unionism's long-standing failure to champion the needs of working mothers, Ruggie places much emphasis upon its strong traditional commitment to free collective bargaining, that is the determination of employment policy through a process of

[79] Marion Shaw, 'The 53rd Women's TUC Congress', in Joy Holland (ed.), *Feminist Action 1* (London: Battle Axe, 1984), 66.
[80] Anne Gibson, 'Women in the Trade Unions: Present and Future Policy on Equal Opportunities', paper presented to the Political Studies Association Women's Group Conference, Bedford College, London, 1980, 8.
[81] Riley, *War in the Nursery*, 136.

bargaining and negotiation between the two sides of industry. As Ruggie writes, in Britain free collective bargaining has been 'sacrosant';[82] intervention by government and the law has been resented and mistrusted. Given the preoccupation with collective bargaining, during the 1960s trade union political energies were largely concentrated on reacting to the attempts to impose prices and incomes policies, first by Conservative and then by Labour governments. However, although such a predisposition undoubtedly helps to explain unions' more general resistance to extensive involvement in the making of social policy in this era, it is not really required to account for their relative silence on the daycare issue. And as we have seen, such inhibitions did not prevent the TUC remonstrating with government on the question of nursery education.

By the 1970s the union stance on child daycare was beginning to change. The numbers of working women and of women in unions continued to grow, as, more slowly, did their representation in leadership positions. Within the unions feminists and feminist ideas were increasingly in evidence. The TUC had long supported the principle of equal pay, originally in order to prevent women undercutting male wage levels and latterly with an eye to ILO and EEC membership requirements. The Equal Pay Act was widely understood to be meaningful only if it implied the need for further legislation against sex discrimination in employment and education. In 1972 the Women's Conference produced its own report on *The Roots of Inequality*. In 1963, at the Women's Conference's behest, the TUC had adopted a six-point Industrial Charter for Women Workers, and with the UN's nomination of 1975 as International Women's Year, the Women's Conference now urged the TUC to update the Charter to include amongst other things the need for expanded child daycare provision. At the same time the Working Women's Charter, referred to above, which had been introduced in the more radical forum of the old London Trades Council and was being taken up by a number of unions, also called for improved childcare. An interesting argument developed at the 1975 TUC Congress about the relationship between these two charters. The General Council clearly deeply mistrusted the Working Women's Charter and it was eventually defeated, but in the process it had to argue that its own Charter's provisions made the other's unnecessary.

In 1976 the General Council established a working party on facilities

---

[82] Mary Ruggie, 'Workers' Movements and Women's Interests: The Impact of Labor–State Relations in Britain and Sweden', in M. F. Katzenstein and C. Mueller (eds.), *The Women's Movements of the US and W Europe* (Philadelphia: Temple University Press, 1987), 250.

for the under-fives, which reported the following year. The TUC endorsed its four principles—to end the distinction between children's educational and welfare needs, to ensure that pre-school services have flexible hours to meet the range of parents' needs, to make them open access, and to make them free. The report acknowledged the growth of women's rights at work and argued that these would be seriously undermined without significant improvements in childcare. In the preface to the TUC Charter that embodied these recommendations, the argument was no longer that mothers of young children should stay at home but that they should be given the choice.[83]

Of course, while these significant, if still quite low-key, shifts were occurring in the national decision-making forum, they constituted demands on government rather than commitments from the union movement itself. Take-up of these demands by individual unions and their local branches was slow and uneven, with little interest at this stage in pressing for childcare measures within the confines of collective bargaining. In comparing the making of policies for working women in Britain and in Sweden, Ruggie emphasizes the contrast between Sweden's highly centralized and cohesive union movement, within which the summit organization, the LO, can speak with authority on behalf of its member unions, with the decentralized, almost centrifugal character of the movement in Britain. Individual unions, typically white-collar and with a large female membership, such as NALGO, whose Equal Opportunities Committee published a step-by-step negotiating guide to setting up a workplace nursery,[84] NATFHE, and NUPE, were swift to adopt the Charter and indeed had been amongst those campaigning for change. Nonetheless the gradual change in the union movement's stance, from one of obstruction and hostility towards the daycare cause to one in which officially at least it stood behind it, seemed to augur well.

RETRENCHMENT UNDER LABOUR

The under-fives lobby I have described was only beginning to emerge by the late seventies. It was fragmented and diverse, and by no means

---

[83] TUC, (Trades Union Congress) *Charter on Facilities for Under-fives* (London: TUC, 1979).

[84] See Anna Coote and Patricia Hewitt, 'The Stance of Britain's Major Parties and Interest Groups', in Peter Moss and Nickie Fonda (eds.), *Work and the Family* (London: Maurice Temple Smith, 1980), 147.

united on the question of working mothers, but it did mean that almost for the first time since the war demands were being voiced at the national policy-making level for improved childcare provision. But just as this lobby was beginning to coalesce, central government acceded to perceived external pressures to cut back on public expenditure, in the wake of the 1973–4 oil crisis.

The new government encouragement to expand day nursery and nursery education had been seized on happily by a number of local authorities. This was especially true for inner-city authorities such as Manchester, or those in inner London, eligible under the 1969 Urban Aid Programme for additional central funding for areas with 'special social need'. But these surges were localized and short-lived; the very modest overall gains of the early seventies were rapidly pared down. As early as 1974 the capital programme for local authority social services as a whole was cut by 20 per cent; a Department of Health circular doubted whether local authorities could now reach their agreed targets for expanded daycare provision by 1982.[85] Central government funding for the nursery education building programme in 1975–6 was half that of the previous year. By 1977 the DES Green Paper contained only two paragraphs on nursery education, warning that 'limitations on resources will confine further expansion of provision in the immediate future to the areas of greatest social deprivation'.[86]

In 1976 David Owen, then Minister of State for Health, presided over a conference in Sunningdale on 'Low Cost Day Provision for the Under-Fives'. The attendance list was an interesting reflection of the range of voices emerging around the under-fives issue. More revealing, however, were the low expectations of those taking part. David Owen opened the proceedings by warning that 'a daunting period of restraint in social expenditure' was imminent.[87] Nearly all those presenting working papers appeared to accept this major constraint, however regretfully, without query or protest, and to fall in with the suggestion that the solution was to expand the role played by low-cost services, especially child-minding and playgroups. The only dissenting voice was Jack Tizard's, who pressed working mothers' needs for full-time childcare of reliable quality and pointed out that 'The cuts are being justified on economic grounds; but they also reflect political priorities'.[88]

[85] Circular LASSL (74) 22, cited in Tizard *et al.*, *All Our Children*, 89.

[86] Department of Education and Science, *Education in Schools: A Consultative Document*, Cmnd. 6869 (London: HMSO, 1977), 15.

[87] David Owen, 'Foreword', in DHSS and DES, *Low Cost Day Provision for the Under-fives* (London: DHSS, 1976), 1.

[88] Jack Tizard, 'Ten Comments on Low Cost Day Care for the Under Fives', in ibid. 43.

It is important, therefore, to realize that the impact of public expenditure constraints long predated the arrival of 'Thatcherism', to be considered in the next chapter. The speed with which childcare expenditure plans were abandoned under Labour was an indication of their low priority. The difference was that under Labour cutbacks were presented as temporary and regrettable deviations from a planned increase in public provision, whilst under succeeding Conservative governments targets for expansion, not only for day nurseries but for nursery education, were abandoned and emphasis shifted from public to private or voluntary services.

In summarizing the overall implications of this chapter, it is helpful to think in terms of two main periods. In the early post-war period it seemed as though in some ways childcare was a non-issue. There was very little active pressure on government to expand daycare provision and it could seem that government policy simply reflected that state of affairs. We saw, however, that when by the mid-sixties such pressure was already being anticipated, the ministries involved and especially the Ministry of Health clearly resisted, suggesting a rather more active role in the construction of policy. It was also noteworthy that this anticipated pressure involved a possible labour shortage, illustrating how the case for daycare assistance for working mothers had always to be justified in terms of labour market requirements.

Increasingly from the mid-sixties a rather different situation emerged in which it was less and less plausible to portray government inertia simply as the passive reflection of demand. Two particular triggers in combination seemed to require a response: the steady growth in female employment, with associated unsatisfactory 'private' childcare arrangements, and a sharpening focus, to some extent the product of government's own research function, on the childhood causes of poverty. These produced a case, based not simply on the requirements of the economy (though feminist arguments still scarcely featured), for some expansion both of daycare and of nursery education, as well as a growing appreciation in theory at least of the need for greater integration of the educational and care aspects of under-fives provision. The manner of the government's response, under both Conservative and Labour administrations, and the response of many inner-city, generally Labour-controlled, local authorities, indicated the extent to which a simple characterization of the British state as 'liberal' at this stage is wide of the mark and needs qualification. Even so, this shift in policy was still quite marginal and the speed with which it was jettisoned from 1974 showed how low a priority it was accorded.

4

Childcare and Neo-liberal 'Restructuring'

What is certain is that by the time of the Conservative victory in May 1979, childcare was established as a public policy 'issue', however low down the policy agenda, and in framing the issue the needs of working mothers, though accorded low priority, were increasingly invoked. What difference did the advent of a Conservative government make to childcare policy and policy-making?

While the precise character of Thatcherism has been much debated, it clearly has to be understood in the wider context of what is often referred to as the process of welfare state 'restructuring'. Already under the Labour government there had been cutbacks in public expenditure, but as noted, these were imposed almost apologetically, and are perhaps better understood as a form of 'retrenchment'.[1] 'Restructuring' implies a more active reconfiguring of the welfare state, through such processes as privatization and deregulation. It can also be seen as in some respects a reassertion of the 'liberal' policy tradition, limiting the sphere of direct state intervention and re-emphasizing the sovereignty of the private sphere. The reframing of childcare policy has to be seen in this light.

This chapter will follow the pattern established in the previous two, in combining a broadly chronological approach with extended discussion of specific issues as required by the developing analysis. Three phases are distinguished: the period covering roughly the first two Conservative government terms in office, from 1979 to 1987–8, was characterized most of all by the minimalism of government intervention or interest, not only in child daycare but in nursery education; during the second phase, from 1988 to 1992–3, the so-called 'demographic time-bomb' galvanized unwonted activity, at least on the daycare front; third, under John Major, following a brief return to minimalism, government interest in child daycare began to re-emerge in the context of government's welfare dependency concerns, and there was a significant new

---

[1] In fact the terms 'retrenchment' and 'restructuring' are often used interchangeably and where they are distinguished there is not necessarily consistency in usage from one author to another, so that the meanings I am presenting here are not always found elsewhere.

nursery education initiative, both of these developments evincing a noticeable shift from supply- to demand-side approaches to provision.

THATCHERITE POLICY PARAMETERS

While it would be a mistake to view the eighteen years under Conservative rule simply as a time of regression or even stagnation in the development either of childcare policy or of the associated policy process, the first two terms, under Mrs Thatcher, were a particularly lean time for childcare developments at national level. The nature of Thatcherism has been much debated:[2] there is little agreement about its coherence, its central values, or whether and how it differed from other manifestations of the 'New Right'. Three observations are relevant to the issue in hand.

First, as an ideology and as a bundle of policies, it was a composite, combining neo-liberal economic themes with moral conservatism. Of these two, however, the neo-liberal element was generally uppermost: in many policy contexts the two did not need to clash but when they did, as over abortion, it was ultimately the liberal approach that prevailed. Attempts to emphasize the moral conservatism of Thatcherism, and specifically to depict it as an anti-feminist backlash, have not been persuasive. The problematic consequences of Thatcherism for women, and specifically in relation to childcare, resulted more from its economic assumptions than from its conservative social values.[3]

Second, it is clear, especially with hindsight, that these developments cannot be seen in isolation from economic and political trends apparent throughout the western world; Thatcherism was an early, ideologically articulate, radical, and forceful variant of a more global phenomenon, associated with the processes of economic liberalization and, as already noted, with welfare state restructuring. This is of relevance when comparing recent childcare policy developments in Britain and elsewhere.

Third, Thatcherism *did* have a policy impact. Accounts that stress its pragmatism or depict it as largely a question of leadership style greatly underestimate its ideological force. Within the literature on welfare

---

[2] For a fuller discussion of these questions, see J. Lovenduski and V. Randall, *Contemporary Feminist Politics* (Oxford: Oxford University Press, 1993), ch. 1.

[3] For an excellent analysis of the limitations of Conservative 'family policy', see Jenny Somerville, 'The New Right and Family Politics', *Economy and Society*, 21:2 (1992), 93–128.

state restructuring, there has been considerable discussion as to whether in practice state leaders have been successful in imposing their restructuring agendas. As Pierson has argued, 'retrenchment is a difficult exercise . . . Retrenchment advocates must operate on a terrain that the welfare state itself has fundamentally transformed'.[4] The growth of constituencies—clients, employees, professionals, suppliers—around the functions and institutions of the welfare state, together with the logic of political party competition, has conspired to hem politicians in. On the other hand, it is sometimes suggested that the British case, at least under Mrs Thatcher, may have been somewhat deviant. Esping-Andersen singles out Britain, together only with New Zealand, as exceptions to the general rule, through the 1980s, of welfare state adaptation through marginal adjustments.[5] Certainly it is correct to recognize the extent to which Conservative policy intentions were in different ways subverted through the process of implementation.[6] But this is not the same as saying they had no impact. To a striking degree Thatcherite government was 'strong, centralised, independent, decisive and initiatory'.[7]

The consequences of Thatcherism for the *process* of the making of childcare policy are discussed in a later section. What of its implications for the direction of policy? It is perhaps interesting to note that the views expressed by Mrs Thatcher herself on the question of childcare were not consistent over time. In the 1950s, not so long after the birth of her twins, she wrote about how exhausting and demoralizing it could be to look after two young children day and night: 'From my own experience I feel there is much to be said for being away from the family for

---

[4] Paul Pierson, *Dismantling the Welfare State?* (Cambridge: Cambridge University Press, 1994), 1–2. In this case Pierson is using the term 'retrenchment' in a broader sense than mine.

[5] See Gøsta Esping-Andersen, 'After, 10. the Golden Age?', in G. Esping-Andersen (ed.), *Welfare States in Transition* (London: Sage, 1996), 10. Although he goes on to question how far they really made a difference, Pierson also points out the particular advantages possessed by the Thatcher government in pursuing retrenchment policies—concentration of power in the executive, severe splits in the Labour Party, and a union movement weakened both by constricting legislation and the effects of rising unemployment. See Pierson, *Dismantling the Welfare State?*, 7. On the other hand, several commentators have argued that in practice, even in Britain, restructuring has been heavily constrained. For instance Taylor-Gooby has characterized the thrust of Conservative rule as tending towards 'a stricter delineation rather than a rolling back of the welfare state'. See Peter Taylor-Gooby, 'The United Kingdom: Radical Departures and Political Consensus', in Vic George and Peter Taylor-Gooby (eds.), *European Welfare Policy* (London: Macmillan, 1996), 112.

[6] See D. Marsh and R. Rhodes (eds.), *Implementing Thatcherite Policies: Audit of an Era* (Buckingham: Open University Press, 1992).

[7] D. Marsh and T. Tant, *There Is No Alternative: Mrs Thatcher and the British Political Tradition*, Essex Papers in Politics and Government, No. 69 (Colchester: Department of Government, Essex University, 1989), 27.

part of the day'.[8] She was vaguer, though, on the childcare arrangements that could make such a reprieve possible, beyond suggesting that a reliable carer was needed and that a sympathetic husband, who did not insist that 'Woman's place is in the home', was a great advantage. In 1990, however, in an interview with Jenni Murray of *Woman's Hour*, she adopted a much more censorious tone, warning against the creation of a 'generation of crèche children'.[9]

A recurrent theme of this study is the location of childcare as an issue at the intersection of a number of more politically salient policy areas. One of these is family policy. To the extent that Thatcherism was characterized by moral conservatism, one might expect its family policy to reflect this. The importance of the family was a central refrain in the Conservative Party's campaign leading up to the 1979 General Election and Mrs Thatcher, Norman Tebbit, and some other leading Conservative politicians publicly attributed the social disorder manifest first in the 1981 race riots and later in football hooliganism to the breakdown of traditional family values consequent on the 'permissiveness' of the 1960s. But in the first place, it was not absolutely clear what this traditional family should look like, and in particular what the mother's place within it should be. Writing in 1990, and as critics based in the Labour-inclined Institute for Public Policy Research, Coote *et al.* claimed that the Conservatives valued the traditional family as a site not only of social but of paternal control.[10] However, instances of such a blatantly patriarchal ideology are hard to find. Second, as Somerville observes, to the extent that Conservatives were committed to the 'family', the content of that term had perforce to be left hazy because the 'family' acted as a unifying symbol for what was in fact an association of disparate ideological tendencies.[11] The different tendencies did not understand the same thing by 'the family', so it could hardly form the basis for an explicit interventionist policy, although family-based rhetoric could sometimes be employed to rationalize policies inspired by other considerations. Of course, as we shall see in Chapter 5, in different national contexts there have been radically different types of 'family policy' with varying implications for childcare; an active family policy could be supportive of or antagonistic towards publicly subsidized childcare provision. The point being made here is that

---

[8] Margaret Thatcher, written for the Conservative publication *Onward*, reprinted in the *Guardian*, 21 Mar. 1990.

[9] Reported in, *Guardian*, 21 Mar. 1990.

[10] Anna Coote, Harriet Harman, and Patricia Hewitt, *The Family Way* (London: Institute for Public Policy Research, 1990).

[11] Somerville, 'The New Right and Family Politics', 123.

Conservative conceptions of the family were not necessarily as unreconstructed as their critics claimed, but nor did they give rise to an active family policy.

More significant for childcare, therefore, was the context of economic policy-making. Although neo-liberal economic approaches can again vary widely, and as we shall see, even in the case of childcare have given rise to quite different policy prescriptions at different times, they have in common their almost religious faith in the wisdom of the market. Under Mrs Thatcher, the government position was not that it was opposed to mothers of young children going out to work but that decisions about work and childcare must be regarded as essentially private. In the words of John Patten, then a Junior Minister in the Department of Health, child daycare must be seen as 'primarily a matter of private arrangement between parents and private and voluntary resources except where there are special needs'.[12]

GOVERNMENT CHILDCARE POLICIES, 1979–1987

Under the Conservative government, the impact of the emerging childcare lobby and of the development of Whitehall thinking about childcare provision was reflected in continuing official recognition of the need for an integrated approach, for monitoring, and for the accumulation of knowledge about childcare issues. The importance of ensuring the *quality* of provision was increasingly emphasized. None the less in practice national policy-making in the childcare field remained an essentially two-track affair, centred in the daycare responsibilities of the DHSS and the nursery education concerns of the Department of Education and Science. The interdepartmental consultative group on under-fives, set up in the early seventies (see the previous chapter), largely lapsed.

Within the DHSS, and in keeping with the new political philosophy, the main practical departure was the 'Under-fives Initiative'. Bypassing local authorities to an extent, this aimed to work directly with a range of voluntary agencies engaged in providing pre-school services in one way or another. The programme, running over four years, 1983–7, entailed an eventual expenditure of £7 million. According to van der Eyken, the first intimation that potential collaborating bodies had of this was when the Secretary of State, Norman Fowler, referred to it in an

---

[12] John Patten, Commons debate, 18 Mar. 1985, cited by Bronwen Cohen and Neil Fraser, *Childcare in a Modern Welfare System* (London: Institute for Public Policy Research, 1991), 9.

adjournment debate in November 1982: at that point the sum mentioned was £20 million. The Department then approached a series of likely agencies, not all of which wanted to take part. Some later complained of a lack of clarity about the aims of the initiative, and van der Eyken observes,

It is a remarkable fact that, at no time during the whole of the Initiative, did the Department produce a single piece of paper setting out either the objectives or the parameters of the Initiative, other than through Press Releases.[13]

In the end fifteen agencies were enlisted. Some care was taken to ensure that their various projects were fairly distributed in terms of geographical spread. More pertinently for this study, only some of these schemes were concerned with full daycare as such—they received around one-fifth of total funding—and the emphasis, in keeping with the Department's traditional approach, was on helping 'disadvantaged' families. Included in this category were families with single parents or in which both parents were obliged to work, families facing stress and isolation, or families in ethnic minorities. The first Initiative was followed by a 'small grants' scheme running for three years from 1987 and involving only six agencies. A further scheme was to run from 1989 to 1992. As Edwards notes, all these schemes tended to be seen by the Department as short term and 'pump-priming', helping particular projects get up and running.[14]

In the meantime local authority child daycare provision received a boost in some cases, above all in the Greater London Council area, under a combination of 'new urban Left' political control and 'municipal feminism'. A number of authorities in London and elsewhere, for instance Manchester and Leeds, were beginning to explore ways of adding to or adapting existing provision to suit it better to the needs of working parents. But even these authorities in the longer term found themselves struggling against central government spending controls. As a result of these financial pressures, together with the total absence of a positive lead from the Department of Health, between 1980 and 1991 the overall number of local authority day nursery places actually *declined* from an already paltry 28,437 to 27,039.

Surprisingly perhaps, given Mrs Thatcher's former responsibility as Minister of Education for the 1972 education White Paper pledging expansion of nursery education, under her government it fared little

---

[13] W. van der Eyken, *The DHSS Under-fives Initiative 1983–1987: Final Report* (London: DHSS, 1987), 20.

[14] R. Edwards, *Beginnings: The Department of Health's New Under-fives Initiative 1989–1992* (London: National Children's Bureau, 1992).

better than child daycare. An early indicator was the 1980 Education Act, which made local authority responsibility for nursery education discretionary only. Rather than encouraging expansion, a 1985 White Paper stipulated that 'plans for local authority expenditure should allow provision to continue in broad terms within broadly the same total as today'.[15] Although despite this, there was some modest growth in preschool education for 3- and 4-year olds, most provision was part-time. The number of nursery schools as such declined. Many children were placed in 'reception' classes for infant schools, prompting concern amongst School Inspectors (HMIs), in particular, that the education received there could be inappropriate for their young needs.

CONTINUING EMPLOYMENT AND FAMILY TRENDS

If policy moved little, the trends in female employment and family formation which had underlain earlier demands for policy change continued unabated. Despite rising overall unemployment rates in the early eighties, the percentage of mothers of young children in the paid workforce grew dramatically from 24 in 1983 to 41 in 1989, although 70 per cent of these were working part time. This partly reflected persistent tendencies in the structure of employment—the decline of traditional manufacturing jobs, continued expansion of the service sector, 'flexibilization', employment of new technology, and expanding employer demand for part-time workers—which were to some degree 'global' in their reach and certainly evident in a range of OECD countries. But it was also facilitated by government policies which weakened institutional barriers that could have provided some check on these forces of economic change. For instance, deregulation included winding down and eventually abolishing the wages councils, which offered the lowest-paid workers some protection. The government fiercely resisted EC Directives aimed at improving the conditions of part-time workers and establishing the right to parental leave. This combination of economic and policy trends simultaneously created new incentives and opportunities for women's employment and contributed to the predominance of part-time work for mothers of young children (the implications of this prevalence of part-time work and its relationship to both childcare demand and supply are considered further in Chapter 5). By 1988, amongst EC countries only the Netherlands had a lower level of full-time employment amongst mothers of under-fives.

[15] Department of Education and Science, *Better Schools*, Cmnd. 9469 (London: HMSO, 1985).

At the same time, if less sharply, the numbers of lone mothers continued to rise. By 1989, 17 per cent of all families with dependent children were headed by a lone parent, nine-tenths of these being women. But the employment rate for lone mothers remained very low: in 1988 6 per cent of lone mothers with a child under 5 were in full-time employment—the lowest rate in the EC—and a further 12 per cent worked part time. In fact, the proportion of lone mothers in employment actually fell by 6 percentage points between 1981 and 1993–4.[16]

Available figures for childcare provision broadly reflect these demographic and employment changes but with a particular and perhaps significant further inflection. Given the continuing shortage of publicly provided daycare places, the primary area of expansion up to the mid-eighties was in childminding. Between 1975 and 1985 the (approximate) total number of places available with registered childminders in England, Scotland, and Wales increased from 87,962 to 138,832—a considerable surge. On the other hand the number of places in registered private nurseries actually fell by nearly a thousand.[17] It was in the next few years that they began to climb again. Between 1985 and 1988 childminding places increased by a further 30 per cent, while places in private and voluntary nurseries grew by around 47 per cent.[18] It is possible that this changing pattern of demand reflects the impact, both on women's childcare needs and on the amounts they could afford to pay, of the general economic recession in the early eighties and of the associated absolute, if modest, decrease in the rate of women's full-time employment from 1980, which did not resume its former level until the latter part of the decade.[19]

THE CHILDCARE LOBBY

If national policies were minimalist during this period, and if potential childcare users for whatever reason were still generally reticent in voicing childcare demands, the various elements of the 'childcare lobby' persisted in their representations; indeed the lobby continued to

[16] See B. Cohen, *Caring for Children: The 1990 Report* (London: Family Policy Studies Centre, 1990), 12–13, and the report issued by the House of Commons Employment Committee, *Mothers in Employment* (London: HMSO, 1995), vi–viii.
[17] Figures from Gillian Pugh, *Services for Under-fives: Developing a Coordinated Approach* (London: National Children's Bureau, 1988), 8.
[18] Cohen, *Caring for Children*, 18, 21.
[19] See J. Humphries and J. Rubery, 'Recession and Exploitation: British Women in a Changing Workplace, 1979–1985', in J. Jenson, E. Hagen, and C. Reddy (eds.), *Feminization of the Labour Force* (Cambridge: Polity, 1988), 85–105.

strengthen and within it arguments based on the needs of working mothers. The first national feminist childcare organization, the National Childcare Campaign (NCC), was founded in 1980. In a sense it was the culmination of more local campaigns of the 1970s. Its members included many veterans of these earlier campaigns, though others, including the convenor, Helen Penn, had a particular concern with the issue of child-minding. Although this was to change, it initially campaigned from an uncompromisingly socialist feminist position: women had the right to work full time and the state should provide the full-time, free, and collective childcare to make this possible. The NCC was one of the organizations selected to collaborate with the DHSS in the first Under-fives Initiative but this helped to precipitate a damaging split in its membership. Later, in 1986, the group set up the Daycare Trust, which had charitable status, acted as an advisory body, and employed full-time workers, leaving the NCC free for campaigning activities.

Another campaigning organization, the Working Mothers' Association, founded in 1984, embodied, as its name suggests, a rather different perspective. It grew in response to the childcare needs of a group of fairly middle-class, young mothers, initially brought into contact with one another through the agency of the National Childbirth Trust. It was not a feminist organisation as such, although its convenor, Lucy Daniels, was sympathetic to feminist arguments, and it was certainly not socialist. Rather, as Daniels herself described, it was oriented to the needs of working mothers, later parents, as 'consumers'.[20]

Besides these new players, support continued to grow in the unions (discussed more fully below) and local authorities and was beginning to appear in the national Labour Party. The Workplace Nurseries Campaign (WNC), set up in 1985 in the first instance to oppose the government's decision to activate a tax on workplace nurseries, included numerous trade unions or their branches in its membership. Closely associated with developments in the unions was the slowly growing consciousness of childcare as an issue and support for expanded provision within the Labour Party. With the flourishing of municipal feminism, local authority childcare initiatives burgeoned, with the GLC setting the pace. Many of these local authorities became laboratories of 'good practice', combining care and education in innovative ways. Though not contributing directly to national policy, they gave rise to new sets of vested interests and professional expertise to inform debate. However, and paradoxically, the ability of local authorities collectively, through their national associations, to influence central government policy was

---

[20] Interview with Lucy Daniels, 20 Mar. 1991.

waning. Already under the previous Labour government the setting up of the Consultative Council on Local Government Finance marked an attempt to shift the focus of consultation from social policy to finance, although the object was still to persuade local authorities of the government's case. But under Thatcher, local authority associations, now unequivocally regarded as 'promoters of profligacy', 'saw their special position slip away'.[21]

But feminist influences were also beginning to be felt in the formulation of national party policy. As Perrigo describes, the immediate consequence of Labour's defeat in 1979 was to strengthen the position of the Left within the party. This leftward turn, together, she suggests, with the rift opening up between the party leadership and some of its traditional trade union allies and the overall weakening of party cohesion and discipline to which this contributed, created an opportunity and space for women to build new political alliances and for the promotion of a socialist feminist agenda. Labour's 1982 Party Programme was the first official party document seriously to address women's needs, amongst which it identified radical expansion of childcare provision.[22] In 1985 the party produced its own Charter for the Under-5s.

Closing a conference on services for under-fives, in July 1988, Gillian Pugh reflected:

There is at present a very vigorous level of debate amongst those who work with and care about young children. Even those of us who feel we've been saying the same thing for 20 years, feel that the momentum is increasing. . . . I feel that the disparate elements of the under fives world have seldom been so united in what their concerns are and how we could move forward,

while observing that what was needed now was a correspondingly vigorous lead from government.[23]

THE POLICY PROCESS

The previous chapter borrowed from policy network analysis to describe the policy process surrounding childcare. But such analysis has

[21] See P. Dunleavy and R. A. W. Rhodes, 'Beyond Whitehall', in H. Drucker *et al.* (eds.), *Developments in British Politics*, 1st end. (Basingstoke: Macmillan, 1983), 128.

[22] Sarah Perrigo, 'Women and Change in the Labour Party', *Parliamentary Affairs*, 49:1 (1996), 116–29.

[23] Gillian Pugh was at this time the Director of the National Children's Bureau's 'Under-fives' Unit. See her 'Closing Remarks', in *Services for Under Fives: Developing Policy and Practice*, Report on NES/NCB Conference.

tended to emphasize the centrality of Whitehall: policy is determined through policy communities that are dominated by the central government departments. Such an approach does not deny the part played by political parties but their contribution is depicted as exogenous, coming from outside the system. In their account of policy network analysis, Rhodes and Marsh acknowledge, in a vivid phrase, that the political party, as the vehicle of ideology, can act as 'the blade for prizing apart the mollusc's shell of Whitehall and the policy networks'.[24] But the experience of Thatcherism has brought home the conceptual dangers of marginalizing political parties as institutional actors, and the effects of party ideology, in frameworks we use for policy analysis.[25] The very centralization of the British state increases the likelihood that if and when the ruling party takes a major new idea on board this will have an impact on policy.

In the previous section we saw how the childcare lobby was growing stronger in terms of its span, internal cohesion, and ideological conviction. But the sources of childcare demands—trade unions, local authorities, socialist feminists and the Labour Left, even child-centred professionals and academics—and their expectations of public funding and provision were deeply antipathetic to the Conservative leadership. Here we need briefly to elaborate what has already been implied, how concerns and organizations that were just beginning to get a toehold in the department-dominated policy process of the 1970s found themselves re-marginalized under the new regime.

The main changes in the central policy process in this period are well known. From the start, Mrs Thatcher was determined to establish control over economic policy, as the key policy area. Actual institutional change at the centre was limited, but the informal process that rapidly developed reflected this objective. Economic policy came increasingly to be determined in consultation with special advisers in the Downing Street Policy Unit.[26] The Treasury's traditional position of 'primus inter pares' amongst the Ministries was reinforced but this did not signify that

---

[24] D. Marsh and R. Rhodes, 'Policy Community and Issue Networks: Beyond Typology', in D. Marsh and R. Rhodes (eds.), *Policy Networks in British Government* (Oxford: Oxford University Press, 1992), 257.

[25] This point is also emphasized by Desmond King in 'The Establishment of Workwelfare Programs in the United States and Britain: Politics, Ideas and Institutions', in S. Steinmo *et al.* (eds.), *Structuring Politics* (Cambridge: Cambridge University Press, 1992), 234: 'Before the 1980s, it has been argued frequently, the civil service in Britain prevailed in public policy-making; this claim has been advanced by many Labour Party politicians. Since 1979 it is the politicians who have assumed the leading role'.

[26] P. Riddell, 'Cabinet and Parliament', in D. Kavanagh and A. Seldon (eds.), *The Thatcher Effect: A Decade of Change* (Oxford: Oxford University Press, 1989), 101–13.

policy was coming from the Treasury, many of whose senior officials Mrs Thatcher for a long time still suspected of being wedded to Keynesianism.[27] Nonetheless the Treasury was expected to oversee strict spending controls: in the words of the 1984 Green Paper, *The Next Ten Years*, 'finance must determine expenditure, not expenditure finance'.[28]

At the same time as there was a drive, however qualified its success, to impose spending controls from the centre, the role of organized interests in policy formulation was increasingly represented as illegitimate and, although this was not true in all policy areas, in practice many of those interests which had come to take their insider status for granted now found themselves largely excluded and even having to resort to 'outsider tactics'. Most obviously implicated in this 'demise of corporatism' were the trade unions, weakened both by rising unemployment and by deliberate government policy. But other potential actors in the childcare field—local government associations, as we have noted, and bodies representing the education profession—found their influence waning.[29]

Contradictory things are said about pressure group politics in the Thatcher era. It is sometimes suggested that the weakening of corporatism left the way clear for a range of less institutionalized pressure groups to proliferate and to exert influence upon the political agenda. Many such groups had grown out of the 'new social movements' of the 1970s and were adept in using the media, especially the expanding medium of television.[30] On the other hand there is little sense that for Thatcher such 'pluralism' enjoyed any more legitimacy than had corporatist forms of interest articulation. More specifically in the field of childcare, such emerging pressure groups were not particularly well placed to exploit the new opportunities, to the extent they existed. One woman involved in public campaigning for childcare told me, ' People now don't realize how tough it was in the mid-eighties to campaign for childcare'. On the one hand government was unlikely to respond positively to any demand for increased public expenditure. On the other hand, as numbers of pressure groups grew so did the competition between them. The most successful were those which had the most professional organizations and media strategy. Campaigning methods

---

[27] M. Holmes, *The First Thatcher Government, 1979–1983* (Brighton: Wheatsheaf, 1985), 29.

[28] Cited in N. Deakin and R. Parry, 'Does the Treasury have a Social Policy?', in N. Deakin and R. Page (eds.), *The Costs of Welfare* (Aldershot: Avebury, 1993), 35.

[29] Ian Holliday, 'Organised Interests after Thatcher', in P. Dunleavy *et al.* (eds.), *Developments in British Politics 4* (Basingstoke: Macmillan, 1993), 307–20.

[30] This is suggested for instance in Somerville, 'The New Right and Family Politics', 99–100.

had to change—it was 'no longer enough getting a lot of women pushing push-chairs into Whitehall'. Or as another campaigner said, lobbying now involved producing 'glossy' publicity and sending faxes. And in the meantime, as campaigning bodies were less able to draw on the idealism of their supporters, volunteers had to be replaced by paid workers.

THE 'DEMOGRAPHIC TIME-BOMB'

By the mid-eighties childcare politics was truly in the doldrums. However, this was to be challenged by three developments: new EC initiatives, the process leading up to the 1989 Children Act, but most of all the so-called 'demographic time-bomb'. Hogwood and Gunn[31] have argued that an issue is much more likely to get on the political agenda if there is a crisis so that the issue can no longer be ignored. More fundamentally, we have seen repeatedly how governments (at least up to the present Labour government) have been most concerned to provide childcare when real or anticipated labour shortages have put a premium on ensuring mothers' availability for paid employment. In May 1988 the Department of Employment released figures, and the National Economic Development Council followed up with a report in December, which indicated a fall of nearly one third in the number of school leavers by 1993. Numbers were predicted to rise again by the mid-nineties but not to the original level. The inference drawn was that government and employers must seek to persuade mothers of young children, especially those with skills in short supply, to resume paid work.

The result was to galvanize activity both in government and on the part of the childcare lobby, which now for the first time since the war included a significant contingent of employers. The new demographic scare at last provided the childcare lobby with a real opening. Childcare-related pressure groups stepped up their campaigns, conferencing, networking, publishing, and exploiting unprecedented media opportunities. The Working Mothers' Association, for instance, found itself inundated with enquiries. The Equal Opportunities Commission brought out a substantial report on the question, *The Key to Real Choice*, which argued the need for a national childcare agency.[32]

As we have seen, childcare was already moving up the trade union agenda. Increasingly in the 1980s, individual trade unions, such as the

---

[31] B. W. Hogwood and L. Gunn, *Policy Analysis for the Real World* (Oxford: Oxford University Press, 1984).
[32] EOC, *The Key to Real Choice* (Manchester: EOC, 1990).

powerful T&GWU, and the Manufacturing Science and Finance Union (MSF), were ready to take up childcare issues as part of their collective bargaining strategy. This reflected the influence of feminist arguments, together with concerns to appeal to actual and potential women members. But it is also relevant that through the decade the traditional prerogatives of trade unions in wage negotiations were being steadily eroded, by changes in the structure of the economy and by unemployment as much as by government policies. This encouraged unions to shift the emphasis of negotiations with employers away from pay to employment conditions, including childcare, but of course it also weakened the bargaining position of unions overall. In 1988 the TUC established an Equal Rights Department. By the end of 1990 its official priorities were equal pay, Europe, and, reflecting the new post-time-bomb sense of urgency, the issue of childcare.

Perhaps the most promising development was the new interest evinced by employers. Individual firms approached organizations like the Daycare Trust and the Workplace Nurseries Campaign in greatly increased numbers to seek advice on setting up nurseries for their employees. The Confederation of British Industry organized its own conference on the question of childcare and its report, *Workforce 2000*, urged the government to give the issue of childcare its most serious attention. Moreover, although, as will be related, the urgency of the time-bomb scenario was soon to subside, the newly kindled interest of the business sector did not diminish to the same extent. In 1993 a pressure group, Employers for Childcare, was formed, with the support of the CBI and including representatives of Midland Bank, Kingfisher, Shell, TSB, and British Gas.

Similarly originating in the momentum generated by the demographic time-bomb scare was an inquiry by the House of Commons Employment Committee, launched in 1992, whose report, *Mothers in Employment*, was published in 1995. Incidentally, of the seventeen MPs who at various times served on this committee, there was only one woman, Angela Eagle, who joined in 1994. The report, while noting that some might question whether having both parents out at work was good for dependent children, refused to commit itself on the issue but preferred to proceed 'on the assumption that it is desirable to increase opportunities for mothers to work, and in particular, to make it easier to combine work with family responsibilities'. Its overall tone was sympathetic to working mothers and it urged 'the formation and implementation of a national strategy for childcare'.[33]

---

[33] House of Commons Employment Committee, *Mothers in Employment* (London: HMSO, 1995), p. v.

Government did appear to respond to the new demographic projections and to the flurry of lobbying activity but on analysis its reaction was less substantial than it looked. Here we must note that there had already been some very small, incremental signs of increasing government interest before the May 1988 Department of Employment report. It is likely that this reflected both the more buoyant state of the economy and the early warning of the population and employment projections. One small indication was government funding for the new Early Childhood Unit within the National Children's Bureau, in 1986. It was around this time, also, that the interdepartmental group on under-fives resumed its meetings.

Significantly enough, the government's public response came neither from the DHSS, nor from the Department for Education. Constituting at least some recognition of the growing currency of equal-rights feminist arguments, from 1986 a cross-departmental Ministerial Group on Women's Issues had been meeting, under the auspices of the Home Office. It was the five-point programme of this committee, chaired by John Patten, which the government announced in March 1989. The programme was described as 'designed to pave the way for the provision of childcare which meets the need of the family' but its provisions implied only minor and incremental change. It included amendments to the Children Bill (discussed further below); encouragement to employers and childcare providers to operate an accreditation scheme that would make information about childcare facilities more widely available, and guarantee their quality; support for the voluntary sector through pump-priming projects (a reference to the under-fives initiatives); and encouragement to employers to use tax reliefs available for providing childcare.

One minor government concession, in 1990, was to waive the tax imposed on workplace nurseries. Under taxation law going back almost forty years, parents were liable to taxation on all forms of childcare facilities provided by employers, as a form of benefit in kind, but this liability was not actually invoked by the taxation authorities until 1984 when a number of parents received back-tax bills, some of them quite substantial, for using workplace nursery places subsidized by their employers. Quite why the government chose that moment to activate this provision in the legislation is unclear, although it is a further illustration of the government's broad indifference to working parents' childcare problems at that time. The move triggered the Workplace Nurseries Campaign mentioned above, although it also provoked dissent amongst childcare activists. For some the issue was a distraction; they maintained that it was of concern only to middle-class parents since others were earning too little to be eligible for tax in the first place.

The raised profile of the issue of child daycare meant that it was given greater attention in the later stages of the deliberations that led to the 1989 Children Act. The Act itself was concerned with a wide range of questions to do with the care and protection of children. Coming in the wake of the much-publicized child sexual abuse episode in Cleveland, it could be interpreted as a hasty attempt by government to defuse and be seen to respond to anxieties which that episode gave rise to. However, its roots went back much further, to successive committees of inquiry beginning with the 1982 All-party House of Commons Social Services Committee, and before that to ministerial and professional concerns crystallizing in the late 1970s.[34] It was the outcome, that is to say, of a growing public and professional interest in the question of childcare in its broader sense. Yet the specific issue of child daycare scarcely figured in this context until the late eighties.

In 1985 the government issued a consultative paper on updating the 1948 Nursery and Childminding Regulation Act, in order to ensure more systematic regulation of the expanding private daycare sector. But the Children Bill, issued in November 1988, took little account of the responses to this consultative paper elicited from the different campaigning organizations. However, in March 1989, as part of the Government's five-point programme in recognition of new demographic concerns, amendments were made to the Bill, strengthening registration and enforcement provisions directed at day nurseries, childminders, and playgroups. More specifically, on the advice of the National Children's Bureau, a clause was introduced late in the committee stage requiring local authorities to review daycare provision in their area every three years.

The Children Act, therefore, did bring some welcome changes. Under section 19, it obliged local authorities to register and inspect childcare services, where before this had been optional, thereby contributing to a stricter monitoring of standards. By requiring the triennial review it set in motion a process of gathering information about the range of services available in each locality. It was the first piece of legislation, as opposed simply to a government circular, nudging different local authority departments into closer collaboration on the issue of childcare. It also helped to bring the different local childcare providers into closer contact with each other and the local authority. In all these ways it prepared the ground for future policy development. Nevertheless, as we shall see,

---

[34] See Nigel Parton, *Governing the Family* (Basingstoke: Macmillan, 1991).

almost as soon as it was enacted, pressures began to mobilize to limit its impact at the implementation stage.

A third development providing advocates of child daycare reform with some modest additional leverage was in the context of the European Community. From the 1970s there had been unfolding a series of EC reports and initiatives through which feminists, whether in the European Parliament or the EC bureaucracy, sought to realize the Treaty of Rome's original commitment to equal treatment for men and women in the labour market. Increasingly it was recognized that this needed to include consideration of the issue of childcare. In 1986, under its Second Action Programme for women, the European Commission established a Childcare Network, with an expert in each member state, to report on childcare provision in their country. The expert for the United Kingdom was Bronwen Cohen and the co-ordinator for the whole network was Peter Moss, based in London at the Thomas Coram Research Institute. The Childcare Network, which took the firm line that 'childcare is an equality issue', produced a report in 1988 which underlined in a comparative European context the inadequacies of childcare provision in the UK. While direct gains from the European initiative were ultimately limited and hopes of persuading the European Commission to produce a Directive on the issue were to prove wildly optimistic, the Network assisted the childcare cause through providing additional funding resources, arguments, and legitimacy.[35]

CHILD DAYCARE UNDER MAJOR

This high point of child daycare advocacy was soon past. Even under the threat of the 'demographic time-bomb', government reaction had been more show than substance. But as the economy entered a period of recession, the daycare issue inevitably lost much of the urgency it had briefly acquired. In the meantime local authorities were beginning to feel the full effects of the financial squeeze from the centre. Although for a long time the more ingenious left-wing councils had found ways around the restrictions, by 1995–6, according to one source, local authority discretion to deviate from a centrally controlled budget was down to less than 5 per cent.[36] In these circumstances, even in well-disposed authorities like Manchester and Leeds, local programmes to

---

[35] Sadly the Network was wound up at the end of 1995.
[36] Paul Wilding, 'The Welfare State and the Conservatives', *Political Studies*, 45:3 (1997), 721.

expand public childcare provision had to be reined in, fees for child-care places were raised, and there were new attempts to involve employ-ers. Authorities seeking to enhance local provision increasingly had to find alternative means of funding. North Tyneside's approach was to set up a childcare business, using the income generated to subsidize places for poorer parents' children. It was successful in its own terms and its experience was widely studied. None the less, those involved recog-nized the limits to which such a model could assist the neediest fami-lies, and since much of the income came from consultancy work for other local authorities, there was also a limit to how far the model could be replicated.

Yet the Major years should not be dismissed as marginal to the devel-opment of childcare politics. On the one hand they saw a resurgence of interest in the nursery education side of under-fives policy, and the vouchers experiment. But there were also developments with significant longer-term implications on the daycare front, in particular the emer-gence of a much clearer government 'discourse' linking childcare with the whole question of lone mothers and welfare dependency, which was to persist into the post-Conservative era.

One consequence of the time-bomb episode was the increased involvement of the Department of Employment. Although this com-pounded yet further the fragmentation of ministerial responsibility, it was on balance a very positive development, since it marked the begin-nings of the institutionalization of childcare policy framed more in terms of the needs of working mothers. An indication that the Department was indeed beginning to develop its own childcare agenda followed the appointment in 1992 of Gillian Shepherd as Secretary of State for Employment. She announced a scheme providing limited funding for after-school provision for children aged 5 and over, and administered through the new Training and Enterprise Councils (TECs), which was to form the basis of continuing expansion under the successor Labour government. It must be added, however, that Mrs Shepherd's successor, Michael Portillo, showed scant sympathy with the recommendations of the House of Commons Employment Committee, referred to above, when they were published in 1995.

Most important for the development of childcare policy was the new emphasis during these Major years on childcare as a factor in the solu-tion of the 'problem' of lone mothers. We have seen that there was a long tradition of viewing the public provision or subsidy of childcare as essen-tially a welfare issue, a tradition articulated by the Department of Health and symbolized by the concentration of responsibility for childcare in that department. In that sense the lone-mother angle represented a retrograde shift in the welfarist direction. On the other hand there was now a new concern with the *employment* of single mothers. Reference has already been made to the growing numbers of lone or single mothers in Britain. They formed a proportionately larger social category in Britain than in any other EC country and in the context of late Thatcherism increasingly gave rise to two convergent sets of anxieties. First and probably foremost were anxieties about the implications for social expenditure. Through the 1980s government had continuously sought to reduce or at least check the growth of public expenditure on social benefits. Policy reviews focused initially on unemployment benefits, then on pensions: eventually attention shifted to lone-parent families. While the numbers of lone mothers with dependent children were rising, the percentage in paid employment actually declined from 45 per cent in 1981 to 39 per cent in 1993–4. It was feared in government circles that this would place an undue burden on the Exchequer. But such fears coincided with a rising strain of 'moral panic' orchestrated to an extent from the Downing Street Policy Unit and influenced in particular by the views of American analyst Charles Murray, who had pinpointed lower-class, never-married mothers, dependent on state welfare, as helping to reproduce a feckless and parasitic social underclass.[37]

The first manifestation of this growing government concern was the setting up, in 1991, of the Child Support Agency, aimed at compelling absent fathers to contribute to their children's upkeep. But this was soon mired in controversy and failed to deliver the expected economic benefits for government. At the same time the media highlighted sensational stories linked more directly with the question of childcare. In 1993 there were two highly publicized 'home alone' cases when first Yasmin Gibson left an 11-year-old daughter at home while she went on holiday to Spain and then Heidi Colwell was found guilty of leaving her 3-year-old daughter at home while she went out to work. While a succession of Conservative Ministers targeted the irresponsibility of lone mothers in speeches during the year, and the 1993 Conservative Party Conference took up the 'Back to Basics' theme which, somewhat confusedly, invoked traditional 'family values', the November Budget introduced a more constructive measure.

Apparently on the suggestion of the Department of Employment,[38]

---

[37] See Charles Murray, *The Emerging British Underclass* (London: Institute of Economic Affairs, 1990). Murray's views on lone mothers are discussed in Sasha Roseneill and Kirk Mann, 'Unpalatable Choices and Inadequate Families', in E. Bortolaia Silva (ed.), *Good Enough Mothering*? (London: Routledge, 1996).

[38] See Patricia Wynn Davies, 'Child-care Allowance was Hunt's Initiative', *Independent*, 4 Dec. 1993.

and closely resembling an allowance introduced under the AFDC (Aid to Families with Dependent Children) scheme in the United States some time before, this measure provided for a childcare 'disregard'. Under this provision, those in low-paid work, receiving Family Credit as an in-work benefit to supplement their income, would be allowed to 'disregard', or discount, up to £40 a week spent on childcare from their earned income, which meant they would be entitled to up to £28 a week additional Family Credit.[39] This was of special relevance to lone mothers since they figured disproportionately amongst Family Credit recipients. The measure was generally welcomed by the childcare lobby, although they argued, and their argument was to be borne out, that in practice it would assist only a very limited number of families. But this approach, of adjusting the benefits system to make it easier for low-paid mothers to afford childcare, was to be taken up and extended by the incoming Labour government of 1997.

NURSERY EDUCATION AND VOUCHERS

Following a pattern frequently noted in this study, while interest in child daycare grew in the late eighties, interest in nursery education seemed to decline. We have seen that from the start the Conservative government under Mrs Thatcher signalled that there would be no significant expansion in this service area. In a further negative development, the 1988 Education Act reduced local education authorities' powers in respect of nursery education.

Advocates of nursery education reform briefly took encouragement from a report issued in 1989 by the House of Commons Committee on Education, Science and the Arts. In a manner strongly reminiscent of the earlier experience of the Plowden Committee back in the sixties, members of the Committee had been persuaded of the importance of nursery education whilst investigating primary education in the early eighties. The evidence provided by the School Inspectors (HMIs) particularly impressed them. As a result of its own subsequent inquiry into *Educational Provision for the Under-5s*, the Committee urged reinstatement of the 1972 target of universal provision, recommending that the government undertake a systematic survey of existing levels of provision and demand.

The Government responded by setting up a committee of inquiry in

[39] This is well explained in Alan Duncan, Christopher Giles, and Steven Webb, *The Impact of Subsidising Childcare* (Manchester: EOC, 1995), 43–7.

the DES under Angela Rumbold. Its brief, however, was confined to issues of *quality* in under-fives provision. The committee considered all forms of under-fives provision, albeit from an educational standpoint, heard evidence from a wide range of interested organizations, and its report, *Starting with Quality*, published in 1990, looked at a number of important and relevant questions, including co-ordination of services and training of service providers. One of the considerations increasingly raised concerned the introduction, under the auspices of the 1988 Education Act, of a National Curriculum for schools. It was suggested that nursery education was needed to provide the proper grounding for Key Stage 1 of the Curriculum. Beyond this discussion, members of the Committee themselves regretted the limitations of their remit, noting in the introduction,

We believe . . . that there is a compelling need to address the issue of quantity; and we would urge those who make provision to recognise the extent to which demand outstrips supply, and to secure a continuing expansion of high quality services to meet children's and their parents' needs.[40]

But at this stage such arguments still cut very little ice with government, as indicated in 1991 when the Secretary of State for Education, Kenneth Clarke, described Mrs Thatcher's original commitment in 1972 to universal provision of nursery education as a 'mistake'.[41]

And yet, pressure was growing both from outside government and from an alternative inside source to reconsider its policy position. Both the Labour Party and the Liberal Democrats included commitments to move towards universal provision of nursery education in their election manifestos in 1992; indeed, the Liberal Democrats famously pledged to pay for it out of the proceeds of an additional 1p in the pound on income tax. With its majority reduced and public support ebbing, the post-1992 Major government was bound to take note. In 1993, moreover, the relatively prestigious National Commission on Education, an independent advisory body established in 1991, devoted a chapter of its report, *Learning to Succeed*, to the question of nursery education, arguing forcefully that 'high-quality publicly-funded education provision should be available for all three and four year olds'.[42]

---

[40] Department of Education and Science, *Starting with Quality* (London: HMSO, 1990), 1.

[41] Cited in Gillian Pugh, 'An Equal Start for All our Children?', unpubl. Times Educational Supplement/Greenwich Lecture 1992, 17.

[42] National Commission on Education, *Learning to Succeed* (London: William Heinemann, 1993), 130. A report issued under the auspices of the Royal Society of Arts, in March of the following year, argued on similar lines: see Christopher Ball, *Start Right: The Importance of Early Learning* (London: Royal Society of Arts, 1994).

Within government, the Home Office traced a link between an apparent upsurge in juvenile crime—most horrifyingly epitomized by the murder of toddler James Bolger by two boys who were not yet teenagers, in February 1993—and the inadequacy of nursery education provision. In the previous chapter we saw that in the 1960s advocates of nursery education cited the beneficial results of America's 'Head Start' programme of pre-school education. Somewhat later, critics claimed that these good results were only temporary, but later still, studies appeared to show there were indeed measurable long-term benefits. In particular, attention focused on the High/Scope pre-school programme, whose effects on an especially disadvantaged group of children were found to offer a dramatic contrast with the intellectual and behavioural development of a control group who had not joined the programme.[43] The Home Office was impressed by the High/Scope results, which seemed to confirm that the right kind of pre-school programme could substantially assist the drive to reduce juvenile crime.

Even then, and to the dismay of nursery education enthusiasts, the 1992 Education Bill made no mention of nursery education. In the House of Lords, Lady Warnock, in consultation with nursery education groups, tabled a number of amendments but these were fiercely opposed by Baroness Blatch, the government spokesperson on education, and voted down. As late as November 1993, the Secretary of State for Education, by this time John Patten, stated that the government could not pursue the aim of universal nursery education because of the prohibitive costs. Just one month later, and taking almost everybody by surprise, the Prime Minister himself declared the government's aim of moving towards universal provision for 3- and 4-year-olds.

This sudden announcement triggered great activity and some confusion in the Department for Education. Two distinct sets of questions were raised. The first was about the feasibility of the target as such. Objections came not only from the Treasury but from within the Department for Education, including Baroness Blatch herself. As a result of their interventions, the policy goals were steadily modified and in October 1994, the Prime Minister indicated that the focus was now to be on 4-year-olds and that nursery education would be provided not only by nursery schools or classes but by reception classes and indeed by playgroups. But even in this amended form the policy needed additional funding and the second question concerned the funding

---

[43] These results are discussed in Kathy Sylva, 'Educational Aspects of Day Care in England and Wales', in P. Moss and E. Melhuish (eds.), *Current Issues in Day Care for Young Children* (London: HMSO, 1991).

mechanism. This occasioned further intense argument within government; the option that eventually won favour, and which was announced in July 1995, was the voucher system.

The use of vouchers, like provision for childcare tax allowances, meant concentrating on the demand rather than the supply end of childcare provision, and reflected the Conservative government's preference for the private and voluntary sectors as child daycare providers, as opposed to the state. The voucher approach also had a particular history within Conservative Party thinking, having long been part of the intellectual armoury of the New Right.[44] Advocates could draw on experience elsewhere, notably the United States.[45] Finally, the notion of vouchers could be seen to chime particularly well with the Major government's growing emphasis on the theme of consumer choice. This theme was prominent in the 1992 education White Paper, entitled *Choice and Diversity*.

The idea of vouchers for nursery education was advanced in the Downing Street Policy Unit, especially following the appointment of its new head, former management consultant Norman Blackwell, and was developed in a publication of the Adam Smith Institute, *Pre-schools for All*, written by David Soskin. Initially there had been interest in the possibility of using vouchers or 'learning credits' in the context of further education, that is education for 16- to 19-year-olds, but this policy option was suspended in 1995,[46] just as the voucher scheme was being adopted for nursery education, and was subsequently abandoned as the practical problems appeared overwhelming.

The decision to adopt a voucher mechanism was thus the culmination of a growing offensive both within the Downing Street Policy Unit and other government policy-making circles and within the Department for Education and Employment (DfEE) itself. It was also supported in principle by Treasury ministers,[47] although they were reported to be in favour of a means-tested scheme rather than the flat-rate voucher pro-

---

[44] The first modern advocate of vouchers was the American free-market economist, Milton Friedman, in 1955. In the 1960s and 70s the Institute of Economic Affairs took up the notion but it was not mooted within government until 1981, when Sir Keith Joseph, as Secretary of State for Education, expressed his interest in using vouchers as a means of extending parental choice.

[45] In the United States, something like the voucher principle had underlain the Food Stamps programme and vouchers also formed a central part of social housing schemes, but most relevantly under the terms of the Child Care and Development Block Grant, enacted in 1990, which made mandatory a voucher system described as facilitating parental choice of forms of childcare. See William T. Gormley Jr., *Everybody's Children* (Washington, DC: Brookings Institute, 1995), 126–9.

[46] See Donald MacLeod and John Carvel, 'Major to Fulfil Nursery Pledge with Voucher Plan', *Guardian*, 14 June 1995.

[47] As reported, for instance, in ibid.

posed. It was widely known at the time, however, that not all government ministers involved were so enthusiastic. Mrs Shepherd's reservations were frequently noted; she regarded the voucher scheme as impractical, as 'cumbersome and bureaucratic'.[48] Overall it seemed as though on this question John Major's personal intervention had been decisive, and that he had first launched the nursery education initiative in a bid to turn round his party's waning electoral fortunes and had then timed the announcement of the adoption of a vouchers scheme to coincide with the party leadership contest and his bid to secure the support of the party's right wing.

Under the scheme parents of all 4-year-olds were to receive vouchers for £1,100 to go towards the cost of nursery education. In spending their vouchers they could, in theory, choose between state nursery places or places in private nurseries or playgroups which offered suitable education. In making these vouchers available, the government would use a combination of £165 million of new funding and £545 million that would otherwise have gone in grants that could be used for nursery education by local education authorities (a further £20 million would be needed for administration and inspection). The intention was that following a brief period of consultation, a series of pilot schemes in twelve local authorities would be launched in February 1996 and the policy would then be fully implemented a year later. In the event, the deadline initially set for local authorities to volunteer to take part in the pilot had to be extended and even then only four authorities eventually signed up. Unsurprisingly three of these were Conservative-held authorities: Kensington and Chelsea, Wandsworth, and Westminster. The fourth, Norfolk, was under joint Liberal–Labour rule but included Gillian Shepherd's parliamentary constituency. Facilitating legislation was passed by Parliament in the early months of 1996.

The vouchers experiment was short-lived but merits discussion both for what it shows about the range and complexity of interests and organizations in which the issue of childcare was by now embedded and because, despite the successor Labour government's rapid repudiation of the voucher principle itself, in many ways the scheme laid the basis for Labour's Early Years Development initiative. The voucher scheme rapidly encountered major difficulties and much criticism, including protest from the Campaign Against Vouchers in Education (CAVE), which set up an active branch in Norfolk. The experience of the four pilot authorities, together with measures taken by other local education authorities in anticipation of the scheme's extension, were carefully

---

[48] See Judith Judd, 'Education Policy Rifts Revealed', *Independent*, 12 Mar. 1996.

monitored by the various interested bodies. The Association of Metropolitan Authorities (AMA), in conjunction with the National Children's Bureau, brought out a highly critical report as early as May.[49] Much more embarrassingly for the government, who had been hoping to use its nursery education policy in the forthcoming General Election campaign, this was followed, in March 1997, by a report of the House of Commons Education and Employment Committee, which, assessing the scheme in terms of its three stated objectives of expanding provision, ensuring quality, and increasing parental choice, fell distinctly short of a whole-hearted endorsement.[50]

Through these and other outlets a number of not always compatible criticisms were made. Firstly, it was widely argued that although administration of the scheme was not particularly difficult to understand or explain, it was costly in terms of both time and public money. Second, there were fears about the scheme's impact on the respective roles in provision of the private and public sectors. One more or less explicit intention behind the scheme was to encourage private and voluntary providers. This was viewed with particular alarm by state educational institutions currently providing nursery education, whether primary schools or nursery schools. They feared that they would lose the money the government was holding back from the local government grant; the value of the voucher, at £1,100, was insufficient to cover the full cost to the authority of a state nursery place and parents might well choose to spend their vouchers on other forms of provision. They also questioned the quality of education 4-year-olds would receive in these private sector settings.

In the pilot schemes, in fact, early indications were that between 67 and 75 per cent of the amount deducted from the Standard Spending Assessment grant was redeemed in the form of vouchers by maintained schools: this might not satisfy the state-based institutions but was hardly reassuring to the private sector.[51] These providers in the private sector were equally afraid of being at a disadvantage. Registered childminders were not normally considered eligible for the scheme. Representatives of the private nurseries accused the primary schools of modifying their admissions policies where necessary and ruthlessly 'hoovering up' all the 4-year olds, who were eligible for vouchers, into reception classes. They pointed out that reception classes were not subject to the same kinds of child–staff ratio requirements that had been imposed on private

---

[49] AMA, *Education Vouchers for Early Years: The State of Play* (London: AMA, 1996).
[50] House of Commons Education and Employment Committee, *The Operation of the Nursery Voucher Scheme* (London: Stationery Office, 1997).
[51] Ibid. p. xv.

nurseries under the Children Act. This put the private nurseries at a disadvantage in terms of the costs of provision. At the same time state educational institutions were better placed to satisfy the educational criteria—formulated as 'desirable learning outcomes'—associated with eligibility for the voucher scheme. Playgroups felt particularly vulnerable, as they lost their 4-year-olds to the state sector, struggled with the complexities of administering the vouchers, and were judged deficient on academic grounds.

There were further concerns about the impact of the scheme on the provision for 3-year-olds and on the broader prospects for the integration of education and care aspects of under-fives services. Severe doubts were expressed about the possibility of ensuring quality. The intention at the time was to allow potential providers to join the scheme if they satisfied certain minimum criteria, but then to submit them to more systematic inspection a later stage. However, there were few currently qualified inspectors and it was argued that there was insufficient time to train the 4,000 inspectors promised by the government.[52]

Indeed, while it is in some ways unfair to judge a scheme which never really had a chance to get going, it did appear ill designed to achieve its stated aims. Although some additional resources were directed into boosting effective demand for nursery education, these did not necessarily translate into supply. In some cases, especially in rural areas, there was simply no suitable provision for parents to spend their vouchers on. Elsewhere primary school reception classes were poised to take in extra pupils without necessarily adjusting teaching provision. It was much more difficult to expand existing private nurseries, in the manner required, without the guarantee of regular future income, let alone to set up new ones. A further constraint upon the expansion of supply was the serious shortage of suitably trained nursery teachers. At the same time there were real grounds for doubting the arrangements to ensure quality control. And effective choice for most parents was narrow at best.

In terms of our wider concern with the provision of child daycare, the vouchers scheme was still less promising. Although ostensibly designed to maximize 'flexibility', the stipulation that the vouchers were to cover five daily sessions of two and a half hours a week posed obvious problems of administration and co-ordination if they were to be integrated into full-time daycare provision catering for the needs of working

---

[52] As argued for instance during the Parliamentary debate by Margaret Hodge (who also sat on the House of Commons Committee). She reported that there were only three suitably qualified inspectors in the DfEE, with a further 200 registered as qualified in the country at large. See Hansard, 22 Jan. 1996, col. 79.

parents. All in all the need to integrate education and care aspects was understated, not only in government pronouncements but in critical responses, although this did appear to be a significant concern of parents in cases where their opinions were canvassed.[53]

THE CHILDCARE LOBBY BY THE MID-NINETIES

One of the effects—it remains to be seen just how long-lasting—of the vouchers episode was on the make-up and cohesion of what I have been calling the childcare lobby. In this last substantial section of the present chapter it remains to trace the development of this lobby in the final years of Conservative rule and to consider implications for policy-making under Labour. As we have seen, while the demographic scare of the late 1980s subsided, its impact on the childcare lobby—both the increased role of employers and the increased emphasis upon the needs of working mothers—tended to persist. Although the childcare lobby did not decline, nonetheless the legacy of a decade of Thatcherism was to alter steadily the terms in which childcare demands were expressed; and at the same time government policies, ostensibly geared to promote healthy 'competition' between service providers, helped to open up new lines of fissure within it.

One arena in which the childcare issue continued to make important gains, with major long-term implications, was the national Labour Party. From the early eighties the cause of childcare had been pressed by feminists associated with the new democratic Left. Perrigo suggests that following the electoral defeat of 1983, a gulf appeared to develop between the political priorities of Labour women and of the party leadership. However, it was the disastrous electoral defeat of 1987 that finally persuaded the party leadership of the need to 'modernize' its organization and image, and this included measures to make the party appear more 'woman-friendly'.[54] In their pamphlet, *Women's Votes: The Key to Winning*, for instance, Patricia Hewitt and Deborah Matinson noted that the 'gender gap', or tendency for women to vote disproportionately for the Conservative Party, had closed for the first time in the 1987 election. They argued that women were more attracted than were men to the

[53] See app. 19 of House of Commons Education and Employment Committee, *The Operation of the Nursery Voucher Scheme*, 'Nursery Vouchers: Parents' View', a memorandum submitted by the National Children's Bureau.

[54] Perrigo, 'Women and Change in the Labour Party', 117. See also Clare Short, 'Women and the Labour Party', *Parliamentary Affairs*, 49:1 (1996), 17–25.

notion of an 'enabling state': 'Increasingly, women are Labour's natural constituency'. Group interviews they had conducted indicated how pre-occupied women were with the difficulties of juggling work and home—amongst other measures, 'Better child-care facilities and other back-up services were also extremely popular'.[55]

In this way, childcare came to be identified as an issue that could simultaneously appeal to the feminist constituency within the party and to potential women voters. Building on this opportunity, Anna Coote, Harriet Harman, and Patricia Hewitt, in their influential publication *The Family Way*, elaborated upon the need for an effective childcare strategy to support the modern family.[56] In fact, while by the end of the eighties, the more strident tone of women-regarding policies had been considerably muted, as demonstrated for example in the 1991 document, *A New Ministry for Women*, the commitment to childcare appeared to be holding firm.[57]

During the Major years, there were signs that childcare was being taken increasingly seriously by Labour Party policymakers. Margaret Hodge,[58] the Labour Party's under-fives spokesperson, chaired a series of 'early years' consultative meetings at Milbank House, bringing together experts, interested national organizations, and local practitioners. Many of the participants at these meetings I talked to clearly saw them as serious attempts to gather information and explore options. In addition to the long-standing commitment to expanded nursery education, party leaders were beginning to see a link between child daycare arguments of feminist origin and their own emerging strategy for combating welfare dependency and unemployment. The outcome of these developments within the Labour Party in policy initiatives from 1997 are analysed further in Chapter 7.

---

[55] Patricia Hewitt and Deborah Matinson, *Women's Votes: The Key to Winning* (London: Fabian Society, 1989), 11.

[56] See n. 10 above.

[57] See Valerie Atkinson and Joanna Spear, 'The Labour Party and Women: Policies and Practices', in Martin J. Smith and Joanna Spear, *The Changing Labour Party* (London: Routledge, 1992), 158–9. Not all feminists in the party regarded the childcare issue with the same enthusiasm. It was suggested to me by one woman activist that many Labour women were suspicious of this pledge, which was in any case couched in a way that tended to fudge the distinction in practice between nursery education and daycare and which they felt was offered in somewhat tokenistic fashion in lieu of a more serious engagement with the women's agenda. Atkinson and Spear themselves suggest rather disparagingly that men within the Labour Party found it easier to grasp more concrete policy questions like childcare than for instance cultural depictions of women (ibid. 159).

[58] She was the former Leader of a council, Islington, known to have prioritized daycare provision. In 1998 she became the Minister directly in charge of the childcare programme within the DfEE.

It has been suggested at various points in this book that the array and articulation of childcare interests cannot be divorced from the way that childcare policy has been institutionalized. Specifically in relation to the process of welfare state restructuring, writers such as Pierson and Taylor-Gooby have reminded us that government leaders may seek to change not only the content of policy but its context. Pierson calls this 'systemic' retrenchment.[59] This is the process by which, through amendments both to policies and to institutional arrangements, government can modify the form and pattern of policy demands, including the language and terms in which policy debate is framed and the relative strengths of different interests and voices involved in the policy process.

One obvious but important effect of the cumulative reinforcement of neo-liberal ideology through this period was the shifting terms within which childcare claims were advanced, and most crucially the growing acceptance amongst childcare advocates that the state would not, and perhaps even should not, play a central and direct role in service provision. Even the National Child Care Campaign had moved by the end of the 1980s from its original commitment to state-funded, free, universal day nurseries to a recognition that it might be necessary to charge fees, and an acceptance of the part to be played by childminders and workplace nurseries.

At the same time, government policies affected the relative strength, organization, and interrelationships of interests involved. An earlier obvious instance was the way in which the trade unions and local authority associations, which had increasingly championed the cause of childcare, were demoted from the seventies onward as players in the process. But the policy context had changed in more subtle ways. The numbers of private day nurseries had been growing from the 1960s; earlier we noted that a slight fall in the early eighties was followed by a surge in the latter part of the decade. Despite this growth, it was not until the 1989 Children Act that a need was felt to give these nurseries a more concerted political voice. Two organizations were formed around the same time: the Childcare Association (CCA) and the National Private Day Nurseries Association (NPDNA). In fact these two organizations were rather different, although it is not clear that this was always recognized by other groupings within the childcare lobby. The Childcare Association was formed to bring together and represent a growing contingent of 'up-market' nurseries, combining an emphasis on staff professionalism with effective commercial management. It saw

---

[59] Pierson, *Dismantling the Welfare State?*, 15–17.

itself primarily as a professional association, promoting early years' services.[60] The NPDNA operated more like a conventional interest organization, representing the interests of a larger and more heterogeneous membership.[61] Prompted by this membership, it was particularly disquieted by the provisions of the Children Act laying down conditions for registration that would be difficult for some nurseries to enforce without making their service prohibitively expensive. Partly as a result of pressures from the representatives of the private day nurseries, directly and through sympathetic MPs, between the Children Act and the issuing of government guidelines in 1991, and again between the appearance of these guidelines and a government memorandum on their implementation in January 1993, the requirements day nurseries had to satisfy before they could be officially registered, and in particular the specified staff–child ratio, were weakened. This generated considerable bitterness amongst the other childcare groups.

The changing political conjuncture, especially the new emphasis on involving voluntary groups together with the government's need to be seen to be responding to childcare needs, also seemed to favour the Pre-school Playgroups Association, originally founded in the 1960s. Despite the growth in childminding and in private nurseries, by the end of the eighties these playgroups still catered for more children than any other category of provision. However, their numbers were levelling off. The fact that playgroups did not provide places on a daily basis and their limited hours made them of little use for working mothers. At the same time they were finding it more difficult to mobilize volunteers because more of the mothers who might have lent a hand were themselves seeking paid work. But now, in the early nineties, the Association found itself viewed with especial favour by the government, which increased its subsidy. Thus encouraged, the Association began to argue that playgroups held the answer to the national childcare shortage. As the focus of government concern shifted from daycare to nursery education, in 1994 the Association, which had changed its name to the Pre-school Learning Alliance, issued a booklet, *The Way Forward*, advancing playgroups as the way to realize the new nursery education targets. This enraged many of the other childcare organizations, who saw the move as both divisive and presumptuous.

As we have seen, the Pre-school Learning Alliance felt severely threatened by the nursery voucher scheme. It was particularly alarmed by the government suggestion during the drafting stage of the bill that

[60] Interview with former Director, Dec. 1997.
[61] Interview with former Chair of London branch, Apr. 1998.

playgroups should receive voucher money at only half the rate of other providers, that is, £550 for an individual child to cover the five weekly half-day sessions instead of £1,100. The Alliance was able to argue that the playgroup movement was the single largest provider for under-fives, constituting an essential component of any viable scheme, and moves to reduce its funding rate were dropped.[62] Even so, implementation of the scheme looked set to hit the playgroups hard.

CONCLUSION

For much of the long period of Conservative rule from 1979 to 1997 childcare policy stagnated at best. When set alongside the progress made in the seventies, or the expansion, spectacular in some instances, of childcare provision in a number of other European countries during this period, this does feel like a terrible wasted opportunity. And in some ways the legacy was more pernicious even than this suggests, in shifting the predominant discourse of *how* services were to be provided and in the damaging discord it sowed amongst providers.

Yet the overall legacy, particularly of the Major years, was not entirely negative. The legitimacy of mothers going out to work was increasingly (though still not fully) accepted. Despite the best efforts of the Conservative Family Campaign, founded in 1986, and, only slightly more serious, the government's 'Back to Basics' drive, it was striking that during a debate on childcare in 1994, nobody impugned working mothers. Both Stephen Dorrell, the minister concerned, and another young Conservative MP, Matthew Carrington, announced that they had recently become fathers and that their wives planned to carry on working.[63] There was, secondly, growing official recognition, in principle, of the importance of the quality of childcare and of the need to integrate care and educational aspects. One further auspicious development in 1995 was the merger of the Departments for Education and Employment, which could help to overcome the functional fragmentation of policy formulation and implementation.

As we have seen, these years have been understood in terms of a concerted push towards a neo-liberal restructuring of the welfare state. Scholars have disagreed as to how far restructuring governments have

---

[62] Judith Judd and Fran Abrams, 'Tories could extend voucher scheme to all school pupils', *Independent*, 7 Oct. 1995, 8.
[63] The debate was initiated by Harriet Harman apropos amendments to the 1994 Finance Bill. See Hansard, *House of Commons Debates*, 19 Apr. 1994.

succeeded in imposing their agenda on the economy and on society. It has been suggested that where interests bound up with the welfare state have been strongly entrenched it has proved difficult in practice to dislodge them. On the other hand, Britain, at least under Thatcher, has been recognized as a possible exception to this observation.

As far as child daycare is concerned, however, there were no powerful entrenched interests to plead its cause. Admittedly Thatcherism greatly weakened the political clout of unions and local government bodies, which were just beginning to champion childcare. But other lobbying groups were weak and the status of the associated professional grouping was low.

The legitimacy and strength of political support for nursery education has always been greater than for daycare. Even so, the government under Thatcher was largely impervious to the demands of its advocates. Once Conservative rule came under greater challenge, and especially once it was running scared in the aftermath of Tony Blair's selection as Labour Party leader, these demands were more difficult to resist. The nursery voucher scheme, for all its ideological quirkiness and the mistrust and conflict it generated amongst the providers, helped lay the foundation for Labour's Early Years Development partnerships and the universalizing of provision for 4- and ultimately 3-year-olds.

But also in these last Major years, there was the beginning of a significant shift in the way that child daycare featured within the 'restructuring' agenda. Whereas under Thatcher it had largely been identified as an extremely marginal welfare service that might be subject to some retrenchment and otherwise properly left to the operation of the private and voluntary sector, it subsequently began to be seen as a possible instrument in the battle to reduce welfare dependency. The very modest childcare 'disregard' introduced in 1994 was criticized by Labour but again constituted the seeds of an approach which has developed since 1997.

5

Mothers, Feminists, and the
Demand for Childcare

The analysis so far has tended to focus on the level of national institutional decision-making. It has demonstrated the extent to which
earlier assumptions and decisions about child daycare were embodied
in institutional arrangements in the early post-war era which constrained both the practical and the imaginable policy options of
later decades. But while there has been a degree of institutional
inertia, there has also been very little effective political pressure challenging the status quo. As we have seen, what I have called the childcare lobby, which emerged in the 1970s, has all along been weak and
divided. Its constituent groups have represented differing and potentially conflicting assumptions about the respective needs of children and
mothers, different interests, and professions. Within their ranks explicitly feminist arguments and energies have played a relatively minor role
(although the impact of second-wave feminism has contributed to a
growing public acceptance of the legitimacy of working mothers' childcare needs).

In the present chapter, I examine first of all the issue of women's
(or parents') demand for childcare. Mothers did not rise up *en masse* to
protest when the war nurseries were being phased out, nor at any time
since have they taken to the streets to demand that government take
on the child daycare question. Is this because they have had no need
of assistance with childcare, or because they have felt unable to articulate the need? What evidence do we have of both the need and the
demand for childcare? In the second part of the chapter, I look more
specifically at feminist involvement in the childcare issue. Feminists
have claimed in some sense to represent women, or women's interests,
so why in general has this involvement regarding childcare been so
limited? I consider the ways in which childcare may be a problematic
issue for feminism.

THE DEMAND FOR CHILDCARE

It seems symptomatic of the overall lack of political urgency which has characterized the issue of childcare in Britain that the DfEE Team responsible, under the new Labour government, for constructing a national childcare policy found itself short of much basic information. Local authorities drawing up their Early Years Development and Childcare Plans in 1998 were encouraged to conduct some form of audit of local need. The authors of a report commissioned by the DfEE, advising on *Local Assessments of Childcare Need and Provision*, observed that 'Basic information on the amount of registered provision for children under eight is fairly easily obtained . . . However sources of information on need and demand are much weaker, and assessed in different ways by different agencies'.[1] Of course indicators such as waiting-lists for day nursery places have for a long time provided evidence of demand. But until the 1970s very little systematic information was gathered at all and even into the millennium knowledge of the extent and forms of need has remained hazy.

This is not to suggest that the concepts of need and demand are straightforward or easy to apply. Beyond what is necessary for human survival, individually and collectively, a strong subjective or cultural element must enter into any estimations of what people need. Holterman, in an appendix to the report mentioned above, suggests that need can be assessed in terms of welfare. Need can be demonstrated where an increase in consumption of the good in question would lead to a significant increase in welfare, or utility, from a level that was previously unacceptable.[2] But this approach still leaves open who is to judge whether there has been an increase in welfare—generally it is assumed this will be the individual themselves, but they might not always be the best judge—and likewise who decides what is acceptable or unacceptable. In the case of childcare, this is hardly nitpicking: there is fundamental disagreement about its welfare implications both for mothers/parents and for children.

Need is not the same as demand: need may not be articulated or even conscious. 'Demand' is usually employed when people articulate a claim on someone and for something. This generally implies that they expect

---

[1] See Peter Moss, Ann Mooney, Tony Munton, and June Stanham, *Local Assessments of Childcare Need and Provision*, Research Report RR72 (London: Department for Education and Employment, 1998), 21.

[2] Sally Holterman, 'The Need and Demand for Childcare—Methods of Assessment', app. 1 of ibid.

their claim to have some force either because of sanctions they can exert or because of its legitimacy.[3]

These real difficulties in defining or conceptualizing need versus demand, together with the patchiness of available information, have compounded the problems in establishing a strong 'objective' case—one that will carry weight with senior politicians and officials—for publicly funded childcare. They have also made it easier for a range of contradictory arguments about childcare to be simultaneously deployed, without the constraining influence of awkward 'facts'.

Chapter 2 described the dispute between the Ministries of Labour and Health over assessing women's need and appreciation of the war nurseries, and the more specific problems in the way of arriving at a 'true' assessment that could disentangle such questions from attitudes to mobilization, the nature of wartime work, and the compatibility of available childcare arrangements with working hours and conditions.[4] After the war women's paid employment, and in particular the employment of married women, soon rose well above pre-war levels. However, a small but growing portion of this work was part-time. More importantly, the employment of mothers of small children remained on a very modest scale. At face value then, mothers' current employment patterns did not suggest an urgent need for child daycare. Similarly, we saw that figures for private nursery places and registered childminders were relatively low, again suggesting limited demand. But it is still difficult to be sure how to interpret these data. To what extent was the dearth of public childcare provision actually preventing mothers of young children from seeking work?

In this context it would be helpful to know more about women's, and specifically mothers', attitudes to paid employment. The previous chapter touched on some of the difficulties in assessing women's attitudes during the war. Summerfield cites one survey produced for the Ministry of Reconstruction in 1943 which found that three-quarters of professional women, but less than half of women doing monotonous work as labourers and packers, wanted to keep their jobs after the war. Also, amongst married women it was the older ones who were most positive, while those aged 34 or less typically did not want to continue in paid employment. This might suggest that younger women who were

<hr />

[3] The EC Childcare Network distinguishes, however, between latent and explicit demand, the latter coming closer to economic or effective demand. See European Commission Childcare Network, *Monitoring and Evaluating Equal Opportunities Policies in the Area of Reconciliation of Employment and Family Life* cited by Holterman, 'The Need and Demand for Childcare'.

[4] See p. 37 above.

or expected to become mothers, especially if they were engaged in manual trades, often did look forward to dropping out of the paid work-force.[5] Peggy Scott's observation, around the same time, tends to support this view and shows the link between attitudes to work and attitudes to nursery provision. She found that whilst many older married women welcomed the nurseries and the emancipation from domestic drudgery they represented, the younger women who had not yet acquired families of their own were less appreciative:

The girls in the service who have never tasted domestic drudgery make it plain in their Brains Trust that they do not want anything communal after the war; neither blocks of flats, nor communal meals, nor laundries, nor nurseries. They want a home with a garden, their own husband and a child.[6]

In the early post-war years, few specific studies of working mothers were undertaken. One small study,[7] conducted by the Christian Economic and Social Research Foundation, concluded that it was often dire poverty, rather than any more positive inclination, which drove mothers of young children into paid work. Two other studies, while tending to confirm the primacy of financial motives (which women may however have emphasized because of their greater social acceptability) noted that some women were also motivated by the desire to overcome loneliness and social isolation and by the satisfaction they could get from their work.[8]

Such partial glimpses of women's attitudes tend to suggest variations according to age and social class or occupation, but also confirm the general finding of limited overall demand for childcare. But demand, we have noted, is not necessarily the full expression of need. We have to recognize that it may have been difficult for mothers to express, even to 'think', about childcare needs in the context of a deepening post-war consensus about the family and women's mothering responsibilities within it, which, while it sought to distinguish itself from previous formulations of the 'ideology of motherhood' and used different arguments, nonetheless incorporated many basic assumptions from the pre-war era. Wilson emphasizes the 'schizophrenic' character

---

[5] Penny Summerfield, *Women Workers in the Second World War* (London: Croom-Helm, 1984).

[6] Peggy Scott, *They Made Invasion Possible* (1944), cited in Sarah Boston, *Women Workers and the Trade Union Movement* (London: David Poynter, 1980), 203.

[7] Christian Economic and Social Research Foundation, *Young Mothers at Work* (1957), cited in Elizabeth Wilson, *Only Halfway to Paradise: Women in Postwar Britain, 1945–68* (London: Tavistock, 1980), 51.

[8] Ferdynand Zweig, *Women's Life and Labour* (1952) and Pearl Jephcott *et al.*, *Married Women Working* (1962), both cited in Wilson, *Only Halfway to Paradise*, 49–53.

of post-war attitudes to women. There was now a general feeling that women should be regarded as the equals of men and have the right to paid work. On the other hand, it was hoped that this more equal status within the home would encourage women to see 'homemaking as a career', the home as a workplace or factory. Such apparent inconsistencies were seemingly reconciled in the dual-role model of women's employment. Whereas between the wars there was a widespread assumption that women should either have a career or be married, now there was a view that married women should only work outside the home before they had children and again after the children had left home, a pattern which, it has already been observed, was in practice beginning to be apparent by the 1950s. Such a prescription was explicitly set out and argued for by two 'feminists', Alva Myrdal and Viola Klein.[9]

These assumptions about a mother's place were diffused through the popular entertainment media. Cynthia White has made a study of women's magazines in the early post-war period. Although initially some of the 'quality' publications urged married women to hold on to the wider work horizons opened up by the war, soon all magazines 'acquiesced in a regressive tendency and later used their influence positively to discourage women from trying to combine work and marriage'.[10] She cites *Woman*'s Evelyn Home: 'No two women have exactly the same capacities and I would never interfere with the right of the minority to prefer outside work. But it is safe to say that most women, once they have a family, are more contented and doing better work in the home than they could find outside it.' *Housewife*'s counsellor warned against mothers working before their children went to school, citing Bowlby on maternal deprivation. In *Woman's Own*, responding to the letter of a reader, Mrs X, Monica Dickens lectured,

I cannot see what else can be more important than your children. To work for them, and play with them, and teach them, and always be there when they need you, is the prime duty of a mother. It does not seem like a duty because it is what a mother most wants to do. . . . Would you prefer your mother to be always at home looking after you and the others, or do you think you would find her more interesting if she went out and gleaned a whole lot of new ideas and connections that had nothing to do with you? . . . I hope that Mrs X does not go rushing out to look for a job. She is not cheating her children by staying at home. She is giving them the supreme gift—herself.[11]

---

[9] Alva Myrdal and Viola Klein, *Women's Two Roles* (London: Routledge and Kegan Paul, 1956).
[10] Cynthia White, *Women's Magazines 1693–1968* (London: Michael Joseph, 1970), 135.
[11] Cited in ibid. 150–1.

To the extent that such views both expressed and reinforced a popular consensus, it would inevitably make it more difficult for mothers of young children to perceive, let alone actively to articulate, a demand for child daycare.

During the 1960s, the growing numbers of mothers in paid work (albeit predominantly part-time), increased recourse to private nurseries and childminders, and lengthening local authority nursery waiting-lists all suggested both growing demand and growing need for childcare. The fact that the increase in mothers' employment was largely in part-time work is also open to more than one interpretation. Was this from choice or were possibilities of full-time employment curtailed by inadequate childcare provision? Certainly by the early 1970s, several studies suggested considerable unmet demand for afford-able child daycare provision. Tizard *et al.* cited estimates derived from interviews conducted in 1974–5 by the Thomas Coram Research Unit in three areas of London. They found that 64 per cent of the mothers of all the children under 5 ($n = 452$) wanted some form of nursery service. Demand increased with the age of the child, reaching 73 per cent for 2-year-olds and over 90 per cent for 3- and 4-year-olds. Moreover, the bulk of demand was for day-long (five hours a day or more) provision. They commented that these estimates were considerably higher than those offered in the Plowden Report.[12]

TWO SURVEYS

A much more extensive survey, published in 1977, was undertaken by Margaret Bone.[13] It was commissioned by the Department of Health and Social Security with the object of establishing the true extent of need but this was need as defined under the Department's criteria, set out in its 1968 circular to local authorities, emphasizing aspects of social disadvantage, including the category of the family headed by a lone parent who 'has no option but to go out to work'.[14] However, Bone chose to supplement this last category with one covering the child with two parents whose father's income fell below a certain

---

[12] Jack Tizard *et al.*, *All Our Children* (London: Temple Smith, 1976), 163–5.

[13] Margaret Bone, *Pre-school Children and the Need for Daycare* (London: HMSO, 1977).

[14] Other categories were that the mother was ill or otherwise inadequate; there was the danger of family break-up; physical home conditions were hazardous; or the child was handicapped.

level or whose mother worked outside the home, whether or not she had to. Using a stratified nationwide random sample of 2,500 children, she investigated mothers' use of and 'desire'[15] for different forms of daycare. She distinguished desire from demand, the latter being cases where the mother was actually trying to get her child into some form of provision, because demand would be limited by information and availability. Overall, and defining daycare very broadly, she concluded that provision was wanted for twice as many children (coincidentally also 64 per cent) as were receiving it. Both desire and use increased with the child's age, but even for 2-year-olds it was wanted for over 70 per cent. Desire, unlike use, also varied very little across social classes.

Bone examined the forms of provision that were preferred. As she astutely observed, what she was registering was only the differences between use and preference 'at a particular period when the full range of facilities was not generally available'.[16] That is, choices were both practically and imaginatively constrained by the existing pattern of provision. Still, she noted that the one exception to the general preference for more of everything was childminders, and that there was a particular preference for educational forms of day provision, especially as children grew older. Day nurseries were preferred by around 7 per cent both of those already using some form of daycare and of those using none. Although absolute figures are small, out of the mothers of the 49 children in day nurseries, nearly a quarter would have preferred a nursery school or class; on the other hand, amongst users day nurseries were found more 'convenient' than any other form of daycare provision.

I have dwelt on Bone's findings because there was a long lapse of time before a comparable survey was undertaken and to date there have only ever been two. What the survey appeared to establish was a substantial and unmet desire, if not demand, for a range of forms of childcare provision, including day nurseries. During the 1980s the percentage of mothers with children under five years of age in paid employment continued to grow; indeed it grew more rapidly than for other categories of women, from 37 in 1984 to 52 in 1993.[17] In addition, the recognition of parents' childcare needs received a further

---

[15] Desire was calculated to include children already receiving daycare provision, which produced a slight overestimate since her analysis indicated that a small percentage of users' mothers would have preferred not to make use of it.

[16] Ibid. 15.

[17] Figures from the Labour Force Survey, cited in Frances Sly, 'Mothers in the Labour Market', *Employment Gazette*, 102:11 (1994), 403–13.

impetus, as we have seen, with the anticipation of a demographic 'time-bomb'.

Howard Meltzer's survey,[18] again commissioned by the Department of Health, was completed in 1990 but, perhaps significantly, not published until 1994, when government was reluctantly beginning to acknowledge that further childcare measures might be needed. Meltzer's national sample was larger than Bone's, at over 3,000 children, but on the other hand was drawn from a wider age group—the under-eights. Chapter 5 of his survey dealt with 'Preferences for Services'. Recognizing, as Bone had, that preferences were likely to reflect current experience of provision, he made a distinction between 'preferred choice' and 'ideal choice'. Preferred choice had to take into account personal constraints like employment and cost, but disregard current availability in their area. Ideal choice in principle should recognize no such constraints. It must be said that while this device revealed some interesting divergences these were relatively marginal and subtle: most of the time there was around 80 per cent coincidence between preferred and ideal choices, indicating no doubt the difficulty of conducting this kind of mental exercise.

Meltzer reported that while only 8 per cent of pre-school children attended a day nursery (like Bone, he did not distinguish between private and local authority provision), for mothers of 26 per cent of children not currently attending day nursery it was the preferred choice. Overall these figures suggested 'a lot of unsatisfied preferences [for day nurseries], particularly among the mothers of one- and two-year olds'.[19] On the other hand, mothers of over a third (38 per cent) of children attending day nurseries would have preferred for them not to be there. Of these, in 60 per cent of cases the preferred option was for them to be in a nursery school or class and in keeping with this preference dissatisfaction with day nurseries was highest amongst mothers of 4-year-olds, at 50 per cent.

The commonest reason given for preferring day nursery provision was to enable the mother to go out to work (48 per cent of children). Mothers of more than half the children attending day nursery wanted them to go more often (in only one-third of cases could they go five days a week). Mothers of over a third also wanted earlier starting times, while only a third of children finished at times convenient for their mothers (only 2 per cent of children attending a day nursery had a latest finishing time of 6 p.m.).

[18] Howard Meltzer, *Day Care Services for Children* (London: HMSO, 1994).
[19] Ibid. 41.

INTERPRETING DEMAND FOR CHILD CARE

Like Bone's survey, Meltzer's focused directly on the issue of childcare, and even more than Bone's it appeared to confirm significant unmet demand not only for a range of childcare services but specifically for day nurseries. However, this has by no means settled the question of how much demand for childcare there really is. This is not because the publication of Meltzer's report was delayed. The demand it documented was real but neither overwhelming nor unambiguous and was not corroborated by any major, popular political campaign for childcare. In fact the extent of demand or need continues to be contested, within the context of wider arguments that are still tacitly about women's mothering responsibilities.

This debate is complex and many-stranded but I shall focus here on two connected questions. The first concerns popular attitudes towards working mothers. Very recently, the feminist author Melissa Benn claimed that 'The "right" of women to childcare is well-established in the public mind'.[20] She suggests that following campaigns such as that mounted in *Cosmopolitan* in the early 1980s, there was a cumulative cultural shift as a result of which 'at some point in the mid to late eighties, the burden of proof shifted from the working to the non-working mother'.[21] To what extent has the legitimacy of mothers going out to work really been established? Although by the 1990s more than half the mothers of children under 5 went out to work, how was this development regarded?

In the 1988 edition of *British Social Attitudes*, Witherspoon[22] investigated attitudes to women's work. She noted that it was perfectly possible for approval of equal treatment for women in the workplace to coexist with more 'traditional' views about women's role in the home. While approximately four-fifths of all respondents supported legislation against sexual discrimination at work, nearly a third agreed with the statement 'Women shouldn't try to combine a career and children'. What's more, 57 per cent believed that a married woman with children under school age should stay at home while a further 22 per cent believed she should only go out to work if she really needed the money. The views of working-age women themselves were somewhat less traditional but the corresponding figures were still 45 per cent and 29 per

[20] Melissa Benn, *Madonna and Child: Towards a New Politics of Motherhood* (London: Vintage, 1999), 22.

[21] Ibid. 33.

[22] Sharon Witherspoon, 'Interim Report: A Woman's Work', in R. Jowell *et al.* (eds.), *British Social Attitudes: The Fifth Report* (London: Gower, 1988).

cent. Although when comparing this hard-line 45 per cent with corresponding figures, from earlier surveys, of 78 per cent in 1965 and 62 per cent in 1980, Witherspoon describes the shift in attitudes as 'tantamount to a sea-change', these figures taken together would still seem to indicate major reservations towards working mothers of pre-school children both in the public at large and amongst women of working age.

In an attempt to shed light on this 'attitudinal lag', in the mid-eighties Brannen and Moss collected survey data for a sociological study of the experience of first-time mothers returning to work. Their sample of mothers had two distinct characteristics: the mothers were drawn from Greater London and they also lived in dual-earner households. None the less the authors were able to use their findings to reflect on wider issues concerning attitudes of and to working mothers.

The study confirmed that only a relatively small proportion of prospective mothers intended to resume full-time employment following the birth of their first child. It also found that amongst the women in the sample who did go back to full-time employment within nine months of the birth, more than a third did not remain in full-time work (not including those women who left work for a second period of maternity leave). On the other hand, between 50 and 60 per cent of all the women interviewed said that ideally they would prefer to be part-time workers. The reasons for these findings were many and complex, but difficulties in arranging adequate childcare were by no means a major explicit consideration. Brannen and Moss attributed this partly to women's attitude to their jobs: their own findings confirmed those of earlier studies suggesting that in dual-earning households at least, the woman was still inclined to regard her employment as of secondary importance to her husband's. This tended to be true even when she was earning as much or more than her husband. The few women who were an exception, in rating their own job more important, were 'hard put' to justify this: 'they appeared to lack a clearly and confidently articulated discourse with which to express their obviously vital contribution to household resources'.[23]

But beyond women's attitude to employment, and in part shaping it, the authors identified the impact of persistent ideologies or 'dominant social meanings available to women'. They suggested that an ideology of full-time mothering endured although its rationale had been subtly changing. Whereas Bowlby and his contemporaries had focused on the *emotionally* harmful effects of 'maternal deprivation', the new

[23] Julia Brannen and Peter Moss, *Managing Mothers: Dual Earner Households after Maternity Leave* (London: Unwin Hyman, 1991), 88.

emphasis, as purveyed by a variety of experts and, increasingly, by a ver-
itable 'child development industry' of manufacturers, retailers, and the
media, was on the mother's role as unfolder of her child's *cognitive*
ability. The mother's constant attention was needed to ensure that her
child reached its optimal level of achievement. The thrust of this kind
of argument is to suggest that the need for childcare is in some sense
understated because the continuing strength of an ideology or discourse
of motherhood, however altered its terms, tends to delegitimize childcare claims and make them difficult to articulate.

The second question to be considered concerns the 'meaning' of
women's part-time work. There is currently quite an argument amongst
feminist social scientists about the general reasons for women's part-
time employment. But here we are most interested in one aspect of this
issue. What does the high rate of part-time employment amongst
women, and specifically amongst mothers of pre-school children, tell us
about mothers' need for childcare?

A striking feature of women's employment in the post-war period has
been the salience of part-time work. Between 1951 and 1981 the total
number of full-time employees fell by 2.3 million whilst the number of
part-time employees grew by 3.7 million. Of these part-time employees,
80 per cent were women. Part-time employment was especially prevalent amongst married women, and above all working mothers. Although
through the 1980s the rate of full-time employment amongst working
mothers with dependent children increased from 17 to 21 per cent, by
1989, 62 per cent of employed mothers were still working part-time. This
compares with 2 per cent of employed fathers.[24] In 1993 64 per cent of
employed cohabiting or married mothers and 65 per cent of employed
lone mothers with children under five years of age worked part-time.[25]
Together with the Netherlands, mothers in the UK work the shortest
hours in the European Union.[26]

In seeking the reason for this pattern, we are confronted first of all
with the difficulties of unravelling factors of demand and supply that
sometimes seem to operate in a circular fashion. But there is also a
difference between accounts that emphasize constraints channelling
mothers into part-time work and those which give greater weight to

---

[24] Figures taken from Anne Harrop and Peter Moss, 'Working Parents: Trends in the
1980s', *Employment Gazette*, 102:10 (1994), 343–52.

[25] Figures from Sly, 'Mothers in the Labour Market', 407.

[26] See European Commission Network on Childcare and Other Measures to Reconcile Employment and Family Responsibilities, *A Review of Services for Young Children
in the European Union 1990–1995* (Brussels: EC Directorate General V, 1996). But note
that the reference here is to mothers with children under 10 years of age. These cross-
national comparisons are considered further in Ch. 6.

their subjective preferences. In considering constraints, some feminist economists stress factors of demand for labour. Thus Olive Robinson argues that the overall increase in part-time working from the 1950s is above all a reflection of the changing pattern of employers' labour requirements. She suggests that the fact that during the 1970s and 1980s there was simultaneous growth of female part-time employment and of male and female unemployment casts doubt on the alternative view that the growth in part-time employment was primarily employers' response to fluctuations in the labour supply.[27] More recently Jean Gardiner has modified the demand argument by suggesting that while there are common factors at work in different countries affecting the level and structure of demand for labour, there is also significant variation in the pattern of demand across different countries associated with their differing national institutional and policy contexts. In this way, 'In Britain a number of government policies in the 1980s contributed to the specific pattern of growth of female employment'.[28] Monetarist policies exacerbated the decline of manufacturing and the expansion of the private services sector, where part-time work was more common. Other contributory policies were the dismantling of national labour standards and agreements, the introduction of subcontracting and compulsory competitive tendering in the public sector, the weakening and final abolition of the wages councils, and the encouragement of localized company bargaining and performance-related pay. Further support for such an argument comes from a comparative study of working mothers in Britain and in France. While again stressing the difficulty of separating out supply and demand factors, the authors conclude that government policies—such as the national insurance systems, and the presence or absence of a minimum wage—have themselves contributed to the much greater propensity to part-time work in Britain, by providing disincentives to French employers to employ workers part-time.[29]

But the constraint argument is not limited to demand for women's labour; it can also be made in relation to women's ability to present themselves for full-time work, that is, supply. Many have argued that the limited availability of affordable childcare is itself a major constraint on the supply of women's labour.

[27] Olive Robinson, 'The Changing Labour Market: Growth of Part-time Employment and Labour Market Segregation in Britain', in Sylvia Walby (ed.), *Gender Segregation at Work* (Milton Keynes: Open University Press, 1988).

[28] Jean Gardiner, *Gender, Care and Economics* (London: Macmillan, 1997), 157–8.

[29] See Shirley Dex, Patricia Walters, and David M. Alden, *French and British Mothers at Work* (London: Macmillan, 1993), Ch. 5.

The alternative approach prefers to emphasize women's active choice to work part-time. A forceful exponent of this view is Catherine Hakim. One of the five 'feminist myths' about women's employment that she claims to have identified and calls into question is that women have the same orientation towards work as men. She observes for instance that the preference for part-time work extends well beyond women with mothering responsibilities.[30] In fact, citing data from the early nineties, she argues that rather than generalizing about the 'typical' woman's attitude to work, we should recognize that women tend to fall into two groups:

The first group of women are committed to careers in the labour market and therefore invest in training and qualifications and generally achieve higher grade occupations and higher paid jobs which they pursue full-time for the most part. The second group of women give priority to the marriage career, do not invest in what economists term 'human capital', transfer quickly and permanently to part-time jobs as soon as a breadwinner husband permits it, choose undemanding jobs 'with no worries or responsibilities' when they do work, and are hence found concentrated in lower grade and lowest paid jobs which offer convenient working hours with which they are perfectly happy.[31]

Elsewhere she has labelled these two groups 'self-made women' and 'grateful slaves' respectively. Although Hakim accepts that the former group has gradually been growing, she still maintains that the two groups are roughly equal in size.

From here, Hakim goes on to query a related feminist 'myth' that part-time work is 'an unwilling "choice" forced on women by the need to cope with childcare responsibilities'. The implication of her argument is that the self-made women will be able to find childcare if they need to; the 'grateful slaves' do not want to work full-time even if they can.[32] In a recent paper, Robert Rowthorn and Shirley Dex (her position appears to have shifted in the last couple of years[33]), estimate that of

[30] One issue discussed in this context is the degree of commitment which working mothers have to their jobs. Evidence is contradictory but according to one recent British Social Attitudes Survey, 'Working mothers with children under 12 do have an unusually high level of work commitment': Katarina Thomson, 'Working Mothers: Choice or Circumstance?', in Roger Jowell *et al.* (eds.), *British Social Attitudes: The 12th Report* (Aldershot: Dartmouth, 1994), 78.

[31] Catherine Hakim, 'Five Feminist Myths about Women's Employment', *British Journal of Sociology*, 46:3 (1995), 434.

[32] Hakim's arguments triggered an extended debate and were contested in particular by ten sociologists in Jay Ginn *et al.*, 'Feminist Fallacies: A Reply to Hakim on Women's Employment', *British Journal of Sociology*, 47:1 (1996), 167–74. Their discussion concludes by reaffirming that 'the evidence that childcare is a major factor in restricting British women's full-time employment seems undeniable' (170).

[33] She is one of the ten sociologists referred to in the previous footnote.

the 42 per cent of mothers with children under 10 who are 'economically inactive', only around one-tenth, or 3–5 per cent of the total, are actually prevented from going out to work by the lack of childcare. On this basis they conclude 'the problem is small' and that current talk of the need to provide affordable childcare is 'unwarranted'.[34] In an interview consequent on this paper, Dex contends,

This shows that mothers shouldn't have childcare forced upon them. They don't necessarily want it. . . . The childcare lobby is driven from the top by articulate, highly-educated women who form a minority but benefit from these policies . . . Their belief that we need more provision has become received wisdom, but nobody has actually bothered to find out what most women want.[35]

The Dex and Rowthorn paper relies on a curious mixture of arguments to sustain their basic position. They criticize the purely economic approach to mother's participation in the workforce but then use it themselves to argue that the need for childcare is marginal. What about making life easier for already working mothers (parents) or indeed for non-working mothers of very young children who just need a break? They also greatly overestimate the extent both of childcare provision and of feminist influence on policy-makers.

Both Hakim and Dex end up dangerously close to the more explicit social conservatism of writers like Melanie Phillips[36] and A. H. Halsey. They appear to lack an appreciation of the historical dynamic through which social preferences change. Subjective preferences are not innate: as one feminist economist put it, 'Women chose to learn to prefer mothering over auto mechanics for the same reason that one would choose to learn to enjoy winter rather than summer sports in a cold climate'.[37]

Even so, it cannot be denied that the messages we receive from mothers of young children both about work and about childcare are quite complex and ambiguous. Combining responsibility for young children with employment, especially full-time employment, *is* difficult and

---

[34] S. Dex and R. Rowthorn, *Parenting and Labour Force Participation: The Case for a Ministry of the Family*, ESRC Centre for Business Research Working Paper No. 74 (Cambridge: Cambridge University Press, 1997).

[35] Zoe Brennan, 'Mothers Spurn Chance of Full-time Childcare', *Sunday Times*, 9 Nov. 1997.

[36] See for instance Melanie Phillips, *The Sex Change State* (London: Social Market Foundation, 1997). She situates childcare demands within a broader discourse of 'female supremacism' that aims to undermine men and turn them into women, force mothers out to work, and so forth.

[37] E. McCrate, 'Gender Difference: The Role of Endogenous Preferences and Collective Action', *American Economic Review*, 78:2 (1988), 237. This is cited in Irene Breugel, 'Whose Myths Are They Anyway?', *British Journal of Sociology*, 47:1 (1996), 175–7.

stressful, especially given not only existing childcare arrangements but the way that work is organized and Britain's slowness to adopt more 'family-friendly' maternity and parental leave policies. Working mothers' favoured form of childcare, while they are away, continues to be informal care, by partner or relatives, but this is in limited supply.[38] Fathers in particular remain singularly unable or unwilling to step in. Mothers' attitudes to more institutional forms of childcare may also be affected by what they know of existing provision, the social stigma traditionally attached to local authority daycare, scare stories about childminders, and so forth.

If the issue of need and demand for childcare is not entirely clear-cut, certain observations are none the less in order. First, it must be stressed that we are talking about the need for more affordable and accessible childcare in a situation where, far from mothers having childcare 'forced upon them', existing provision is extraordinarily meagre. Surveys such as Bone's and Meltzer's have established significant unmet demand. It is not necessary to prove that most mothers of young children want to work full-time in order to make the case for more childcare. Even as we enter the new millennium, and despite growing if still qualified public acceptance of the principle of childcare assistance for working mothers, there is ludicrously little available.

Second, given the present organization of the economy and family life, women who choose not to work, or to work part-time, following the birth of their child *do* suffer economically. Heather Joshi, in particular, has investigated the considerable opportunity costs associated with childrearing, including lower rates of pay, lost training, and promotion possibilities, all of which have consequences for earning power and will mean lower earnings-related pensions.[39] Although many women may be willing to incur these cumulative disadvantages, they do raise serious issues of gender equality.

Third, while mothers' subjective preferences must be respected and the emphasis must be on providing them with the opportunity to exercise 'choice', it must also be recognized that choices are never entirely free. We have seen how, even when encouraged to envisage an 'ideal' situation, mothers' choices have tended to be shaped by existing practical constraints, by their own experience, and beyond this by prevailing assumptions about the maternal role. This observation chimes closely with the broader emphasis of this analysis of childcare policy-making

---

[38] Thomson, 'Working Mothers: Choice or Circumstance?', 72–4.

[39] See for instance Heather Joshi, 'Sex and Motherhood as Handicaps in the Labour Market', in Mavis Maclean and Dulcie Groves (eds.), *Women's Issues in Social Policy* (London: Routledge, 1991).

on the constraining consequences of the way that childcare provision
has been institutionalized in the past. It is true that there has been no
clamour for increased provision from actual or would-be working
mothers to counteract the inertia embodied in inherited policy and practices. But this at least in part must reflect in turn the effects of policy
and practices in fashioning conceptions of what is practicable. I return
to these questions in the concluding chapter.

A final observation leads into the second part of our discussion. To
the extent that there *is* a need for childcare whose articulation has,
however, been muffled by the kinds of discursive and practical constraints we have identified, there has been a corresponding need for
feminism both as a movement and as an influential social analysis to
supply or reinforce that articulation, to express the childcare demand
forcefully and unequivocally. Contrary to the accusations of Hakim and
Dex, such advocacy, with the partial exception of very recent developments, has not really happened and we must now ask why.

FEMINISM AND THE CHILDCARE ISSUE[40]

Of course not all accounts agree that second-wave feminism in Britain
has failed to prioritize childcare. Looking back over the seventies, Coote
and Campbell, for instance, claimed that 'child care has been a major
preoccupation of the women's liberation movement'.[41] But this and
other references to an 'extensive debate' within the movement on motherhood and childcare seem to have little factual basis. Rather, with New
and David, we must ask, 'Why is it that feminists have had so little to
say about the future of motherhood and child care?'[42] Before attempting to answer that question, it is necessary briefly to summarize and
supplement what has been said in earlier chapters about feminism's
involvement in the issue.

Child daycare remained a highly marginal concern for first-wave
feminists but in the 1960s and 70s it seemed to have a much more immediate and personal relevance. As Rowbotham recalls, 'The contradictory
situation of the mother with small children, expected to care and yet

---

[40] The following section draws heavily on the analysis presented in my article, 'Feminism and Child Daycare', *Journal of Social Policy*, 25:4 (1996), 485–505. I am grateful to
Cambridge University Press for allowing me to reproduce parts of it here.

[41] Anna Coote and Bea Campbell, *Sweet Freedom* (London: Picador, 1982), 38.
Cited in Caroline New and Miriam David, *For the Children's Sake* (London: Penguin,
1985).

[42] New and David, *For the Children's Sake*, 17.

denied an environment in which this was possible, was one of the factors that brought many women into the movement'.[43] One of the four initial movement demands announced by the first women's liberation conference, in 1970, was for 'twenty-four hour nurseries'. According to Val Charlton, the demand was formulated by the Women's National Coordinating Committee and was 'intended to cover the immediate needs of the most hard hit women, including night workers',[44] and not, as some might conclude, to make it possible for children to be left for twenty-four hours at a time in a nursery.

The demand gave rise to a brief and troubled attempt to mount a national campaign. It also generated a debate in the early movement literature. But already by 1973, Charlton was referring to the national campaign as 'abortive', although there were a number of more localized campaigns under way. At the same time, even at this stage, the attention devoted to the childcare issue in different movement publications and fora was limited.[45] Charlton herself observed: 'Considering the centrality of the issue, attention given to it has been both incidental and underdeveloped with few exceptions'. Moreover, in these early discussions the difficulties and differences raised by the childcare issue (and discussed further below) were already apparent.

In the longer run the demand for childcare remained strikingly underexplored and undertheorized. But local initiatives persisted and some, such as the Dartmouth Park Children's Community Centre, opened in 1972, which became the Market Nursery in Hackney, enjoyed some success. Nor were these confined to London. These local schemes helped to build up a new, more solid momentum behind a national campaign. At the same time socialist feminists associated with the Working Women's Charter set up a Nursery Action Group in anticipation of cuts in local authority provision as early as 1974. Out of this came the London Nursery Campaign, which in turn fed into the National Childcare Campaign of the 1980s.

The NCC's uncompromisingly stated objective was 'To build a mass national child care campaign around the demand for comprehensive, flexible, free, democratically controlled childcare facilities funded by the state'. Its policy statement also insisted that this was a feminist issue:

[43] Sheila Rowbotham, *The Past is Before Us* (London: Penguin, 1990), 129.
[44] Val Charlton, 'The Patter of Tiny Contradictions', *Red Rag*, 5 (1973), 5–8.
[45] But see Liz, 'Games Children Play', *Shrew*, 3: (1971), 6–8; 'More than Minding', *Shrew*, 3:2 (1971); J. Cullen, 'Nurseries' (written in 1971), in M. Wandor (ed.), *The Body Politic* (London: Stage 1, 1978); Charlton, 'The Patter of Tiny Contradictions'; Sue Cowley, 'Thatcher's Nurseries—Expansion or Containment?', *Red Rag*, 4 (1973), 3–5; Myra Garrett, 'Girls and Boys Come Out to Play', *Red Rag*, 5 (1975), 6–8; Annette Muir, 'Laissez-faire Parenthood?', *Red Rag*, 3 (1973).

'We would like to see a National Child Care Campaign that says loud and clear that women do work, need and want to work, and that child-care facilities are absolutely necessary and central to women's equality'. This represents in a sense the high-water mark of the feminist articula-tion of the childcare issue.

However, the NCC was a small organization. As described in the pre-ceding chapter, it split in 1983. The reasons were complex but included the general strains of working as a campaigning body in the Thatcher era, and related to this the relative weight to be given to considerations of democracy and efficiency within the organization. There were also arguments over whether to accept a large grant from the DHSS under its 'Under-5s Initiative'. The DHSS grant meant that the NCC, or what remained of it, could expand in organizational terms, but it also helped to change its character. In 1986 the members of the governing collect-ive constituted themselves as a charitable organization, the Daycare Trust, while the NCC persisted as a voluntary body. The Trust got funding for several workers and its role became one of giving infor-mation and advice about setting up childcare provision to parents, em-ployers, and other interested groups. Its work inevitably tended to marginalize the more direct campaigning of the NCC. At the same time the broad outlook of the combined Daycare Trust and NCC gradually shifted: the demand that childcare be provided free of charge was early abandoned as was resistance to the idea of workplace nurseries, while there was less and less tendency to frame childcare demands in terms of sex equality.

A number of former members of the NCC joined the Workplace Nurseries Campaign (which later changed its name to Working for Childcare), formed in 1984 in the first instance to oppose the tax on workplace nurseries. From the start more conventionally structured and hierarchical than the NCC, and more comfortable with the idea of a 'mixed economy' of childcare provision, it worked particularly closely with and through the trade unions.

The other significant national organization campaigning for childcare was the Working Mothers' Association, founded in 1985. It was never explicitly feminist although it saw itself as reflecting the needs of young mothers, and it was a more middle-class organization than either the NCC or the WNC. By 1991 the burgeoning association had around 145 local branches. Despite initial reservations about 'male' organizational forms, it had come round to more formal procedures. Moreover, it approached the question of childcare primarily from the perspective of the mother as 'consumer'. It was not directly concerned, as the NCC had been, with the possible exploitation of childminders and never had any expectation that childcare should be free. Reflecting the wider process of deradicalization, in 1994 it changed its name to Working Parents' Association.

In addition to single-issue organizations, the second main way in which feminists mobilized around childcare issues was through their growing presence in the labour movement, both trade unions and the Labour Party. Feminist activism in the labour movement had been growing before, and intensified with, the advent of the Thatcher government in 1979, as, on the one hand, socialist feminists reconsidered their rejection of 'mainstream' institutions as a site of struggle and, on the other, both party and trade union leaders appeared more receptive to feminist arguments. The first manifestation of this pressure was in the context of the blossoming of 'municipal feminism', that is the proliferation of women's committee's, women's units, women or equality officers, and so on, at local level. The GLC led the way. First the Women's Committee, set up in 1982, gave funding to existing childcare centres and set up new ones. By 1984–5 it was providing 140 grants to childcare organizations. Overall, it accounted for over 12 per cent of all full-time childcare places in London, a massive contribution unrivalled before or since. Second, the Popular Planning Unit was authorized to award grants up to a maximum of £750 to local childcare campaigns and finally, of course, the GLC provided childcare for its own employees.

This precedent was followed by a significant expansion of childcare programmes in other local authorities where feminist ideas had made some inroads. For instance, in 1986 Manchester City Council adopted as its new policy objective that child daycare 'should be universal, affordable, provision offering quality, continuity, and flexibility, for all children whose parents want it'.[46] It aimed to build a series of Children Centres which would differ importantly in their admissions criteria from the traditional day nurseries, reserving a smaller proportion of places for children falling into the different categories of need and otherwise making them available to children of all parents living in the neighbourhood.[47] At the same time, feminist activists, as we have seen, were helping to push the childcare issue onto the agenda of the national Labour Party, and through their agency it was also being taken up by individual trade unions and the Trades Union Congress.

The most striking feature of this history of feminist mobilization is

[46] Manchester City Council, *1995–96 Children Act Review* (Manchester: Manchester City Council, n.d.), 3.
[47] In the event, fewer of these centres were built than originally intended. The existing day nurseries were redesignated Children's Centres and their admissions criteria modified but not to the same extent.

simply to its relatively limited scale. We have seen that in the 1970s, while there were numerous initiatives, these were locally based and fragmented; they also frequently ran into difficulties. The 1980s saw more sustained attempts at national co-ordination and lobbying, together with the increasing absorption of childcare as a campaigning issue into the feminist-influenced labour movement, but this was accompanied by a process of deradicalization. There was a continuing shift away from a more radical, with a small 'r', demand for free state or community-based childcare as a fundamental woman's right, to the demand for some mixture of state, voluntary sector, and employer provision, including childminding, for which charges could be made, and all of which was justified no longer in terms of women's rights but by reference to the need for choice or the requirements of the national economy. Under New Labour, despite the input of individual feminists, such as Harriet Harman, the feminist discourse of childcare has been still further attenuated.

This pattern of feminist mobilization on childcare can firstly be contrasted with mobilization around other feminist-identified issues such as abortion, male violence, and pornography. It is true that feminist activism on all these issues showed some tendency towards greater 'moderation' and pragmatism in the 1980s, though to a lesser extent than with childcare. Even so, they are issues which have prompted mass campaigns, inventive direct action, and dramatic slogans, taken up reams of column space in the movement literature, and generated the debate through which feminist thought has developed and diversified. The same cannot be said of childcare. Up to a point, and as discussed further in Chapter 6, the British experience also contrasts with the role of feminism in childcare politics in other countries, for instance Australia and New Zealand.

EXPLAINING FEMINIST RETICENCE

There is no one single cause for this less than whole-hearted involvement of the feminist movement in campaigning for childcare, but we may go some way toward an explanation by seeing it as resulting from the interaction of three elements: the character of early second-wave feminism in Britain, the 'political opportunity structure', and the problems posed for feminist ideology by the childcare issue itself.

The specific character of the women's movement in the late sixties and seventies was not necessarily conducive to mobilization on childcare. It is always somewhat invidious to separate out and label different strands of feminism, thereby obscuring the range and subtlety of people's actual positions. There were, even so, real and often fierce conflicts between groups identifying themselves with particular tendencies within the women's movement in the 1970s. The more 'reformist', liberal kind of feminism played quite a minor role at this stage. To begin with, socialist feminists, whether aligned with Marxist organizations and thinking or identified with the new libertarian Left, predominated. Soon a distinct radical feminist position emerged which, though tending to incorporate socialist economic and political assumptions, firmly gave these second place to the power struggle between the sexes. While the conflict between socialist and radical feminists was especially bitter, the socialist feminists took on board much of the radical feminist agenda, and both saw themselves as in some sense 'revolutionary', opposed to the 'system' and the existing capitalist, patriarchal state.

This hostility and mistrust affected not only attitudes to participation in mainstream politics, through parties, pressure groups, and the like, but perceptions of the welfare state as dispenser of benefits and services. The first full-length feminist analysis of the welfare state, by Elizabeth Wilson, though pioneering and perceptive in many ways, tended to present it largely negatively as instrumental to advanced capitalism in ensuring the reproduction of the labour force both physically and psychologically. To this end, welfare state policies and ideology shored up the traditionally conceived family and women's maternal, caring role within it.[48] Though succeeded by critiques from a range of feminist positions,[49] until recently more positive feminist assessments of the British welfare state were hard to find.

In practice, of course, and from the start, feminists engaged with the state, especially the 'local' state, in numerous ways. The more aligned or Marxist feminists were in any case not anti-state as such but anti the specific form of the British state. They were state-centred, attacking the state but demanding concessions from it.

Nor can we entirely divorce the ethos of the women's movement from its political and institutional context or 'opportunity structure'. In the Introduction it was suggested that despite its 'liberal' characterization, the British political system has been relatively centralized and difficult for outsider groups, such as those associated with the feminist movement, to penetrate. In addition there was no obvious home for feminists

---

[48] Elizabeth Wilson, *Women and the Welfare State* (London: Tavistock, 1977).
[49] As usefully summarized in Fiona Williams, *Social Policy: A Critical Introduction* (London: Polity, 1989), ch. 3.

within what might count as the institutionalized opposition. Not only the Conservative but the Labour Party,[50] and the trade union movement, as we have seen, tended towards social conservatism in the postwar period. By the same token, the greater willingness of feminist activists in the 1980s to work in mainstream political channels, and especially the influx of socialist feminists into the Labour Party and trade unions, was in part a response to a shift in the political opportunity structure, in the sense of an increased receptivity of the trade unions and Labour Party to feminist arguments and initiatives.

While, therefore, early feminist hostility towards the state can up to a point be seen as a response both its relative impenetrability and its social conservatism, as far as childcare is concerned, the timing of feminist involvement was to say the least unfortunate.[51] As we have seen, by the early 1970s a (mainly non-feminist) head of steam was gradually building in favour of expanding nursery education and childcare, and of integrating them more closely, but this was largely cut off by the public expenditure squeeze of the late 1970s and by the time a national feminist childcare campaign got going in the 1980s it was faced with a particularly unhelpful Conservative government. In the longer run, feminist influence within the Labour Party *has* contributed to a change in national childcare policy under the 'new' Labour government from 1997. Nor should one discount the more diffuse and longer-term cultural effects of the feminist movement in altering public attitudes to working mothers, as we have traced above. None the less it is

---

[50] Jenson links Labour's social conservatism with the fact that Labour formed the first post-war government and was heavily identified with the dominant, and paternalist, conception of the welfare state. See Jane Jenson, 'The Modern Women's Movement in Italy, France and Great Britain: Differences in Life Cycles', *Comparative Social Research*, 5 (1982), 341–75. It may also have reflected Britain's system of parties alternating in office: for approximately half the period from 1945 to 1979 Labour was in power.

[51] Watson has argued that because feminist activists only began to get involved in mainstream politics in substantial numbers in the 1980s, crucial opportunities may have been lost. Although she concedes that it is 'impossible to assess' what might otherwise have been achieved, she suggests both that 'the "against the state" discourse has been disempowering, and that it has meant that once feminists began to intervene intervention inevitably took on a marginal character'. See Sophie Watson, 'Unpacking "the State": Reflections on Australian, British and Swedish Feminist Interventions', in M. F. Katzenstein and H. Skjeie (eds.), *Going Public* (Oslo: Institute for Social Research, 1990), 135–7. Arguing that effective feminist politics requires both a sufficient feminist presence in mainstream political institutions and a vibrant grass-roots movement, Chamberlayne suggests that by the time British feminists got over their mistrust of state institutions, the grass-roots movement was going into decline. See Pru Chamberlayne, 'Women and the State: Changes in Roles and Rights in France, West Germany, Italy and Britain, 1970–1990', in J. Lewis (ed.), *Women and Social Policies in Europe* (Aldershot: Edward Elgar, 1993). Both Watson and Chamberlayne seem to be saying that in terms of having an impact on policy British feminism somehow 'missed the boat'.

worth asking why the women's movement in the crucial early to mid-seventies period was less than enthusiastic about or galvanized by the childcare issue.

No issue is straightforward for feminism. All issues touch on questions that divide feminists, or women as a whole, or which are not properly acknowledged or thought through. But childcare, which at first glance would seem one area where feminists could agree and be clear, has proved one of the least straightforward. It brings together some of the most difficult questions for feminists: the role of the state; the significance of motherhood; differences between women, especially class differences; and how all these relate to strategies for short- or long-term change.

Childcare and the state   The Women's Liberation Movement's largely negative attitude to the state was nowhere clearer than on the question of childcare. The twenty-four-hour nursery demand was a recognition of the immediate needs of the 'hardest-hit' women, but there was almost at once a concern with what quality of provision could be expected from the state. Here feminists were partly responding to reality; that is, to the general shortcomings of local authority child daycare at that time. But they were also afraid that such daycare would reflect the patriarchal and capitalist values of the state. As Charlton writes, 'Women in Women's Liberation were confused, suspicious, uncertain. They didn't want nurseries for everyone if the nurseries remained hot-beds of sexist ideology and authoritarianism'.[52] A feminist infant school teacher deplored the authoritarian ambiance of her school and asked: 'Do we really want our children to go to nurseries or childcare centres for even longer periods where they will be treated just as they are being treated now'.[53] Sue Cowley dismissed the announcement in 1973 of a modest expansion in the nursery education programme as a 'hollow' victory, and a 'small but meaningful attempt to intensify the influence of bourgeois ideology on the working class'.[54]

At most, they were prepared to countenance an expansion of state-controlled nurseries run on traditional lines, for 'hard-hit' working-class women, but these had 'very limited appeal for those with a remnant of choice, both in and out of the movement'.[55] What were the alternatives? Exceptionally, the 'local' state might buck the national trend and offer 'a decent nursery with a fairly progressive outlook and atmosphere'.[56]

[52] Charlton, 'The Patter of Tiny Contradictions', 5–8.
[53] Liz, 'Games Children Play', 13.   [54] Cowley, 'Thatcher's Nurseries', 3.
[55] Charlton, 'The Patter of Tiny Contradictions', 6.
[56] Cowley, 'Thatcher's Nurseries', 3.

Or groups of parents might obtain space and funding from a council to set up their own nursery. But according to Charlton, for some feminists even this degree of reliance on the local council was unacceptable.

Childcare and motherhood But the childcare issue also raised the crucial and vexed question of motherhood. At the outset, I would refute one argument that has been advanced in this connection. This is the suggestion that feminist activism has been guided by narrow self-interest. Not all women, not all feminists, are mothers; furthermore not all are mothers of young children for any extended period of time. It is also possible that mothers were particularly under-represented in the early WLM. Thus Dena Attar has contended:

Strip away the anecdotal detail and this is the picture—feminists have failed to campaign for childcare because mothers, who need it, don't have enough of it to find the time for campaigning, and others, who don't think they need it, don't have the motivation—some are even hostile.[57]

These differing personal needs doubtless contributed to variations in campaigning effort and focus but the link with motherhood is not this simple. After all, the same point could be made about other issues. Not all women need an abortion or get raped but there has been a much greater recognition amongst feminists, and one that they have communicated more effectively to women at large, that these are issues which in an important sense touch us all.

More significant has been the general attitude amongst feminists to motherhood and, especially in the early WLM and amongst radical feminists, the negativity of these views. Shulamith Firestone, a 'founding' American radical feminist, wrote that 'the heart of women's oppression is her child-bearing and child-rearing role'.[58] The family was seen as an overwhelmingly oppressive institution and in so far as motherhood was the means through which women were subordinated within the family, it too was rejected. As Katherine Gieve has written, if the WLM was centrally concerned with liberation and autonomy, then motherhood was seen as 'the antithesis of liberation'.[59] Not all feminists shared this view: many came into the movement with more complex feelings derived from their own mothering experiences but often found it difficult to give voice to them in the face of a prevailing orthodoxy. As one recalls:

---

[57] Dena Attar, 'The Demand that Time Forgot', *Trouble and Strife*, 23 (1992), 27.
[58] Shulamith Firestone, *The Dialectic of Sex* (London: Paladin, 1970), 73.
[59] Katherine Gieve, 'Rethinking Feminist Attitudes towards Mothering', *Feminist Review*, 25 (1987), 38.

I remember a group meeting where we discussed motherhood, and had decided to interrogate each of the mothers present (they were in a minority) about their reasons for having children. They all said it had not been consciously or deliberately chosen. That let them off the hook. They obviously had the rest of us figured out—that version of events gave them some lever to demand support, whereas any woman confessing she'd deliberately opted to have a child could expect to be left to get on with it.[60]

One consequence of this implicit rejection of motherhood was that feminists were reluctant to engage with the issue of childcare for fear of guilt by association. They did not want to have to think about something that represented all they were trying to get away from, and they also feared that if they did it would only confirm sexist stereotypes. As another feminist agonized, 'All articles on childcare are directed at women. Are we reinforcing this by even discussing this subject in a journal of women's liberation?'[61]

By the late 1970s a shift was discernible: feminists were talking more openly and positively about motherhood. One underlying factor may simply have been the 'biological clock', or what Heron referred to as a 'latterday feminist baby boom'.[62] But associated with this to some extent was also the emergence of a different kind of radical feminist voice, one that was 'pro-woman' and positively celebrated women's child-bearing capacities. Although none of its main literary exponents were British,[63] these ideas did filter into the broader feminist consciousness through women's magazines and other channels, contributing to a surge of 'maternal revivalism', to use Lynne Segal's term.[64] But the rediscovery of motherhood did not presage a new appreciation of the childcare question, or at least of the need to help existing mothers cope with childcare responsibilities.[65]

[60] Attar, 'The Demand that Time Forgot', 26.

[61] Muir, 'Laissez-faire Parenthood'. Not all feminists were happy with this apparent collective amnesia. One anonymous and untitled article deplored the 'rottenness' of a crèche laid on at a one-day workshop: 'Why do we do this? Why are we so thoughtless about children?'. *Shrew*, 3:5 (1971), 10.

[62] Elisabeth Heron, 'The Mystique of Motherhood', *Time Out*, 21–7 Nov. 1980.

[63] An early formulation was the American feminist writer Adrienne Rich's *Of Woman Born* (London: Virago, 1977). The idea was taken up by other Americans, including Sara Ruddick and J. B. Elshtain. The only possible exception to the rule of non-Britishness is Dale Spender.

[64] See Lynne Segal, *Is the Future Female? Troubled Thoughts on Contemporary Feminism* (London: Virago, 1987).

[65] Rich's position was at best ambivalent. She was extremely critical of the role of 'mass childcare', both state-sponsored and commercial, under conditions of patriarchy, but at the same time acknowledged that in society as currently constituted many working mothers had a desperate need for childcare. Pro-woman feminists also discussed how far men, or fathers, should be allowed to play a larger role in child-rearing but this all tended to be at a fairly theoretical level.

Why is this? It seems that feminist attitudes to motherhood and to children may be rather more complex than the simple maternalist line suggests, that the revaluation of children may have had something to do with questions of female autonomy and power. Ann Oakley notes that although motherhood as a social structure has been oppressive to women, 'at the same time it can be one in which women can experience autonomy and wholeness'.[66] Pro-woman and other feminists have perhaps half-consciously recognized this. The autonomy held out by women's liberation proved exhausting and elusive to achieve. Segal links 'maternal revivalism' with

feminists' disappointment that our aspirations to engage in creative and rewarding work, to struggle for social change, to build warm and supporting communal spaces and friendship networks—as well as to choose to have children—have proved so often difficult, stressful and transitory.[67]

Having children in this context could be seen almost as a healing restorative experience; it could bring a new kind of freedom or confidence based on a grounded identity and sense of connectedness.

Put in rather less flattering terms, however, motherhood can be a source of powerlessness but also power. New and David have speculated that one reason feminists have been less than enthusiastic to take up the issue of how childcare should be organized in the future is that it is too 'threatening':

The more we look into this, the easier it is to see that the future of child care is an uncomfortable subject, not because it is to do with liberating mothers, but because it is also to do with empowering children. As things are, mothers play the most decisive part of all in changing children.[68]

In similar vein, Ruth Wallsgrove suggested that many of the feminists opting for motherhood in the eighties 'want to have some area of life, childcare, where they'll have the last word, where the importance of their position—as one and only Mum—is assured'.[69]

We saw that in the late nineteenth century, one dimension of feminist activism concerned the assertion of women's rights as mothers in the face of husbands' claims, especially in the context of child custody disputes. Feminists were much more exercised by this question of rights in children than by the issue of childcare. Though the

---

[66] Ann Oakley, 'Feminism and Motherhood', in M. Richards and P. Light (eds.), *Children of Social Worlds* (Cambridge, Mass.: Harvard University Press, 1986), 79.

[67] Segal, *Is the Future Female?*, 145.

[68] New and David, *For the Children's Sake*, 19.

[69] Ruth Wallsgrove, 'Thicker than Water', *Trouble and Strife*, 7 (1985), 28.

circumstances are quite different and mothers' rights in many respects much more secure, there may yet be some parallels in the present times, when in particular the group Families Need Fathers has mobilized on the issues of child custody and, more recently, child support. Christine Delphy surely exaggerates when she charges the women's movement with 'transforming itself into a fight for the ownership of children'[70] but this power dimension may help to explain why the new maternalist strand of radical feminism did not translate into a practical interest in the question of child daycare provision. As we have seen, all the impetus and public campaigning over the last twenty years has come from quite a different quarter, within the movement and without.

Childcare and women's employment   Another reason why feminist energies did not initially pour into the childcare campaign may be the WLM's deep ambivalence, to put it mildly, about the real value of paid work. Again this was partly a response to the reality of women's plainly disadvantaged position in the paid workforce and the limited range of employment available. But it also reflected the movement's student Left beginnings.

Rowbotham distinguishes two strands of early feminist thinking about work, which broadly correspond to the division between aligned and libertarian socialist feminists. Those in the aligned camp, with its emphasis on class struggle and the need for connection with the labour movement, had inherited the Marxist assumption that, for all the hardship entailed, work outside the home increased women's financial independence and furthered their emancipation. They dutifully picked up on demands for equal pay and equal rights at work made by increasingly militant women workers from the 1960s. Even so, these remained rather remote issues for 'most of the young middle-class members of women's liberation . . . many of whom were students, young mothers or had only just started work'.[71] And this approach 'coexisted and collided' with the libertarian perspective, the 'Great Refusal', which rejected work within the capitalist system. Feminists of this persuasion could argue 'that all the problems of caring for children in the isolation of their own home were preferable to the daily grind of some rotten job, given that money wasn't the deciding factor'.[72]

Such ambivalence towards paid work had implications for childcare.

[70] Christine Delphy, 'Mothers' Union?', *Trouble and Strife*, 24 (1992), 12.
[71] Rowbotham, *The Past is Before Us*, 166.
[72] Charlton, 'The Patter of Tiny Contradictions', 6.

It was recognized that childcare was a pressing need for working-class mothers who had no economic choice but to take such paid work as they could find—'the immediately hard-hit'. It was often also recognized that all mothers needed time to themselves, time to discover themselves and 'time to discover who stops us from living'.[73] But there was less approval, at this stage, for women positively opting to participate in the capitalist system, and less readiness to recognize childcare in the context of an equal rights or equal opportunities agenda.

Such categorical rejection would of course be much more unusual these days. Feminist social scientists and others quite rightly continue to point out the limited prospects and unattractive conditions of much part- or flexi-time female employment.[74] But the increasing influence of equal opportunities and trade union perspectives within the public voice of feminism has tended to enhance the positive connotations of paid work, both for the independence it helps to confer and for its own sake. This has been taken to an extreme under New Labour. As Minister of Social Security, Harriet Harman, one of the most feminist of New Labour women, declared, 'Work is not just about earning a living. It is a way of life'.[75]

Childcare and class   The discussion so far suggests one further aspect of the childcare issue which was potentially problematic for feminism, the way in which, partly as a consequence of the way that policy has institutionalized childcare provision, both the supply of childcare and demand for childcare have varied in form and degree along social class lines. Like so many social movements, the WLM was predominantly middle class. Influenced by the existing pattern of provision, its activists saw state-funded childcare as necessary for working-class women but not something they would want for themselves. One childcare activist suggested that this created a further class divide between feminists and the women workers who provided childcare. In particular, she argued, feminists, even those involved in trade unions and the Working Women's Charter, had been strangely slow to take up the cause of nursery nurses. These were, for the most part, young working-class women, often

[73] Taken from 'The Four Demands', as drawn up in *Women's Newspaper*, 1 (1971), republ. in M. Wandor (ed.), *The Body Politic* (London: Stage 1, 1978).

[74] See for instance Diane Perrons, 'Labour Market Transformations and Employment Policies: The Organisation of Work, Care and Leisure in the UK', paper presented to workshop on 'Labour Market and Social Policy—Gender Relations in Transition', Brussels, 1999.

[75] Cited in Ruth Lister, 'From Equality to Social Inclusion: New Labour and the Welfare State', *Critical Social Policy*, 55 (1998), 219.

recruited direct from school at 16, with minimal training, low in status and very poorly paid.[76] On the other hand feminists within the National Child Care Campaign were very conscious that childminders could be exploited, expected to work long hours for very low rates of pay, and for that reason only gradually relinquished their objection to child-minding as a form of childcare.

In some ways the very fear that, given the way that childcare has been institutionalized in this country, the provision of childcare could entail the exploitation of one (poorer) group of women by another, more afflu-ent and middle-class group, has further inhibited feminists' enthusiastic endorsement of the need for childcare. These are very legitimate con-cerns but have tended to discourage feminist involvement rather than encourage a direct engagement with issues about the staffing and remu-neration of childcare work. Melissa Benn's recent observation that 'The fundamental contradiction of childcare in Britain today is this: for those who can afford it childcare can be a family's major expense . . . Yet they are paying wages for one of the lowest-paid occupations in the country'[77] in some ways illustrates the rather paralysing, if well-meaning, way in which this class-related dimension of the childcare question can be formulated.

The burden of the discussion so far has been to suggest why the issue of childcare, as it was framed in the British context, was problematic for the idealistic feminism of the Women's Liberation Movement. Perhaps this could be summed up in terms of the tension that existed between the vision of a transformed world for which feminists understood them-selves to be struggling and the practical exigencies of the existing reality they had to deal with. Goals like an end to male sexual violence, or 'women's right to choose' whether to have an abortion, were inspiring because they collapsed together more instrumental and transcendent considerations. For radical and socialist feminists the demand for child-care, even publicly provided childcare, could not occupy the same log-ical space. Although it might seem instrumentally desirable in helping women struggling to combine mothering responsibilities with public and especially economic roles, it did not prefigure in a clear way the kind of future world feminists hoped for. There were grave misgivings about the kind of service state-run nurseries did or could provide, and the way they functioned to support a capitalist, patriarchal system. Beyond this there was confusion about how parenting and work *should* ideally be organized and reconciled.

---

[76] See Garrett, 'Girls and Boys Come Out to Play'.
[77] Benn, *Madonna and Child*, 143.

The increasing salience of childcare as an issue for feminists coincided to an extent with the 'de-radicalization' of the movement and its integration into mainstream institutions—the professions, unions, parties. Childcare has assumed greater urgency in association with a range of more partial agendas—needs of women workers, or of working parents, or of equal employment opportunity—without having to be situated in a grander vision of transformed social relations.

CONCLUSION

This chapter has tried to analyse why there has not been more pressure for change both from women themselves and from within the feminist movement. Evidence of demand for increased child daycare provision has not been overwhelming or free from ambiguity. Feminists have been relatively slow to take up the issue in a sustained national campaign. While the reasons for this hesitancy are complex, it has been apparent that two important shaping influences have been firstly the nature of childcare as an issue itself and second the consequences of the way that childcare policy has been institutionalized. The issue of childcare—who looks after small children?—raises questions about women's responsibilities as mothers, the relationship between mothers and fathers, mothers' rights in their children—which remain socially contentious and emotionally and morally highly charged. It signifies a lot of serious and unfinished business for women and for feminism. But the manner in which childcare has hitherto been provided compounds these complexities by encouraging a negative, stigmatizing view of state day nurseries, and by embodying class differences in ways that foster antagonisms and insecurities.

One conclusion which might be drawn at this point is that childcare should not be a priority either for mothers or for feminists—that, as things stand, it is impossible to pursue the goal of increased childcare provision without unacceptable political compromise and the betrayal of children and other women. It is certainly the case that child daycare cannot be a consummate goal—it is not an intrinsically desirable ideal, except in some very limited form. It is a means of enlarging women's choice in a situation heavily constrained by the structuring of economic opportunity and the continuing imbalanced gender division of labour within the home. As such it could be seen as propping up the present 'system' rather than encouraging change in an ultimately desirable direction. But we have to be realistic about what we can and cannot change and the likely speed of change. Or as one former councillor who spent much of her working life campaigning for nursery education succinctly put it, 'You have to start from where you are'.

6

British Childcare Policy in
Cross-national Comparative Perspective

One way of trying to understand the making of childcare policy in Britain is to compare it with the experience of other industrialized democracies. The sheer number of societies this comprises means shifting gear from a relatively detailed, local exploration to a more strategic overview of what seem to be the most salient dimensions. From relative neglect, the topic of childcare has in recent years enjoyed increasing, though still highly uneven and selective, international coverage, both a cause for celebration and a further reason not to attempt any kind of comprehensive account. Instead the approach will be to organize discussion around questions or suggestions derived from the British case.

We must begin by reiterating what is to be explained—the pattern of Britain's childcare provision, with particular emphasis on the very limited contribution of either public provision or public funding. Table 2 shows figures for publicly funded services for children up to six years of age taken from the most recent report of the EC Network on Childcare, in 1995,[1] shortly before it was disbanded. As might be imagined, there are all kinds of problems comparing provision rates in these countries, not least the variation in the age of compulsory schooling. Countries collect figures on different bases.[2] None the less some contrasts emerge quite starkly. Britain is clearly amongst the worst laggards; whereas the amount of provision for children aged 3 and over (though largely part-time) is quite substantial and will have increased significantly since 1995, provision for under-threes, at 2 per cent, is pathetic. Contemporaneous figures are not readily available for the Old Commonwealth countries of Australia, Canada, and New Zealand, or for the

---

[1] See European Commission Network on Childcare and Other Measures to Reconcile Employment and Family Responsibilities, *A Review of Services for Young Children in the European Union 1990–1995* (Brussels: EC Directorate General V, 1996), 148–50.

[2] Some calculate provision in terms of the number of places available, others in terms of children attending. Definitions of 'publicly funded' also vary. In compiling the table I have sought to take these differences into account.

TABLE 2. *Provision of publicly funded childcare services in EU member states, 1995*

Country	Age at which school begins	Year	Provision for children aged 0–3 (%)	Provision for children aged 4–6 (%)
Austria	6	1994	3	75
Belgium	6	1993	30	95+
Denmark	7	1994	48	82
Finland	7	1994	21	53
France	6	1993	23	99
Germany	6	1990	2 (West)	78 (West)
			50 (East)	100 (East)
Greece	6	1993	3	70[a]
Ireland	6	1993	2	55
Italy	6	1991	6	91
Netherlands	5	1993	8	71[a]
Portugal	6	1993	12	48
Spain	6	1993	2 (approx.)	84
Sweden	7	1994	33	72
UK	5	1993	2	60[a]

[a] Includes some children in compulsory schooling.

Source: European Commission Network on Childcare and Other Measures to Reconcile Employment and Family Responsibilities, *A Review of Services for Young Children in the European Union 1990–1995* (Brussels: EC Directorate General V, 1996), 148–50.

United States. However, figures compiled for all of these, excepting New Zealand in 1987, show greater similarity to Britain.[3] Canada, Australia, and especially the United States also have a much higher rate of 'for-profit' childcare provision than any European countries.

Diane Sainsbury suggests that national childcare systems can be located in relation to two extreme poles or childcare models—the maximum private responsibility model and the maximum public responsibility model. 'The private responsibility model prescribes state intervention as a last resort in situations of need and to promote social protection of children at risk. . . . The public responsibility model views children as a common resource and concern, and the financial burden

[3] See Janet C. Gornick, Marcia K. Meyers, and Katherine E. Ross, 'Supporting the Employment of Mothers: Policy Variation across Fourteen Welfare States', *Journal of European Social Policy*, 7:1 (1997), 45–70. Australia is shown as having 2% of children aged 0–2 in publicly funded child care and 26% of children between the age of 3 and entry to school; for Canada the corresponding figures are 5% and 35% and for the United States 1% and 14%.

of having children as one to be shared by all members of society'.[4] While such modelling certainly captures what is perhaps the crucial variable dimension of provision, there are other features, such as the extent to which educational or care aspects are emphasized, the scope for local (or in federal systems, state-level) variation, and the way that childcare arrangements mesh with other measures to help mothers/parents reconcile family and work, notably those for parental leave, which are not strictly detemined by, though often associated with, positioning on the private–public-responsibility continuum. The analysis that follows will focus primarily on the private–public axis but seek also to address other relevant variations.

COMMON PATTERNS IN THE DEVELOPMENT OF CHILDCARE

While the emphasis of this chapter is on the variations in childcare policy, it is important at the outset to stress how much the histories of childcare policy have had in common, which in a way makes the differences the more remarkable. Many aspects of the British experience are far from unique but rather serve as an illustration of a more general pattern.

This is evident firstly in the way that childcare originated as an issue of public concern and to that extent as a policy issue. It was not only in Britain that the processes of industrialization and urbanization contributed to a heightened awareness both of the vulnerability and of the indiscipline of working-class children left to fend for themselves in the city streets, though of course these very processes occurred at varying times and in varying ways. A widespread initial response to this problem took the form of charitably endowed crèches or infant schools (at this stage the distinction was not as clear-cut as it later became), although subsequent development was more diversified. Another common experience from the late nineteenth century was the impact of the kindergarten movement, originating with Froebel's pioneering efforts in Germany but extending as far as the United States, Australia, and New Zealand. The kindergartens themselves tended predominantly to cater for middle-class children but the practices and ideas associated with them influenced developments more widely.

---

[4] Diane Sainsbury, *Gender, Equality, and Welfare States* (Cambridge: Cambridge University Press, 1996), 95–6. She is drawing on a distinction made by Yasmine Ergas in 'Child-care Policies in Comparative Perspective', in OECD, *Lone-parent Families: The Economic Challenge* (Paris: OECD, 1990).

The distinction and institutional separation between custodial or care aspects of childcare and more educational aspects, which has become such a marked and tenacious feature of British childcare policy, likewise is not unique to this country. Almost everywhere, as the issue came to be addressed, care aspects were seen as largely remedial, that is as required only for children in unfortunate circumstances whose mothers were unable or entirely unfit to care for them themselves. Along with this went the assumption of the mother's primary responsibility for childcare, part of a more deeply embedded conception of women's domestic role. Such maternalism indeed was tending to enjoy a kind of revival, as in Britain in the late nineteenth century, though the timing varied considerably. Gradually, in addition to this grudging acceptance of public responsibility in the last resort for the care of very young children, there developed a more positive recognition of the value of educational aspects of provision for very young children. The main exception to this pattern of divorcing care and educational aspects seems to have been France (discussed further below), where the *écoles maternelles*, as they evolved from the nineteenth century, came to combine both caring and educational functions.

Moving forward somewhat in time, another feature not entirely peculiar to Britain was the tendency for the state to be much more 'proactive' in the provision of child daycare facilities at times of war, when mothers' energies were required to contribute to the war effort. The 'war nurseries' of Britain in the 1940s had their counterpart in the United States,[5] and to a more limited extent in Canada.[6] They were even to be found in Sweden.[7] But this was everywhere regarded, by government at least, as a purely temporary measure. In the early post-war years the importance of home-based maternal care was rearticulated. The influence of Bowlby's arguments extended well beyond British shores, in many cases supplemented by more local exponents of the dangers of 'maternal deprivation'.

Furthermore, and while the varying complex of policy pressures and responses is precisely the issue to be explored further below, from the

---

[5] See Susan E. Riley, 'Caring for Rosie's Children: Federal Child Care Policies in the World War II Era', *Polity*, 26:4 (1994), 655–75; also Jill Norgren, 'In Search of a National Child Care Policy: Background and Prospects', *Western Political Quarterly*, 34:1 (1981), 127–42.

[6] Alan R. Pence, 'Canada', in Moncrieff Cochran (ed.), *International Handbook of Child Care Policies and Programs* (Westport, Conn.: Greenwood Press, 1993). In practice the combined federal-provincial childcare initiative was only pursued in Ontario and Quebec.

[7] See Mary Ruggie, The State and Working Women (Princeton, NJ: Princeton University Press, 1984), 255.

1960s there has been a strong tendency for the increased salience of childcare as a policy issue to be associated with the growth in the employment rate of mothers with young children. Even in Sweden and Norway, 'the behaviour of mothers began to change well ahead of any welfare reforms facilitating their entry into the labour market'.[8] This is what has helped to create what officials and the general public are prepared to accept as a childcare 'problem'. A further relevant trend, despite cross-national variations, has been the rising numbers of single mothers. Although in this respect Britain, where by the end of the 1980s around 17 per cent of all families with children under 18 were headed by a lone parent (and everywhere the great majority of these are mothers), is exceeded only by the United States (21 per cent), Sweden and Denmark have been close (15 per cent), with Australia, Canada, Finland, and Austria at 13 per cent.[9] The emergence or revival of various forms of feminist activity and, at least as important, the public diffusion of a range of feminist values and arguments has also generally played some part in the identification and framing of the childcare issue, though again variations have been important and are discussed further below.

EXPLAINING THE DIFFERENCES: THE STATE TRADITION ARGUMENT

Given these convergent features, how do we explain such divergent outcomes? As outlined in the Introduction, a major explanatory theme both in the relevant literature and in this study concerns what could be called 'state characteristics', the cluster of issues focusing on the underlying philosophy of state action, the style of policy-making, and the 'type' of welfare regime associated with different states. We are interested, that is, in assessing how far differences in childcare policy are associated with different traditions of state intervention.

Britain has usually been classified as a 'liberal' state, characterized by limited state intervention and correspondingly generous scope for 'private' market and family spheres. It stands in contrast to a number of continental European states with a much stronger tradition of state

---

[8] Arnlaug Leira, 'The "Woman-friendly" Welfare State?: The Case of Norway and Sweden', in J. Lewis (ed.), *Women and Social Policies in Europe* (Aldershot: Edward Elgar, 1993), 57.

[9] Figures taken from Jane, Millar, 'Mothers, Workers, Wives: Comparing Policy Approaches to Supporting Lone Mothers', in Elizabeth Bortolaia Silva (ed.), *Good Enough Mothering?* (London: Routledge, 1996), 99.

intervention. These have been variously classified but one highly influential approach has been advanced by Esping-Andersen. As noted in the Introduction, in drawing up his typology he focuses on the extent of 'decommodification', or 'the degree to which individuals, or families, can uphold a socially acceptable standard of living independently of market participation'.[10] Referring primarily to social security provision, he distinguishes not two but three kinds of welfare regime. While decommodification is least extensive in liberal welfare states, there is a further distinction between conservative corporatist and social democratic welfare states. In conservative regimes, for instance Germany, Austria, and France, despite the interventionist state tradition, welfare policies, rather than reflecting an ethos of social egalitarianism, have tended to build upon private and voluntary provisions, through the 'subsidiarity' principle, and to incorporate existing social status distinctions. It is in the social democratic states of Scandinavia that the process of decommodification has gone furthest.

We shall begin, then, by comparing childcare policy in Britain with policy in Sweden. Sweden to an extent epitomizes the social democratic type of welfare regime (which is also often referred to as the Scandinavian model). It is generally depicted as being in the vanguard of social democratic reform in Scandinavia: 'Typically Sweden has led the way'.[11] And it is also through the Britain–Sweden comparison that Ruggie developed her original analysis, albeit prior to the more recent attempts to classify welfare state systems.[12]

Sweden's interventionist state tradition has deep historical roots. Some accounts trace it back to the system of national administration developed under absolutism from the sixteenth century. The state bureaucracy played a vital role in modernizing a nation that was at the beginning of this century still 'agrarian and pre-democratic',[13] generating a long-standing tradition of 'faith in the benevolence, capability and

[10] Gøsta Esping-Andersen, *The Three Worlds of Welfare Capitalism* (Cambridge: Polity Press, 1990), 37.

[11] Gøsta Esping-Andersen and Walter Korpi, 'From Poor Relief to Institutional Welfare States: The Development of Scandinavian Social Policy', in Robert Erikson *et al.* (eds.), *The Scandinavian Model: Welfare States and Welfare Research* (New York and London: M. E. Sharpe, 1987), 47.

[12] See Mary Ruggie, *The State and Working Women: A Comparative Study of Britain and Sweden* (Princeton, NJ: Princeton University Press, 1984). I have also provided a rather longer comparative analysis than is possible here of the British, Swedish, and French cases in 'Comparative Childcare Policy and the Public–Private Divide', in Susan Baker and Anneka van Dooren-Husikes (eds.), *Women and Public Policy* (Aldershot: Ashgate, 1999).

[13] Arnold J. Heidenheimer, Hugh Heclo, and Carolyn Teich Adams, *Comparative Public Policy*, 3rd edn. (New York: St Martin's Press, 1990), 21.

responsibility of the state'.[14] Along with this state tradition, Sweden has developed a characteristic policy style. Describing it, Ruin distinguishes between norms of policy-making and actual 'standard operating proced-ures'. He argues that in everyday decision-making, policy-makers seek agreement amongst participants, aiming to build consensus and avoid conflict, but at the same time, there has been 'an emphasis on trying to direct events rather than letting events dictate policy, on being active and innovative rather than reactive'.[15] Finally, social democratic values have become strongly institutionalized in the policy process as embod-ied above all in the Social Democratic Party's long-standing domina-tion, from the 1930s to the 1970s, both of the party system and of the institutions of government.

As Ruggie writes, 'The story of modern day care in Sweden begins in the 1960s'.[16] Up to that time child daycare was seen as essentially a welfare function, as it was elsewhere; provision was not only meagre but quite traditional and fragmentary. However, the childcare issue emerged in a particularly favourable context, in which interventionist family and labour market policies and policy discourses, which could not only accommodate but help to sustain childcare demands, were already institutionalized.

Both these national policy concerns can be traced back to the 1930s. In that decade, firstly, Sweden had the lowest fertility rates in Europe, leading the Social Democrat government to set up a Royal Commission on the Population Problem. This Commission was especially impressed by the evidence advanced by Alva and Gunnar Myrdal that lower-income families tended to have fewer children and their argument in consequence that young couples must be encouraged to have children by ensuring that their income did not suffer.[17] Pro-natalism, that is, com-bined with social egalitarianism to produce a strong and explicit family policy, with an emphasis on material support for the family and on the child's well-being. The 1930s also saw the start of an active, inter-ventionist labour market policy. This originated in Social Democrat commitment to combatting unemployment through government expenditure. Though the various economic policies initiated at this stage were not directly concerned with women, they established a precedent

[14] Maud Edwards, cited in Linda Haas, *Equal Parenthood and Social Policy* (New York: State University of New York Press, 1992), 51.

[15] O. Ruin, 'Sweden in the 1970s: Policy-making becomes Difficult', in J. Richardson (ed.), *Policy Styles in Western Europe* (London: Allen Unwin, 1982), 141.

[16] Ruggie, *The State and Working Women*, 255.

[17] Carolyn Teich Adams and Kathryn Teich Winston, *Mothers at Work: Public Policies in the United States, Sweden and China* (New York: Longman, 1980), 184.

for government intervention to remove obstacles to labour force participation that would prove very helpful to women later. These policies also coincided with a significant and heated debate about women's employment, which eventually resulted in the acceptance in principle of the working woman's right to have a family.[18]

The upsurge of women's employment in the 1960s occurred at the same time as a serious national labour shortage. A relevant question here is why Sweden did not make more use of immigrant labour, as in Britain in the 1950s. Accounts differ: according to Broberg and Hwang, the first response was to look to Finland and southern Europe for new supplies of workers but not enough were forthcoming.[19] Haas, on the other hand, suggests that the problem with imported labour was more to do with assimilation.[20] The latter interpretation implies a more complicated relationship between women's employment and national labour requirements, one mediated by the 'exclusive' tendencies of Swedish culture. At any rate, Swedish women were the beneficiaries and the growing numbers of working mothers finally led to serious questioning of existing childcare policy.

Representatives of industry, the unions, the press, child-centred groups, and women's groups began to draw public attention to the issue and to demand reforms. In response, a series of commissions were established to review different aspects of the problem. Here childcare policy benefited from the way in which Swedish policy-making has typically proceeded, once government has identified an important issue area. Usually government appoints a commission to investigate the issue and make policy recommendations. Commissions marshal and review evidence systematically and their recommendations have tended to be largely accepted by Parliament. Their membership has included senior 'experts' and more junior researchers from the state bureaucracy, as well as representatives of labour, business, other affected interest groups, and MPs.[21] The prevalence of this traditional mode of determining policy has meant that childcare needs and provision, once these were perceived to

[18] See Barbara Hobson, 'Feminist Strategies and Gendered Discourses in Welfare States: Women's Right to Work in the United States and Sweden', in S. Koven and S. Michel (eds.), *Mothers of a New World* (London: Routledge, 1993). She describes how in 1934, at the height of the economic crisis, at least 9 motions were presented in the Riksdag designed to prevent married women going out to work. But the Swedish Parliament turned them down and instead set up a commission (4 of whose 6 commissioners were women) which in its 1938 report counselled against any such discrimination.

[19] A. Broberg and C. P. Hwang, 'Daycare for Young Children in Sweden', in E. C. Melhuish and P. Moss (eds.), *Daycare for Young Children* (London: Routledge, 1991), 93.

[20] Haas, *Equal Parenthood and Social Policy*, 26.

[21] Ruin, 'Sweden in the 1970s', 141–2; Ruggie, *The State and Working Women*, 283–5.

be an important dimension of both family and labour policy, have been carefully assessed and monitored.

Thus proposals from a 1962 Family Commission for a new type of 'child centre' and recommendations from a 1965 Family Commission investigating childminding formed the basis of new legislation. Then in 1968 a Royal Commission on Child Centres was established which served to integrate and systematize preceding policy changes, reporting in 1972. Ruggie notes the matter-of-fact, non-judgemental way in which the Commission presented its findings about working mothers. It proposed completely reorganizing the system of childcare. Recognizing that while all children needed some form of pre-school provision, the need for daycare was itself directly related to the needs of working parents, it demanded a public commitment to meet all these pre-school needs, both quantitatively and qualitatively. The Commission's proposals formed the basis for a Pre-school Act, passed in 1973, followed by further supplementary legislation in 1975 and 1976. Policies were to be implemented by local authorities but their active co-operation was to be facilitated by generous funding from the centre. Although the Commission had noted the harmful effects of dividing childcare services between caring and educational functions, it took rather longer for appropriate policy changes to ensue, but subsequently the Board of Health and Welfare, responsible for child daycare at the national level, worked increasingly closely with the Board of Education. In its 1987 report, *Pre-school Educational Programme*, the Board of Health and Welfare went so far as to identify education as the primary task of child daycare.[22] Other political parties in the Riksdag did not oppose the Social Democrat government's legislation. There were, and have continued to be, differences of emphasis in the parties' approach to the question of childcare but these have taken second place to a recognition that mothers for one reason or another may have to work outside the home, and that the state needs to assist in the provision of child daycare.[23]

Childcare policy in Sweden has not stood still and we shall come back later to the most recent developments. But enough has been said to show how, in Sweden's case, the social democratic state tradition has combined with particular population and labour shortage concerns to provide a highly propitious context, comparatively speaking, for the evolution of childcare policy. The provision of childcare services has

---

[22] Cited in Broberg and Hwang, 'Daycare for Young Children in Sweden', 82.
[23] Maud Edwards, 'Towards a Third Way: Women's Politics and Welfare Policies in Sweden', *Social Research*, 58:3 (1991), 677–705.

moreover been part of a broader swathe of policies aimed at reconciling employment and parenting responsibilities, including very generous parental leave provision, amounting from 1989 to 450 weekdays
with income replacement. There has been less progress over measures
to ensure that fathers take up their share of the leave allowance:
even so, in 1995, new legislation established the 'father's month' (*pap-
pamånaden*), earmarking 30 days' worth of leave to the father which is
forfeit, rather than being transferrable to his partner, if he fails to take
it up.[24]

But whilst Swedish experience appears to lend strong support both
to the state tradition thesis and to Esping-Andersen's model, there have
been significant variations in the making and outcome of childcare
policy amongst the Scandinavian states. Thus Langsted and Sommer
argue that although levels of childcare provision in Denmark may if
anything exceed those in Sweden, and as in Sweden, policy really took
off in the 1960s when even conservative parties could be persuaded of
the need to draw in women workers in the context of a severe labour
shortage, there has never been anything like a systematic family policy
in Denmark; rather, provisions have emerged piecemeal.[25]

But the really deviant case is Norway. Arnlaug Leira in particular has
cited differences in the history and provision of childcare in Norway and
Sweden which call into question the existence of a common Scandinavian model, at least where policies to do with reproduction (including
social reproduction) are concerned. In Norway the issue of childcare did
not really emerge until the 1970s, partly because Norway was slower to
industrialize and urbanize but also, she suggests, because of a particular
cultural preference for the traditional model of the male breadwinner
family.[26] Even after the 1975 Daycare Act, quite basic political disagreement persisted in Norway on the related questions of working
mothers and state funding for childcare.[27] By the late eighties the
employment rate for mothers of young children was higher than in most

[24] See Christina Bergqvist, 'Still a Woman-friendly Welfare State?', paper presented to
the Council of European Studies, Baltimore, 1998, 21.

[25] Ole Langsted and Dion Sommer, 'Denmark', in Cochran (ed.), *International
Handbook*.

[26] Arnlaug Leira, 'The "Woman-friendly" Welfare State?', 59. She points out that even
when a labour shortage was believed to be impeding post-war reconstruction the possibility of increasing the employment of married women was not canvassed. The notion
of the male bread-winner model is discussed further below.

[27] Such disagreement was still much in evidence during my period as a guest researcher
at Bergen University in the autumn of 1998, when it was one of the main issues stalling
approval of the state budget.

EC countries, though predominantly part-time. But while parental leave and provision for older pre-school children has been substantial, in daycare provision for under-threes ' "social democratic" Norway is more similar to "liberal" UK than to its "social democratic" neighbour'.[28] In 1989 only 10 per cent of children under 3 had access to public childcare, with much greater reliance than in other Scandinavian countries on private and informal care.

The case of Norway suggests that while there are considerable family resemblances across the social democratic Scandinavian countries, as regards childcare policy the 'Scandinavian' model cannot on its own explain significant residual policy variation. A similar conclusion emerges when we address Esping-Andersen's second category: the conservative corporatistic welfare state. Here we have a strongly interventionist state, for instance as far as the economy has been concerned, but without or with much less of the social egalitarian impulse. Such regimes are also typically shaped by the Church and 'hence strongly committed to the preservation of traditional family-hood', as a result of which 'day care and similar family services are conspicuously underdeveloped'.[29] An examination of the cases of Germany and France demonstrates that the conservative corporatist category of states contains extreme contrasts in childcare policy.

Assessing first (West) Germany's record,[30] daycare provision for under-threes has been especially lacking. As late as 1986, publicly-subsidized crèche care was available for only 3 per cent of this age group. Combined with the private daycare sector, including childminders, and family daycare, this still only covered 5 per cent. Monika Jaeckel's survey for the European Network in 1995 concludes that 'public acceptance of services for school-age children and children under 3 years in west Germany is still very low'.[31] From the 1970s, there was growing government support, based on recognition of their educational value, for predominantly church-run kindergartens catering for pre-school children aged 3 and over. By 1986 79 per cent of the eligible age group participated. But most of these kindergarten sessions were half-day, excluding lunch, and thus ill suited to the needs of working

---

[28] Leira, 'The "Woman-friendly" Welfare State?', 64.

[29] Esping-Andersen, *The Three Worlds of Welfare Capitalism*, 27.

[30] Obviously the re-unification of Germany has complicated the situation. The former GDR, in its bid to encourage—or viewed more negatively, to pressurize—women to combine motherhood with full-time employment, had made generous public childcare provision.

[31] Monika Jaeckel, 'Germany', in EC Network on Childcare, *A Review of Services for Young Children*, 42.

mothers. At the same time, provisions for maternity pay and parental leave have improved steadily.[32]

The social, or more precisely gender-role, conservatism implicit in these policies is mirrored in the relatively low though growing work-force participation rates not only of mothers of young children but of married women altogether. Ostner[33] traces this back to the circumstances of the Federal Republic's formation, the felt need to emphasize and sustain the (traditional) family as a basis for the restoration of normality and a site that had been relatively 'uncontaminated', though much interfered with, by the Nazi state. But one might want to add here, anticipating the contrast with France below, that potential arguments from the Left that married women, and even mothers of young children, have, if not a right, then at least a need to go out to work, have been muted both by the constitutional and ideological constraints on organized communism and by invidious comparisons between such arguments and the practices of neighbouring communist states.[34] Certainly, when faced with labour shortages, Germany turned to 'guest workers' rather than its womenfolk. This negative attitude to paid female employment, and the assumption that women are responsible for unpaid caring work, has in turn tended to be absorbed by West German feminists.

CHILDCARE IN FRANCE

Childcare policy in France stands in remarkable contrast to the German story. Indeed, on many criteria, France has been a world leader in this policy area. The tradition of state intervention in France goes back to Napoleonic times, if not earlier. Although in the nineteenth century liberal ideas were current, Ashford amongst others observes that France never embraced them whole-heartedly: 'However slow the actual progress of the welfare state in France, reconciling the needs of state and society was a constant preoccupation of nineteenth century French

[32] Figures taken from Rudolf Pettinger, 'Germany', in Cochran (ed.), *International Handbook*, 223.

[33] Ilona Ostner, 'Slow Motion: Women, Work and the Family in Germany', in J. Lewis (ed.), *Women and Social Policies in Europe*.

[34] See Myra Marx Ferree, 'Making Equality: The Women's Affairs Offices in the Federal Republic of Germany', in Dorothy McBride Stetson and Amy G. Mazur (eds.), *Comparative State Feminism* (London: Sage, 1995). She writes, 'More so than in other Western European countries, FRG policymakers saw full employment for women and support for childcare as dangerously communist' (97).

political philosophers'.[35] This interventionist tradition has been reflected in aspects of the national policy style. Hayward suggests that whilst French policy-making displays a predominantly reactive, short-term, and piecemeal approach to problem-solving, at the summit of the French state there is an informal network or nucleus of executive power capable of challenging routine norms and attempting to impose an active, longer-term, comprehensive style of policy-making and implementation.[36] The possibility of this 'heroic' style of policy-making has been one element contributing to much higher levels of public childcare provision.

On the other hand, French national policy has been driven by certain overriding priorities, which have combined to create a relatively favourable context for the subsequent development of child daycare. Most important amongst these have been long-standing population concerns which have contributed to a quite strongly redistributive family policy. As in Scandinavia, there have also been periodic labour shortages, during which, though not without controversy, France has turned to its housewives and mothers. A further relevant feature of French policy-making may have been a concern with the preservation of diverse socially or geographically peripheral groups' and their assimilation into the national culture, and thence with the potential role of nursery education in the early socialization of children. We should also note that while French political culture lacks the social democratic egalitarianism of the Scandinavian countries, radical and secular left-wing discourse has been much more prominent and combative than in West Germany. These points will be elaborated.

As elsewhere, the origins of French childcare policy lie in the nineteenth century. Although industrial change was linked with the doctrines of economic and political liberalism, they never commanded the same authority as in Britain. While late nineteenth-century Britain remained largely confident in her imperial destiny, across the Channel was a growing preoccupation with the 'déclin francais'. Disease, emigration, war, and especially defeat by Germany in 1870 and the loss of Alsace-Lorraine had contributed to stationary population levels that seemed to leave France economically and militarily vulnerable. As Jenson writes, 'within the concern about depopulation was an analytic link to the economic system, which people thought to be

---

[35] Douglas Ashford, *The Emergence of the Welfare States* (Oxford: Basil Blackwell, 1986), 36.

[36] Jack Hayward, 'Mobilising Private Interests in the Service of Public Ambitions: The Salient Elements in Dual French Policy Style', in Richardson (ed.), *Policy Styles in Western Europe*, 116.

guaranteeing neither reproduction of the labour force nor a powerful nation state'.[37]

These fears encouraged and sanctioned official concern with the need to improve the health and welfare of children and mothers, resulting eventually in a series of national policy initiatives. One of these was to build on the existing system of *salles d'asile*, which had developed from the 1820s as charitable bodies providing daycare for children aged 2 to 6 and were progressively brought under the auspices of the Ministry of Public Instruction. In practice many of these, while hygienic, provided a harsh regime and were increasingly criticized for their atmosphere of the barracks or prison. However, in contrast to the British experience, the decision taken by policy-makers was to raise standards rather than dissolve these existing institutions. Norvez describes how, over the period 1880–1900, they were refashioned into an 'entirely original institution', the *écoles maternelles*, combining both caring and educational perspectives. A central role in this process was played by Pauline Kergomard, appointed chief inspector of the *asiles* in 1879.[38]

This is a very important development, even though for a long time their intake was relatively modest and largely confined to working-class children. While Jenson tends to attribute the emergence of the *maternelles* to public concern to reconcile women's paid work with childcare, this may be most relevant both to the very early years and to the expansion in take-up after World War II. But a significant part of the explanation for the consolidation or institutionalization of the *maternelles* under the Third Republic may lie in the value attached to their educational role, understanding that term in its broadest sense. As Ashford notes, 'Perhaps more than any other democracy, France saw education as a central policy concern of the state, more accurately that education was such an important attribute of the state that it was conceptually inseparable'.[39] Eugene Weber has argued that French national identity and unity by the early twentieth century were the outcome not of tradition but of a centrally imposed process of national integration. He cites Sanguinetti—'France is a deliberate political construction for whose creation the central power has never ceased to fight.[40] At the same time there was a struggle between republicanism and the Church

[37] Jane Jenson, 'Representations of Gender: Policies to 'Protect' Women Workers in France and the United States before 1914', in Linda Gordon (ed.), *Women, the State and Welfare* (Madison, Wisc.: University of Wisconsin Press, 1990), 159.

[38] Alain Norvez, *De la naissance à l'école*, INED, Travaux et Documents, Cahier no 126 (Paris: PUF, 1990), 21.

[39] Ashford, *The Emergence of the Welfare States*, 56.

[40] Eugene Weber, *Peasants into Frenchmen* (Stanford, Calif.: Stanford University Press, 1976), 113.

to influence the nature of French identity. The *maternelles* were enlisted in the struggle to create a republican image of the state. Indeed one of their subsidiary functions was seen to be the education of parents (*les couches populaires*) via the children.[41]

But even given these educational interests, we need to ask why fears for the health of infants and mothers did not, as in Britain, lead to greater disapproval for an institution which might seem to encourage mothers to go out to work and neglect their infants. While conservative arguments advocating the 'mère au foyer' have all along been heard, they were countered by the socialist contention that, however desirable this might be as an ideal, for many working-class women and their families the income from their wages was so essential that it was not a realistic option. Here it is notable that during the first three decades of the twentieth century, while in Britain the percentage of married women in paid employment was somewhere around 10, in France it was closer to 40.[42] This is partly of course a reflection of the more protracted process of industrialization: French women workers were predominantly in the agricultural sector. The sheer fact of such a relatively large married female workforce may have served to weaken principled objections to the *maternelles* (although this tends to contradict the link implied above in the case of Norway between late industrialization and the persistence of more traditional attitudes to working mothers).

It was not until the 1960s, as growing numbers of middle-class women began entering professional jobs, that the take-up of *maternelle* places really soared. By now, not only over 90 per cent of French children aged 3–6 but also one-third of 2-year-olds attend these schools.[43] But in addition to the *maternelles*, working parents have benefited from France's distinctive family policy. Those who framed the original policies in the late nineteenth century were often inspired by humanitarian concerns themselves, but had to cite demographic and national power considerations as a justification for overriding the liberty of the individual. In so doing, they were also able to exploit the consensus between the dominant and otherwise mutually antagonistic tendencies of social Catholicism and republican nationalism on the importance of the 'family'. The actual elaboration of family policy was left to the officials.[44]

[41] Norvez, *De la naissance à l'école*, 399.

[42] See Shirley Dex, Patricia Walters, and David M. Alden, *French and British Mothers at Work* (London: Macmillan, 1993), ch. 3.

[43] F. Leprince, 'Day Care for Young Children in France', in Melhuish and Moss (eds.), *Day Care for Young Children*, 11.

[44] Norvez, *De la naissance à l'école*; see also Remi Lenoir, 'Family Policy in France since 1938', in J. S. Ambler (ed.), *The French Welfare State* (New York: New York University Press, 1991).

In the context of continuing population concern in the inter-war era and the aftermath of the Second World War, family policy became institutionally inscribed, with its own dedicated ministry—variously named—and range of associated agencies.[45] A system of family allowances was established under the 1939 Family Code. This was intended to stimulate population growth. Although it is also sometimes suggested that it was designed so as to encourage mothers to stay at home, most specifically through the additional allowance for 'la mère au foyer', this is misleading. Rodgers maintains that its post-war rationale was increasingly to prevent families with children from being unduly disadvantaged in income terms: it provided a means of horizontal redistribution between families with children and those without.[46] Hantrais likewise contends that the motivation was basically gender-neutral. She points out that the allowance was actually introduced in the immediate post-war period when 'the shortage of skilled labour rather than of jobs was the main problem'.[47] At any rate, it meant that as women, including married women, entered the paid workforce in increasing numbers from the 1960s, and in the context of renewed fears about a falling birth rate, the institutional fabric and resources earmarked for family policy were potentially available to channel into increased childcare provision.

Though the influence of women's rights arguments should not entirely be discounted, the expansion of childcare provision in the 1970s also reflected official awareness of changing family needs, itself partly a consequence of state-sponsored research 'mounted with the express purpose of providing information that would enable family policy, and family benefits in particular, to be related more closely to the changing situation and expectations of families'.[48] Much of the rethinking of French family policy took place in the General Planning Commission, which emphasized professional training for women, childcare, and pre-school instruction. Legislation in 1972 provided simultaneously for an

[45] Pedersen draws a contrast with Britain: 'French family policy is defined and protected by powerful ministries and semi-public institutions while this advocacy role in Britain is performed—as best it can be—by the voluntary lobbying organization, Child Poverty Action Group': Susan Pedersen, *Family Dependence and the Origins of the Welfare State: Britain and France, 1914–1945* (Cambridge: Cambridge University Press, 1993), 13.

[46] Barbara N. Rodgers, 'Family Policy in France', *Journal of Social Policy*, 4:2 (1975), 113–28.

[47] Linda Hantrais, 'Women, Work and Welfare in France', in Lewis (ed.), *Women and Social Policies in Europe*, 120. For a fuller discussion of attitudes to working mothers in the 1950s see Claire Duchen, *Women's Rights and Women's Lives in France, 1944–1968* (London: Routledge, 1994), ch. 4.

[48] Rodgers, 'Family Policy in France', 125.

increased allowance for home-based mothers with young children and a new childcare allowance for working mothers. The actual decision of whether to go out to work was left with the mothers, thus to an extent side-stepping the continuing differences between traditionalist and more 'liberal' views of the family. This childcare allowance was mainly implemented through the local bodies responsible for administering the family allowance—the CAFs (Caisses des Allocations Familiales), in conjunction with local government. And indeed as Leprince notes, 'since 1970 CAFs have been increasingly involved in funding the capital and running costs of day care services, reducing the proportion of costs borne by local authorities; day care provision for young children has become one of the main objectives of CNAF'.[49]

To summarize, the existence of a tradition of state intervention in 'corporatistic' France has significantly shaped the possibilities for childcare policy. But this has been in conjunction with a particular set of national policy priorities, centring on the creation, survival, and integrity of the nation state, stemming from France's troubled recent history. Against a background of fairly continual population concerns, a degree of national consensus crystallized at an early stage on the need for a strong family policy, as also on the broadly educational value of the *maternelles*. This helped, first, to give official policy-makers both the authority and the freedom from party or ideological interference in which to elaborate major policy initiatives absorbing sizeable public resources and, second, to ensure considerable continuity in the development of these policies and their adaptation to changing patterns of employment and family life. While feminist pressures have also had some impact on policy, discussed further below, this was in the context of a generally supportive national policy framework.

The discussion so far indicates both the relevance and the limitations of the state tradition thesis, and more specifically of Esping-Andersen's threefold typology. It is clear that a strong state tradition, while it may be a prerequisite, is in itself no guarantee of extensive public support for childcare. But in addition, not all social democratic welfare states have been to the fore in terms of childcare policy and not all conservative corporatist states have been laggardly. How are these exceptions to be explained?

Esping-Andersen's typology has been extensively criticized by feminist writers on social policy for largely neglecting women. It is argued that the model presupposes a social class perspective that ignores

---

[49] Leprince, 'Day Care for Young Children in France', 15. The CNAF is the national body for the CAFs.

gender relations. The pivotal criterion of decommodification likewise has a gendered meaning: it is valued for what it signifies for the male worker, whereas for women its meaning could be different. For instance, it may be that for many women paid work holds greater promise of emancipation. Alternatively it is charged that the Esping-Andersen approach fails to give a sufficiently central place to the activity of 'caring',[50] which of course includes childcare itself. Citing these and other arguments, some have argued that the approach is too flawed to be useful: it may be time 'to embrace fully another theoretical agenda'.[51] But this seems premature. There are two great virtues of Esping-Andersen's approach. First, it provides a set of criteria which, however 'gender-blind' or reprehensible, constitute significant features of those welfare regimes against which to orient more gender-related questions. Secondly, it does attempt some kind of historical explanation for these significant differences between regimes, based on the role of working-class mobilization and political coalitions in the process of establishing the welfare state together with the historical legacy of its early institutionalization. It is wiser, therefore, at any rate for the present analysis, to follow the example of O'Connor *et al.*, who see their work as building upon rather than replacing Esping-Andersen and other such 'mainstream' accounts.[52]

In that spirit, Jane Lewis originally developed the concept of the 'male-breadwinner' model, in which wives were excluded from the labour market, firmly subordinated to their husbands for the purposes of social security entitlements and tax, and expected to undertake the work of caring (for children and other dependents) at home without public support.[53] This model was to a greater or lesser extent inscribed in all the western welfare states that became fully institutionalized in the wake of the Second World War. Since the model was to begin with almost universal, as Lewis writes, 'the interesting question . . . becomes when, how and to what extent countries moved away from the male breadwinner model'.[54] If we want to elucidate the difference between childcare policy in Norway and Sweden we can refer to the stronger hold in Norway of the male-breadwinner model. It is more difficult to

[50] For a very helpful summary of these criticisms see Jane Lewis, 'Gender and Welfare Regimes: Further Thoughts', *Social Politics*, 4:2 (1997), 160–77.

[51] Jane Jenson, 'Who Cares? Gender and Welfare Regimes', *Social Politics*, 4:2 (1997), 187.

[52] See Julia S. O'Connor, Ann Shola Orloff, and Sheila Shaver, *States, Markets, Families* (Cambridge: Cambridge University Press, 1999), 19.

[53] Jane Lewis, 'Gender and the Development of Welfare Regimes', *Journal of European Social Policy*, 2:3 (1992), 162.

[54] Lewis, 'Gender and Welfare Regimes: Further Thoughts', 168.

go further and explain exactly *why* the model had a greater hold, though relatively late industrialization is likely to be relevant. Similarly, amongst the corporatist welfare regimes we can say that the male bread-winner has been much more strongly entrenched in Germany and Austria than in France. Indeed Susan Pedersen argues that already in the inter-war period, rather than incorporating the male breadwinner model, French family policy was coming to rest in what she calls a 'parental' logic: 'Parental policies do not assume that women are nec-essarily dependent, nor that men always have 'families to keep'; rather, they presume the dependence of children alone and hence redistribute income primarily across family types and not along gender lines'.[55] Again, however, to explain these differences we must look beyond the presence or absence of male-breadwinner assumptions to factors like population policy.

CHILDCARE VARIATIONS IN THE LIBERAL STATE

We have seen that Britain, however unsatisfactorily, has been classed amongst the liberal welfare states, which are usually also taken to include Australia, Canada, New Zealand, and the United States. Another way of exploring how far Britain's minimalist childcare policy is a consequence of the liberal-state ethos is to compare it with child-care developments in these other countries. From a study of the mate-rials available, a number of common features do emerge but it is also immediately apparent that childcare policy and the political struggles and debates surrounding it have taken markedly different forms. While liberal assumptions and their institutionalization in the process and for-mulation of policy *have* hindered childcare possibilities, the ascendance of such assumptions has not been constant but has varied cross-nation-ally and also (especially in the three federations) more locally and over time. This is itself partly connected to the strength and political influence of the Left and the labour movement. But there have been other relevant differences, including the strength and cohesion of the childcare lobby and the impact of feminism.

Taking these liberal welfare states as a group in distinction to the social democratic or corporatistic welfare states examined earlier, it is certainly true that there is a common thread to their pattern of child-care provision. Altogether provision has been left much more to the

[55] Pedersen, *Family, Dependence and the Origins of the Welfare State*, 17.

incentives of the free market, rather than the agencies of either the state or the voluntary sector. It is difficult to find figures, or estimates, that are strictly comparable. But in the United States, it is generally reckoned that around half of care provided in day centres is 'for-profit' or commercially based.[56] Of these for-profit centres, according to Gormley, approximately one-sixth are actually owned by chains: the largest and best-known, Kindercare, is sometimes referred to as 'Kentucky fried children' and by 1993 ran around 1,200 centres, catering for 141,000 children.[57] For Canada, where however there is significant variation between provinces, we are told that roughly 40 per cent of all childcare places are commercially provided; the corresponding figures for Australia and New Zealand are 25 per cent and 10 per cent respectively.[58] On the other hand it is unusual for the state, at whatever level, directly to provide daycare itself as opposed to helping to fund it.

In debates about the need for childcare, opponents in particular regularly invoke the public–private distinction, deploying arguments about both the need to protect the family from state intrusion and the virtues of the (private) market. In the United States, state-provided child daycare has sometimes been depicted as tantamount to incipient communism: 'Day care is powerful. A program that ministers to a child from six months to six years has over 8,000 hours to teach beliefs and behaviour. The family should be teaching values, not the Government or anyone in day care'.[59] And there is considerable resistance to state regulation of the private sector, including family daycare (childminding). Gormley reckons that 82–90 per cent of family daycare in the United States is unregulated.

Along with these features reflecting the limited role of the state, we tend to find that those involved in childcare work suffer from exceptionally low status, poor working conditions, and abysmal pay. In the United States, after controlling for education and experience, childcare workers are the second-worst-paid occupational group—the first is the

---

[56] Deborah Phillips, 'Day Care for Young Children in the United States', in Melhuish and Moss (eds.), *Day Care for Young Children*, 165.

[57] William T. Gormley, *Everybody's Children* (Washington, DC: Brookings Institute, 1995), 68.

[58] Figures taken from Katherine Teightsoonian, 'Neo-conservative Ideology and Opposition to Federal Regulation of Child Care Services in the United States and Canada', *Canadian Journal of Political Science*, 26:1 (1993), 117; Deborah Brennan, 'Australia', in Cochran (ed.), *International Handbook*, 24; and Helen May, 'Changing Policies, Changing Politics: Early Childhood Care and Education in New Zealand', in Susanna W. Pflaum and Frank Pignatelli (eds.), *The Yearbook of Bank Street College of Education Thought and Practice* (New York: Bank Street College, 1994).

[59] Norgren, 'In Search of a National Child Care Policy', 139; the statement is by a member of a coalition of New Right groups.

clergy![60] The same is reported for Canada and Australia, though in New Zealand there was a successful campaign to raise the pay of trained childcare workers.[61] This raises the further point that training for childcare workers has tended to be either minimal or highly diverse and unsystematized, left to local or provincial initiative.

But this general picture conceals significant variations. In many respects the United States, and then Canada, stand at the laissez-faire extreme, with the state having a larger childcare role in New Zealand and Australia. There is considerable public support and government funding for (half-day) nursery education or kindergartens in the Antipodean countries: indeed Brennan reports that in most states in Australia, they are almost universally available.[62] In addition, and in rather similar stop–go fashion, there has been a degree of success in getting the national government to recognize its responsibility for daycare, although more has been achieved at the level of policy agreement than implementation.

In New Zealand, partly in response to growing feminist pressures, the Labour government in 1974 introduced a limited fee subsidy for parents who could not afford childcare. It subsequently commissioned a report which appeared in 1981 recommending that childcare be incorporated into the education service and that government fund up to 50 per cent of its cost. But the incoming National Party government shelved it. Again, from 1984 to 1990 the Labour government identified early childhood policy as a central issue. In 1988 it introduced a greatly improved and systematized set of training programmes for childcare workers. A 'Before Five' package was also eventually assembled which provided for substantially enhanced levels of government funding for child daycare provision. Once more the incoming National Party government soon began to 'trim' these commitments but there was still the sense that developments under Labour in the 1980s had raised childcare awareness and provision onto a new plane.[63]

Similarly, childcare moved onto the national agenda in Australia in the 1970s. The Labour government under Gough Whitlam (1972–5) introduced the 1972 Child Care Act, which substantially raised the level of federal funding for all kinds of children's services. Brennan notes that the intention was that such provisions should cater for all children rather than being targeted to the 'needy', but that, because it

---

[60] Phillips, 'Day Care for Young Children', 170–1.
[61] Helen May, *The Hand that Rocks the Cradle* (Department of Early Childhood, Waikato University, 1993), 13.
[62] Brennan, 'Australia', 24.
[63] May, *The Hand that Rocks the Cradle*.

relied on submissions from community groups rather than centrally directed allocation, government policy in practice tended to benefit the wealthier, better-organized groups and areas. The Labour government was succeeded by the Liberal–Country government under Malcolm Fraser (1975–83), which emphasized the role of families and private enterprise in childcare provision. Total funding was reduced by a third in real terms. Then in 1983 a new Labour government, under Bill Hawke, took up the issue again but this was now related closely to economic concerns and objectives, most of all the determination to reduce welfare dependency but also fears, in the mid- to long-term, that the ageing population profile would give rise to a labour shortage. Through the eighties there was considerable expansion of childcare provision, presented under the rubric of 'facilitating work force participation': around 80 per cent of funding under the Children's Services Programme went to support non-profit services that provided work-related care. In the early nineties the (still) Labour government proposed further expansion.[64]

If the childcare experience of Australia and New Zealand seems to diverge most sharply from what might be expected under the liberal welfare state model, one apparent reason may be that in both cases the 'liberal' label needs qualification. There is general agreement that 'The concept of the state as a vehicle for social justice and the civilizing of capitalism has been embodied in the state experiments of Australia and New Zealand since the 1890s'.[65] New Zealand's Social Security Act of 1938, for instance, helped blaze the trail for welfare reform elsewhere. Castles[66] attributes this particular variant of the liberal-state format to the combination of the level of affluence already achieved by the turn of the century and the political strength of organized labour. It is, or has been, moreover, the Labour Parties which have most embodied and promoted this more statist tradition. It is abundantly clear from the preceding summaries that it has been under Labour governments in both countries that publicly funded or subsidized childcare programmes have made most headway. So if Australia and New Zealand have witnessed more state intervention in the childcare field this may be because they have been less liberal.

---

[64] Brennan, 'Australia'; see also Suzanne Franzway, 'Childcare', in S. Franzway, Dianne Court, and R. W. Connell, *Staking a Claim* (Cambridge: Polity Press, 1989).

[65] Marion Sawer, ' "Femocrats in Glass Towers?" The Office for the Status of Women in Australia', in Stetson and Mazur (eds.), 24.

[66] Francis G. Castles, 'Needs-based Strategies of Social Protection in Australia and New Zealand', in Gøsta Esping-Andersen (ed.), *Welfare States in Transition* (London: Sage, 1996).

So far, therefore, the analysis of some divergence from the liberal norm in Australia and New Zealand is not really incompatible with the overall state tradition thesis. But is this the whole story? A factor that one might expect to be relevant is whether we are dealing with an essentially unitary or federal state structure. In Britain, the unitary structure has reinforced the centralized character of the policy process, though even then allowing for significant variations in policy implementation amongst the local authorities. Federalism could mean a more open policy process, with more points of entry and opportunities for state-level innovation. But it could also mean a more fragmented childcare lobby, as well as impeding the emergence of an effective *national* policy. The available evidence is not entirely conclusive. In both Canada and the United States, state governments have wide discretion and levels and forms of childcare provision vary considerably. Opponents of the expansion of federal childcare programmes frequently invoke the argument of states' rights. In Canada, for instance, they resented the 'Ottawa knows best' implications of the 1988 Canada Child Care Act, on the regulation of childcare.[67] Such objections seem to be more deeply rooted and carry more weight in Canada, however, than in the United States, where, Teightsoonian argues, they are more likely to be the rationalization of what are primarily socially conservative sentiments. And in Australia, federalism has not been an insuperable obstacle to national policy-making.

But also relevant have been the strength and cohesion of the child-care lobby, and within this the role of feminism. As the British case suggests, these cannot be seen as entirely independent of the national policy-making context but neither are they simply determined by that context. Both in Australia and in New Zealand substantial, nationally concerted campaigns for child daycare have been sustained for considerable periods, although these have been rather differently constituted. In New Zealand, expansion of the kindergartens (nursery education) in the early post-war period led to the formation of the Kindergarten Teachers' Association (KTA). During the 1960s the feminist and Labour Party activist Sonja Davies established the New Zealand Association of Childcare Centres.[68] Even then, in the early seventies, according to May, there was little consensus amongst the different groups involved in early years issues, on the need for daycare. The great variety of early years services also meant that at times these different groups could seem to

---

[67] Described in Teightsoonian, 'Neo-conservative Ideology and Opposition', 113.

[68] Her involvement in the daycare movement is interestingly described in her autobiography, *Bread and Roses* (Masterson, NZ: Fraser Books, 1984), esp. ch. 11.

be in competition for resources. An important development was the successful unionization, in which Sonja Davies was again instrumental, of child daycare workers into the Childhood Workers' Union, registered in 1982. This combined with the KTA in 1989 to form the Combined Early Childhood Union of Aotearoa (CECUA—'Aotearoa' is the Maori word for New Zealand), which spearheaded the drive to ensure that the Labour government delivered on its electoral childcare pledges.[69]

In Australia, according to Franzway, 'traditional' early years groups rather than feminist organizations helped bring about the 1972 Act. Thereafter feminists and the pre-school lobby were in some contention over the way policy was developed. One survey in the 1980s found that a majority of trainee Early Childhood teachers still firmly believed that mothers and babies should be together at home.[70] However, feminism, specifically the 'femocrats' working within government, became for a time at least a decisive influence in the way that childcare policy was defined and framed. Feminists also helped to move the childcare issue slowly up the trade union agenda. In the 1980s the Australian Council of Trade Unions in particular took up, first, together with a number of public sector unions, the issue of workplace daycare, and second, with the Federated Miscellaneous Workers' Union, the question of childcare workers' pay and conditions.[71]

Given the importance of feminist influence in the Australian case, we need to consider in a little more detail how feminism responded to the childcare issue. Franzway suggests that, as in Britain, although the feminist movement that burgeoned from the late 1960s identified childcare as a critical issue for women, and was soon demanding that it be provided free, universal and twenty-four hours a day, it was 'slow to go beyond the slogan, to recognise its implications'. However, in Australia, in contrast to Britain, in the seventies there were a growing number of 'femocrats', or individual feminists who had moved into mainstream positions within state institutions.[72] Working in conjunction with feminists outside the bureaucracy involved in community daycare schemes, they challenged the more traditional perspective of the pre-school lobby, albeit with mixed success. Under Fraser such femocrats, together

[69] May, *The Hand that Rocks the Cradle*, 9.

[70] Survey by Jan Kelly, 1986, cited in Franzway, 'Childcare', 64.

[71] See Deborah Brennan, *The Politics of Australian Child Care*, 2nd edn. (Cambridge: Cambridge University Press, 1998), ch. 7.

[72] Franzway, 'Childcare', 62–5. See also the discussion in Sophie Watson, 'Unpacking "the State": Reflections on Australian, British and Swedish Feminist Interventions', in M. F. Katzenstein and H. Skjeie (eds.), *Going Public* (Oslo: Institute for Social Research, 1990).

with arguments for publicly subsidized daycare, were largely marginalized, though femocrat interventions persisted at state level: Franzway
cites here for instance the report produced by Marie Coleman in South
Australia, which led to a reorganization of childcare services in that
state. Again, under Hawke, while neither Franzway nor Brennan see
feminism as directly shaping the childcare agenda, femocrats were posi-
tioned to influence its precise formulation. Thus in 1986 the government
commissioned a review of social security arrangements, supervised by
feminist policy analyst Bettina Cass, which helped focus attention on
childcare provision as a means of enabling welfare recipients, especially
lone mothers, to take up paid work. Still later, in 1993, the Prime Minister's femocrat advisers were credited, at least by their opponents, with
obtaining extensive new childcare commitments.[73] Overall Brennan sees
the impact both of women and of feminism as a major feature distin-
guishing Australia's childcare experience, and setting it apart from
either the intense public responsibility model of the Scandinavian countries or the private responsibility model identified with the US and
Britain: 'Women have been crucially involved . . . —as lobbyists, bureau-
crats and policy makers as well as users and providers'.[74]

THE FEMINIST INPUT

Perhaps one implication of this discussion of the other 'liberal' states is
the potentially important role of feminism (inside and outside the state),
and especially in conjunction with the trade unions. It is suggested that
in the United States, organized feminism has played little part: on the
one hand, those feminists who 'somewhat glibly' demanded universal,
free daycare 'did virtually no lobbying',[75] whilst those more prepared to
work within the 'system' were unlikely to look directly to the state for
childcare provision. Moreover, the main labour organization which has
taken up the issue, the powerful AFL-CIO, influenced by the arguments
of their teacher members, has urged that responsibility for childcare be
given to primary (state) schools, thereby antagonizing other sectors of
the weak and fragmented childcare lobby. In Canada, where childcare
regimes have varied amongst the different provinces, the state has
played a more interventionist childcare role in Ontario. Colley describes
the campaign in the early eighties of the Ontario Coalition for Better

---

[73] Sawer, '"Femocrats in Glass Towers?"', 38.
[74] Brennan, *The Politics of Australian Child Care*, 5.
[75] Norgren, 'In Search of a National Child Care Policy', 134.

Day Care, which included both women's groups and the Ontario Federation of Labour. She argues that 'Without the leadership, commitment and resources of the trade union movement such an achievement would never have been possible'.[76]

In discussions of childcare policy in those European countries where public provision has been relatively generous, there is often an implication that these measures were largely the by-product of the state's prior concerns with the economy and population levels, with pressures from the women's movement counting for very little. For instance Lewis finds it 'noteworthy that in both France and Sweden women played little part in securing such advantages as accrued to them from the respective welfare regimes'.[77] This is also implied, if not explicitly stated, in Sainsbury's very systematic account of women-friendly welfare policies in Sweden.[78] The analysis earlier in this chapter reinforces the argument that variations in state characteristics and policy priorities *have* been of enormous relevance. However, these variations may themselves bear the imprint of earlier feminist mobilization, and at any given time policy-makers may need to take fresh account of feminist pressures and concerns, depending on the effectiveness of mobilization and the specific political conjuncture.

Focusing to begin with on the Scandinavian countries, in Sweden, as Bergqvist notes, 'not much has been said about the role of women in formulating policies. There has rather been a tacit understanding that welfare policies to a large extent have been designed by men'.[79] But as she describes, individual feminists—for instance Eva Moberg and Alva Myrdal—significantly helped to frame the gender equality debates of the 1960s, out of which eventually emerged the cross-party commitment to extension of childcare facilities. Moreover,

Women strongly dominated political documents and debates leading to decisions in Parliament of an extension of public child care. In the large public commissions on child care there were many women who had a positive attitude to the extension of child care facilities, not only for reasons of equality but also for social and pedagogic reasons.[80]

In 1976, when the Social Democrat government was proposing to extend the period of paid parental leave, without including the com-

---

[76] Susan Colley, 'Free Universal Day Care: The OFL Takes a Stand', in Linda Briskin and Linda Young (eds.), *Union Sisters: Women in the Labour Movement*, 2nd edn. (Toronto: Women's Press, 1985), 311.

[77] Jane Lewis, 'Gender and Welfare Regimes', *Journal of European Social Policy*, 2:3 (1992), 170.

[78] Sainsbury, *Gender, Equality, and Welfare States*.

[79] Bergqvist, 'Still a Woman-friendly Welfare State?', 5.   [80] Ibid. 13.

pulsory father's month, as the Social Democrat women's organization had recommended, there was a 'revolt', in which 18 of the 36 Social Democrat women MPs tabled a motion demanding reinstatement of the *pappamånad* (overtaken when their party lost the general election of that year). In Sweden then, while 'structural' conditions may have been paramount we should not underestimate the role of feminism in developing childcare policy.[81]

Feminism has made altogether fewer inroads into the mainstream of French politics and there is little evidence of direct feminist intervention on the childcare issue. Even so, given the existence of a strong family-policy tradition, feminist influences may have helped to ensure recognition for the childcare needs of working mothers. In the aftermath of the upsurge in feminist activism associated with the student revolt of 1968, policy-makers became more sensitive to women's rights issues. Though disowned by the women's movement, feminists within the Socialist Party (PS) succeeded in pushing women's issues up the party agenda. Although the Ministry for Women's Rights, established by the Socialist government in 1982 under the somewhat autocratic leadership of Yvette Roudy, was not directly concerned with childcare and moreover only enjoyed power for a very few years, Roudy 'can be credited with having substantially raised the level of awareness and political involvement in women's affairs'. In 1983 the CNAF initiated a new 'nursery agreement' with local authorities aimed at increasing nursery and organized childminding provison for under-threes. The objective was to create 20,000 new places a year, although what was achieved fell far short of this. The successor conservative government, despite its pro-natalism, largely built on the policy foundations of its predecessors; an official report in 1987, rather than expecting mothers to stay at home, accepted the need for childcare to be adapted so as to allow parents a choice.[82]

On the other hand, and without straining this argument too far, it can be said that the freedom of policy-makers in (West) Germany largely

---

[81] However, Borchorst tells a different story for Denmark: 'Women played a role as professional pedagogues, as philanthropists and in political parties, but apart from the 1950s when a social democratic women's organisation worked to increase the number of child facilities, the women's organisations did not play a major role in the establishment of child care facilities, among other things due to class based differences in solutions to child care problems': Anette Borchorst, 'The State and the "Social Pedagogic" Universal Child Care Services—Danish Child Care Policy and Gender Equality', paper presented to the National Institute For Working Life workshop on 'Labour Market and Social Policy—Gender Relations in Transition', Brussels, 1999, 9–10.

[82] Hantrais, 'Women, Work and Welfare in France', 125–6. See also Jane Jenson and Mariette Sineau, *Mitterrand et les Françaises: Un rendez-vous manqué* (Paris: Presses de la Fondation Nationale des Sciences Politiques, 1995).

to ignore the need for public childcare provision has been enhanced by the failure of feminists in that country to take up the cause of working mothers. Though containing the usual diversity of strands, the German movement has included a powerful strain of 'maternal feminism'. In the 1970s the influential 'Mothers' Manifesto' urged a perspective beginning with the needs of mothers and of children, rather than demanding employment equality with men. For a time there was also widespread support for 'Wages for Housework' as a means of establishing the value of women's domestic labour.[83] In the longer term the movement has continued to differ from feminism in other European countries 'in that it has always been very reluctant to identify independence with employment'. As Ostner notes, this attitude has been 'very much in harmony with state policy'.[84]

A comparison of childcare policy-making in Britain and in other western industrialized societies, and especially with other 'liberal' welfare states, suggests that state traditions and priorities to an extent independent of feminist influence have been strongly correlated with types of childcare policy. But the cases of Norway, France, and also perhaps Australia and New Zealand caution us against assuming too deterministic a model. The strength of 'male-breadwinner' assumptions is not entirely reducible to type of welfare regime. Moreover, feminist mobilization and pressure, particularly through the medium of left-wing parties and trade unions, have also been able to make some difference. The question we must finally turn to concerns more recent developments. Given these markedly different trajectories of childcare policy, to what extent and in what ways have the political and economic forces associated with 'restructuring', discussed in the previous chapter, affected the evolution of policy? Has there been any tendency towards cross-national 'convergence' in more recent approaches to childcare provision?

CONVERGENCE?

Put very crudely, over the last ten to fifteen years the societies in question have been subject to the same broad demographic and employment

---

[83] See Edith Hoshino Altbach *et al.* (eds.), *German Feminism: Readings in Politics and Literature* (Albany, NY: State University of New York Press, 1984), especially Altbach's introduction and the readings in pt. 8, 'Motherhood and Housework'.

[84] Both quotations from Ostner, 'Slow Motion: Women, Work and the Family in Germany', 94–5.

trends (though from very different bases and at differing rates): the continued growth of female employment, an increasing tendency for such employment to be part-time, and the growing numbers of lone parents, meaning largely mothers. Mothers' or parents' recourse to the range of childcare services available has continued to rise. At the same time these societies have been exposed to the same intensified forces of global competition, fuelling internal political arguments about the need to deregulate, reduce public expenditure, and so forth. On the other hand there has been a growing, if uneven, tendency for feminist arguments for gender equality to be absorbed in some form into the official discourse of governing institutions. We could envisage a possible scenario in which, on the one hand, the 'big spender' states which have provided relatively generous public child daycare would be under pressure to cut back while the 'scrimpers', given trends in female employment, welfare dependency, and feminist-inspired expectations of gender equality, would be under pressure to move from almost no provision to somewhat more. Without suggesting that such movement would ever produce actual convergence, the tendency could be in that direction.

We can only begin to explore the complex issues raised by this question here. Starting with the Scandinavian countries, trends in childcare policy and closely related fields have not all pointed the same way but overall it has to be said that the scale and indeed the trend towards expanding public provision have borne up well. Although governments, in response to economic pressures but also according to their ideological complexion, have pursued a range of retrenchment measures, cuts in child daycare, at least by the mid- to late nineties, did not appear to be part of them. In Denmark, conservative governments from 1982 to 1993 sought to reduce expenditure by increasing the intake and lowering the ratio of staff to children in publicly funded childcare facilities, but without cutting the overall numbers of such facilities. The incoming Social Democratic government in 1993 aimed to guarantee, through the municipalities, provision of childcare for all who needed it, though this has yet to be fully implemented.[85] Likewise, in Finland municipal daycare provision has actually been extended since 1985.[86]

Sweden also saw an expansion of public childcare provision through

---

[85] Borchorst, 'The State and the "Social Pedagogic" Universal Child Care Services', 9.

[86] The 1985 Child Home Care Allowance Law obliged local authorities as of January 1990 to provide day care for children under 3 to any parents returning to work after parental leave who wanted it. In 1991 and 1995 this was extended to children under 4, and then 7, respectively. (In Finland children begin school at seven years of age.) See Eeva Huttunen and Merja-Mararia Turunen, 'Finland', in Cochran (ed.), *International Handbook*, 173.

these years, although as in Denmark this was accompanied by some dilution of the previously very generous staffing levels. The political consensus on childcare persisted for a long time. Only in the late 1980s did
non-socialist parties even begin to question the need for further expansion. The 1991 general election, which also incidentally saw a reduction
from 38 to 33 per cent in women's representation in Parliament, brought
a coalition of non-socialist parties to power, which introduced legislation for a 'care allowance'. This would have provided an allowance to
parents of children aged between 1 and 3, ostensibly to increase their
freedom of choice about how their child would be looked after. But the
measure was stoutly opposed by the Social Democrats, who saw behind
it continuing assumptions about separate spheres for men and women,
and on their return to power in 1994 it was revoked.[87] Sainsbury argues
that the continuing commitment in Sweden to a range of public services,
even while cuts are being imposed on a range of social benefits, signals
the determination to protect the basic contours of the welfare state.[88]
Public childcare may be seen as part of a strategy to prevent the brunt
of retrenchment falling on the economically most vulnerable groups,
though it also reflects the strength of institutionalized feminism.

Turning to France, according to Fagnani the modest but steady expansion of crèche childcare places continued at least up to 1996, again suggesting that retrenchment has not dented the basic scale of public
provision. She is, however, concerned by what she sees as the socially
divisive implications of recent developments in childcare policy. The
1994 Family Law, passed under a right-wing government headed by
Balladur, reinforced and extended measures first introduced under an
earlier right-wing government in 1986. These included, firstly, doubling
the allowance for childcare in the home, AGED, which despite the
accompanying rhetoric of 'free choice for parents' and 'diversification
of childcare arrangements' tended to favour well-off families employing houseworkers. A second measure (AFEAMA) provided a tax
allowance to the employer of a registered childminder, the effect again
being to help better-off families. But third, this is in conjunction with a
child-rearing benefit (APE), originally available to parents after the
birth of their third child but in 1994 made available after the second
child, whose effect, Fagnani argues, is to encourage women who have
been economically active to stay at home. The Socialist government
under Jospin, which came to power in 1998, has softened but not abandoned these approaches. These measures in combination tend to imply

[87] Bergqvist, 'Still a Woman-friendly Welfare State?', 19–20
[88] Sainsbury, *Gender, Equality, and Welfare States*, 220–1.

a two-tier childcare regime for women: on the one hand better-off, and presumably more highly educated and highly skilled, women are assisted to remain in the paid workforce, while on the other, poorer, less educated women, who are not in a position to avail themselves of the new allowances for employing childcarers in the home or childminders and who, despite expanded provision, face an overall shortage of subsidized crèche places for under-threes, are strongly tempted by the childrearing benefit option. The point then is not that there should not be a choice for mothers whether or not to stay at home to look after their very young children, but that the choice is much less meaningful for poorer women. The reason for these seemingly contradictory and divisive policies, according to Fagnani, is 'the growing hold that employment policies have over family policy' in a context in which severe unemployment has become a burning political issue.[89]

Developments in Scandinavia, and, with some qualifications, in France do not yet suggest any serious diminution in public childcare funding and provision in response to pressures for economic restructuring. Can we on the other hand detect any sustained trend in the liberal welfare states of North America and Australasia, where subsidized childcare has been extremely scarce but female employment continues to rise, towards a greater public contribution to childcare provision? Here again the picture includes contradictory elements. As in Britain, there has been a drive to reaffirm the market and neo-liberal economic principles but this has itself been subject to more than one interpretation depending to a large extent on which party is in government, with significant implications for childcare.

In the United States, under the Republican presidency of Ronald Reagan from 1980 to 1988, as part of the drive to curb social spending, federal subsidies to childcare progammes were cut in real terms by around 25 per cent and the amount that could be claimed for childcare expenses under the AFDC programme was reduced. Kamerman and Kahn identified childcare as the 'prototypical illustration of "privatization" as an explicit policy of the Reagan administration'. The federal government also ceased to set minimum standards for federally funded daycare. At the same time tax allowances for childcare were raised, thereby helping better-off families and encouraging the growth of

---

[89] Jeanne Fagnani, 'Who should Take Care of the Child? The Ambiguities of French Family Policy', paper presented to the National Institute for Working Life workshop on 'Labour Market and Social Policy—Gender Relations in Transition', Brussels, 1999; quotation from p. 10. Martine Felix also stresses the French political preoccupation with reducing unemployment in her contribution to EC Network on Childcare, *A Review of Services for Young Children*, 61.

private provision.[90] However, overall federal expenditure on childcare has continued to grow (by the early 1990s it was estimated at around $12 billion) and from 1988 there has been some shift away from tax relief for middle- and upper-income groups back to the childcare needs of AFDC and the working poor.[91]

Australia had a succession of Labour governments from 1983 through to 1996. As we have seen, the second, under Hawke, began in 1984 with a strong commitment to expand publicly subsidized childcare provision: the initial pledge was for 20,000 additional places to be created over the following three years. However, the Labour government was divided: the Finance Minister, Peter Walsh, in particular argued that the programme was much too expensive. As a kind of compromise the government introduced new funding arrangements. Fees were to be raised but, more serious in the eyes of the childcare lobby, it was decided to delink subsidies to centres from the pay levels of childcare workers—even the Fraser government had not proposed such a move. It prompted the kind of popular outcry that, sadly, would be unthinkable in Britain:

Protest rallies and demonstrations against the government took place around Australia. At the height of the campaign, the Prime Minister was reported to be receiving 600 letters per week on the issue—more than on any topic other than the killing of kangaroos.[92]

But to no avail. Divisions persisted in the 1987 government: those, including Walsh, who simply wanted to cut back childcare clashed with those who saw it as 'an integral component of the government's economic and social justice policies'. Walsh failed in his attempt, supported by the growing number of commercial providers represented by the Australian Federation of Child Care Associations, to move the funding of childcare onto a voucher basis. None the less by the early 1990s, Brennan argues, a fundamental shift had occurred. In the 1993 election all the major parties highlighted the issue of childcare. But first, it was perceived ever more narrowly as an instrument of economic and labour force policy and second, there was growing encouragement to commercial providers and employers to supplement the non-profit sector. The shift towards the for-profit sector has been sustained through the

[90] Sainsbury, *Gender, Equality, and Welfare States*, 203; Sheila B. Kamerman and Alfred J. Kahn, 'Child Care and Privatization', in S. B. Kamerman and A. J. Kahn (eds.), *Privatization and the Welfare State* (Princeton, NJ: Princeton University Press, 1989); quotation from p. 236.

[91] Gormley, *Everybody's Children*, 47–8.

[92] Brennan, *The Politics of Australian Child Care*, 183. My discussion of Australia relies heavily on the last three chapters of her book.

nineties, assisted by the election of a National/Liberal government in 1996, and by the turn of the century it is estimated that non-profit, community-based services will account for only 15 per cent of childcare provision.

While this analysis of recent developments in childcare policy is inevitably somewhat impressionistic it does make clear the difficulty of identifying any overriding single trend. But it also shows how both the momentum of already institutionalized policies and to a lesser extent the impact of more contingent factors—party politics, feminists, and the childcare lobby—tend to mediate pressures arising from contextual processes of demographic and economic change. By the same token it calls into question any simple convergence thesis.

CONCLUSION

By examining the development of childcare policy in a range of comparable states, this chapter has aimed to shed further light on the British case. A major question has been the extent to which British childcare policy can be accounted for by the broadly 'liberal' character of its state and policy-making tradition. In many ways the analysis offered above has confirmed the relevance of this state tradition. Britain's childcare policy accords much more closely with that found in other 'liberal' welfare states than with policy in the social democratic states (though Norway comes nearest). The comparison with the conservative/corporatist states is, however, complicated by the fact that they do not exhibit a single predominant pattern themselves, which in itself suggests the explanatory limitations of this kind of typology as far as childcare is concerned.

What the instances of the Scandinavian countries and France do suggest is that a strongly interventionist state tradition has been a necessary though not a sufficient condition for extensive public childcare provision or funding. But in addition there needs to be a set of national policy priorities which at some point combine to favour an extensive system of public childcare. While labour market concerns (both labour shortages and state intervention to combat unemployment), population fears, social egalitarianism, and cultural or educational concerns have all played a part, the exact nature and mix of policy priorities has also varied. Thus in Denmark, we are told, family policy has played little part; in France, I speculate, cultural concerns may have been particularly relevant. The development and institutionalization of these policy commitments has had a long history, in some cases extending back to the late nineteenth century. They have been researched, authorized, and propelled forward through distinctive policy mechanisms—for instance, the Royal Commission in Sweden and the more technocratic planning commission in France—and childcare itself has been incorporated into this relatively synoptic policy process. A striking example of the possibility for comprehensive policy-making in these circumstances was when, as we saw, the 1968 Swedish Royal Commission proposed a complete reorganization of the existing childcare system.

The absence of this facilitating institutional and policy legacy has clearly prejudiced the possibilities for childcare development in Britain. It has made it easier for policy-makers to marginalize and privatize the question of childcare. It has also meant that there have been fewer institutional and discursive 'buffers' to protect such limited public childcare provision as exists from the winds of neo-liberal restructuring. However, the European cases themselves suggest that these national policy-making traditions cannot entirely explain childcare policy differences— policy emphasis has been affected most notably by shifts in party control and also by feminist influences. The need to understand childcare policy-making as a more open-ended process is confirmed when we examine the other 'liberal' cases.

Of course part of the effect of introducing the liberal cases is to demonstrate the need for subtler ideological distinctions within the social democratic–liberal state polarization. Australia and New Zealand, and even Canada, have more of a state interventionist tradition than the USA. But there have also been variations between governments, both nationally and at the level of the states (provinces), which, it could be said, have their own 'mini'-state traditions. In the British case too we need to go beyond the overly static and monotonic liberal-state thesis to recognize a much more dynamic and variegated picture.

This very variability has at times produced opportunities in which arguments for childcare based on labour market requirements, the need to address social inequalities, and even women's rights could be made to resonate with policy-making objectives. In such conjunctures, the strength of the childcare lobby, as well as the policy influence of feminism (with Australia's femocrats as the outstanding case) and its ability to galvanize trade union support, have helped determine the possibilities for childcare policy. Sometimes, in the right combination, they have been able to make a real difference, even if policy gains never seem all that secure and have to be vigilantly defended.

7

Conclusion and Prospects

The central issue running through this study has been the meagreness of child daycare provision, especially of publicly run or funded provision, in Britain—both the why and the how. Successive chapters have examined the historical legacy, the development of policy in the post-war period to the transition from Conservative rule in 1997, the demand from mothers for childcare and the feminist response, and the experience of childcare policy in other western democracies. This concluding chapter will firstly try to draw together the strands of the argument up to this point in order to suggest some of the main reasons why childcare policy in Britain has been as it has. Second, it will consider the policy changes, in some respects quite remarkable, under the Labour government from 1997, drawing on the earlier analysis to assess their significance and likelihood of success. The final section will argue that for all its complexities and ambiguities, the issue of childcare remains crucial for equality in this country, both gender equality and equality amongst women.

THE 'LIBERAL' STATE TRADITION . . .

Childcare arose as a public issue, in Britain as elsewhere, in the context of urban and industrial growth. This meant some increase in the numbers of mothers working away from home but also rendered their unsupervised children more visible and potentially disruptive. Though Britain's policy-makers were very slow to perceive this as a problem requiring any public, as opposed simply to charitable, action and then defined state provision as a welfare function for cases of extreme need, this was again not too dissimilar from experience in most other western industrializing societies.

During both the First and especially the Second World War, there was a striking departure from this pattern, with a hugely expanded scale of public provision. Whatever the shortcomings of this provision, it did suggest that the British state had the capability, at very short notice, to transform childcare arrangements when there was the political will to make the resources available. But it was made clear that this was a temporary measure and in the aftermath of the war central government in some ways encouraged, and certainly made no attempt to prevent, the closing down of the war nurseries. It is the way in which policy has developed from the 1960s that serves most to mark out Britain from many of her European neighbours, and that finds strong parallels in the Old Commonwealth. Despite the expansion of female employment, and specifically the employment of mothers with young children; despite the growth of an admittedly very heterogeneous childcare lobby and government moves in the early seventies to increase nursery education and, on a much more limited scale, public day nursery provision; in practice little changed and through the 1980s, though there was a modest increase in part-time nursery education, public child daycare actually declined.

Such a cross-national comparison points to the crucial relevance for childcare of the state tradition, that is the assumptions and conventions governing state intervention in social and family spheres and in the market. The liberal tradition emphasizes the public–private distinction and requires careful justification for any intervention in the private, family sphere. By favouring the market over state intervention in the economy it also militates against redistributive policies. In both these ways, state liberalism has provided an inhospitable environment for public daycare policies.

Although childcare has been construed as a policy problem in many different ways, I have argued that it contains certain elements of 'contingent fixity'. Childcare is about responsibility for children and thus about family relationships. Within the liberal tradition, the family has traditionally been seen as quintessentially private. But secondly, childcare is, or should be, a redistributive issue: to be affordable for all who need it, good quality childcare requires some degree of public subsidy, which again runs counter to a liberal policy approach.

The argument here is however 'two-tier'. It is not that those countries, especially Sweden, Finland, Denmark, and France, where publicly subsidized childcare provision has been much more generous were already providing extensive under-fives services by the 1960s; as noted, their provision and the assumptions governing it had much in common with the British pattern. What was different was that, in the context of a more interventionist state tradition, certain policy priorities had become institutionalized—focusing in varying combinations on the family, the labour market, reduction of social inequalities, cultural assimilation—which then, in the changed circumstances of increasing rates of female employment, provided resources, structures, and arguments with could help to underpin the expansion of public child daycare.

By contrast, in Britain, first, there has been no active 'family policy' in the sense that it has featured in Sweden or France.[1] Policy-makers have not been concerned in any sustained way with maintaining or increasing population levels. Population fears in the immediate post-war period were relatively short-lived but to the extent that they, and a new emphasis on family stability, contributed to an intensified 'familism' in the 1950s this did not generate a systematically researched and generously resourced pro-active policy to support the family.[2]

Neither has there been a tradition of explicit intervention in the labour market, although of course the welfare state, through its benefits and taxation policies, and still more through its role as an employer, inevitably had some impact. The post-war government was committed to the principle of full employment but still 'it was assumed that, with the dismantling of controls, the labour market would resume its "natural" functions in allocating manpower to where it was needed'.[3] From 1964 there was a growing interest in different kinds of training programme. However, it is really only under the Blair government of 1997 that more deliberate attempts to shape the labour market through the various 'New Deals' have been evident.

In Britain government recognition of women's childcare needs, at least up to the 1990s, was largely in response to labour shortage scares. In the extreme situation of the two world wars this actually resulted in increased provision. During the 1950s the favoured solution to labour shortages in key health and transport sectors was however to turn to the former colonies for new supplies. Briefly in the 1960s officials anticipated another shortage in which it would be necessary to encourage mothers back to work, but none of the Ministries was eager to take this

[1] We have noted earlier the difficulties in defining what constitutes 'family policy'. Most governments, certainly post-war governments, in Britain have given great rhetorical emphasis to the importance and value of the family. But this has not been associated with giving it substantial state support. See Lorraine Fox Harding, *Family, State and Social Policy* (London: Macmillan, 1996), ch 6. Land and Parker similarly argue that in Britain family policy has been implicit and reluctant rather than comprehensive. See Hilary Land and Roy, Parker, 'United Kingdom' in S. B. Kamerman and A. J. Kahn (eds.), *Family Policy: Government and Families in Fourteen Countries* (New York: Columbia University Press, 1978), 331–32.

[2] Thus Riley notes 'the careful distancing' of English pro-natalism in the late '40s, not only from eugenic Nazi policies but more generally from European family allowance programmes: Denise Riley, 'War in the Nursery', *Feminist Review*, 2 (1979), 102.

[3] Sarah Vickerstaff, 'Industrial Training in Britain: The Dilemmas of a Neo-corporatist Policy', in Alan Cawson (ed.), *Organised Interests and the State* (London: Sage, 1985), 51.

task on and the sense of relief as the pressure died down was almost palpable. In the late 1980s the demographic time-bomb threat had a much higher profile; government felt bound to be seen to react but its response was largely a matter of re-packaging and bringing forward measures that were already under consideration. While these instances demonstrate the force of labour market considerations in focusing attention on childcare, they also reveal government reluctance to do more than it absolutely had to.

In social democratic Scandinavia there has been a long-standing policy commitment to reducing social inequalities (often using family or labour market policies to this end). The Introduction noted problems in classifying Britain as a 'liberal' welfare state, and these are discussed further below. The welfare state, as it was consolidated in the post-war period, did bear some imprint of social egalitarian ideas, especially in relation to social class. And it was in the context of such ideas that attachment grew within the Labour Party and union movement to the ideal of universal nursery education. Still, the policy orientation within which nursery education provision began to be re-examined in the late 1960s had less to do with promoting social equality or even reducing inequality than with the more limited objective of specifically combating poverty.

So to the extent that Britain has conformed to its 'liberal' label, this has been associated with the failure to develop strong national interventionist policies around the family, the labour market, or social equality that could have provided a propitious context for the later emergence of public childcare provision. It may also, of course, be the case that the British government has not faced such pressing population and labour problems as Sweden or France. But the interventionist tradition in these countries is itself not just a consequence of specific economic and population crises—it has a much longer history.

. . . AND THE POLICY PROCESS

This study has examined the political process through which the 'liberal' tendency to marginalize and even privatize childcare as an issue has been enacted and sustained, that is, to show *how* childcare policy has been made. In keeping with the liberal model, policy-making has been incremental and largely reactive rather than proactive. Reflecting its marginal position in the policy pantheon, national responsibility for childcare has been divided between several Ministries, for a long time primarily between those of Education and Health, and within these has been accorded low status. Further fragmentation and inertia have been achieved by ostensibly devolving decisions to local authorities as to how much childcare to provide without devolving corresponding financial resources or autonomy.

This fragmentation has a long history, with the basic institutional arrangements in place by 1918, a continuity reflecting the absence of any kind of synoptic or even reforming initiative but also helping to impede such initiative. The limitations of this pattern of intitutionalization were tacitly recognized when, during World War II, it was the Ministry of Labour that had to take the initiative and keep up the pressure to expand provision (although this also showed that existing institutional arrangements, while obstructive, were not an insuperable obstacle). Problems of co-ordination at national level were again tacitly acknowledged in the 1980s, during the demographic time-bomb scare, when responsibility for putting together a package of childcare measures was located in the Ministerial Group on Women's Issues. Given the growing interest of the Department of Employment in issues of women's employment and specifically in after-school childcare provision, the merger of the Departments of Education and Employment in 1995 represented a promising development. It is only under the Labour government of 1997, however, that the bulk of childcare functions have been brought together within the DfEE.

Up until the 1980s, at least, the national policy-making process was dominated by the two main policy communities—education and social services/welfare—in which departmental concerns (which rarely focused directly on childcare) tended to set the agenda, although professional groupings, local authorities and their associations, and other recognized 'experts' were routinely consulted. This all contributed to policy inertia or at best extreme incrementalism. Paradoxically the explicit reassertion of liberalism under Thatcher, because it represented a push for radical change, involved some movement away from this incremental, consensual policy style, although the organizational matrix was left intact. There was more policy intervention from the party in government, and a reduced role in policy-making for trade unions, other professional associations, and local authority associations. The effect of these changes in the policy process was further to reduce the political influence of those arguing for public childcare provision or subsidy.

The long-standing division of the childcare field into the two areas of child daycare, with strong welfare connotations, and nursery education, posed problems of co-ordination at local level. By the late seventies, as pressure grew for greater co-ordination and integration of services, this fragmentation was often a source of conflict between departments and between the corresponding council committees and professional groups. There were questions about which department should be given ultimate responsibility, though where there was the political will, these could up to a point be surmounted by organizational innovation. Where, in exceptional cases, individual local authorities in the eighties and early nineties tried to go further in offering a truly integrated childcare service, they encountered major difficulties over comparability of pay, working conditions, and training qualifications of nursery nurses and nursery teachers.

Fragmentation has also encouraged conceptual confusion. There has often been a lack of clarity as to what the term 'childcare' comprises and the difference between daycare and nursery education. This, one suspects, has not been entirely unwelcome for officials and politicians. Not only Conservative but also Labour spokespersons have at times played on this ambiguity to imply that expanded nursery education, albeit part-time, is the equivalent of increased child daycare provision.

On the other hand, politicians have sometimes found it useful to present daycare and nursery education as in competition for scarce resources. We saw an early example when at the end of the last war, winding down the war nurseries was made more acceptable by the strong implications that resources, including premises, that were thereby released would be used to expand nursery education. In the event this expansion failed to materialize. A more recent instance was in the London Borough of Wandsworth, in 1992, where severe cutbacks in local authority day nursery services were justified by referring to a simultaneous plan to extend nursery education to all 3- and 4-year-olds whose parents wanted it.[4] This zero-sum representation of expenditure for daycare and nursery education is, of course, quite misleading. Although they are both ultimately in competition, along with the whole range of local government activities, for local and central funding, available statistics show that far from displaying an inverse relationship, levels of daycare and nursery education provision are quite highly correlated.[5]

. . . AND THE CHILDCARE LOBBY

While government has been slow to acknowledge the need for childcare, the childcare lobby has also been weak and fragmented. It might

---

[4] Melissa Benn, 'Wandsworth—A Cut Above the Rest', Guardian, 26 Feb. 1992.
[5] See, for instance, figures provided in Peter Moss, 'Day Care Policy and Provision in Britain', in Peter Moss and Edward Melhuish (eds.), *Current Issues in Day Care for Young Children* (London: HMSO, 1991), 91–2.

be argued that meagreness of childcare provision was less a reflection of state liberalism than of the absence of political pressure. But while its causes have been complex, and include the nature of the childcare issue itself, we should not underestimate the impact of state institutions and policies in shaping the field and setting the terms of childcare politics.

We have seen how, through a kind of vicious or self-confirming circle, the low scale of provision, the lack of importance attached to childcare by policy-makers and associated low levels of pay and inadequate training arrangements, and the overall fragmentation of under-fives services gave rise to corresponding professional groupings that were numerically weak, low in status, and internally divided. It was argued in Chapter 5 that, to the extent that the pattern of provision reified a certain rather depressing and stigmatized welfare conception of childcare, this may in turn have influenced the attitudes of parents and even of feminist activists engaging with the issue. Similarly problematic for the latter was the way that child daycare and childminding, as currently organized, appeared to entail the exploitation of predominantly working-class women by middle-class women. As demand for childcare grew, the weakness of public provision left the way clear for a growing private sector, which, especially in response to moves to tighten government regulation, was organizing politically by the late 1980s and further complicated the cohesion of childcare advocacy. The voucher episode of 1995–7 fostered further bitter divisions between the range of service providers, a legacy which has outlived the end of Conservative rule.

Childcare advocates were constrained by the manner of institutionalization of childcare policy as to how they could intervene to influence policy. One of the ongoing problems for those wishing to make the case for childcare was the lack of systematic information about demand for childcare, itself a reflection of low government priority. Another difficulty was the terms on which they could offer advice. From the late 1960s the lobby, or well-known figures within it, were increasingly incorporated into a process of consultation with the two main departments concerned, and even in such formal interdepartmental consultation as occurred. Government also set up the National Children's Bureau in 1963 and helped fund other bodies like the Thomas Coram Research Institute and even the Daycare Trust. In this sense members of the lobby became 'insiders' but also had to accept the constraints of existing compartmentalization and policy (although in the long run the various 'experts' *did* increase officials' awareness of the importance in principle of integrating education and care aspects of provision).

Childcare advocates were further constrained in terms of the kinds of arguments and cross-connections they could make. Bacchi, we saw in the Introduction, stresses the need to examine how a potential issue such as childcare becomes framed as a 'problem' within the perspective of differing policy concerns.[6] In certain European countries childcare came to be associated with both a proactive family policy and policies affecting the labour market. In Britain, child daycare was for a long time seen by national policy-makers as an aspect of welfare policy for mothers and children at risk. Nursery education enjoyed greater legitimacy, in theory at least, because of its association with education. This is one area in which liberal policy-makers have traditionally been more ready to recognize a need for public intervention in the family and for expenditure of public resources. But nursery education provision was organized to follow the schools calendar, largely on a part-day basis, rather than to reflect the needs of working parents. In the 1960s the 'rediscovery' of poverty provided a new policy context in which to press the claims of childcare. Subsequently, with the demographic time-bomb threat, labour market concerns offered a new opportunity, and one in which the focus was actually on the needs of working mothers, although this coincided with the de-emphasis on public provision. A further policy opening was offered by the growing concern to check the welfare dependency of lone mothers, which lay behind the move, through the 'disregard', to increase their effective demand for childcare. There has, then, been a limited though changing range of policy concerns and commitments within which childcare proposals could be located. Alternatively phrased, childcare advocates have in large measure lacked an important kind of 'discursive resource', in the sense that Hobson has elaborated, that is 'ways of formulating public debate that allow for linkages to other policy concerns and hegemonic ideologies'.[7]

LIMITS OF THE LIBERAL STATE THESIS

But the liberalism thesis cannot tell the whole story. Not only, as noted in the Introduction, is liberalism a broad encompassing doctrine that has assumed a multitude of different forms—as in the evolution from the 'classical' liberalism of the early nineteenth century to the 'social' or

---

[6] Carol Lee Bacchi, *Women, Policy and Politics: The Construction of Policy Problems* (London: Sage, 1999).

[7] Barbara Hobson, 'Feminist Strategies and Gendered Discourses in Welfare States: Married Women's Right to Work in the United States and Sweden', in S. Koven and S. Michel (eds.), *Mothers of a New World* (London: Routledge, 1993), 408.

'new' liberalism increasingly prevalent from the turn of the century to the 'neo'-liberalism emerging in the 1980s. The concept of a liberal welfare state is also, as we have seen, a blunt instrument for registering the coexistence of contrasting and competing political approaches. In the previous chapter we saw how, amongst and within the 'liberal welfare state' cases, childcare policies have varied according to the ideological complexion of the party in government. Generally they have fared better, at least from the 1970s, under social-democratic-inclined governments, better under Whitlam and Hawke than under Fraser in Australia, for example.

In Britain, until very recently, this has been less the case at national level. Labour governments have been no more inclined than Conservatives to expand childcare provision substantially. The limited programme to increase both nursery education and public daycare in the early seventies was adopted by a Conservative government. (I shall return to this point shortly.) Locally, however, an analysis of data for English local authorities shows a strong statistical correlation between Labour Party control and public daycare provision in the 1970s, though this disappears in the 1980s and 1990s, partly, we may presume, because of central government's tightening financial grip.[8] So the blanket term 'liberal' conceals the extent of social democratic forces and arenas that *could* be advantageous for childcare.

The concept of the liberal state likewise leaves unexamined the specific consequences of political centralization. In the Introduction, we noted that the British system of government has been relatively centralized. Analysis of the experience of the federal liberal states, in the previous chapter, permitted no firm conclusion as to whether having a federal system was in itself an advantage as far as childcare provision is concerned. None the less centralization has in some ways constituted a further impediment for childcare advocates in this country. There have been *ad hoc* grass-roots campaigns, particularly those demanding or defending nursery education, which doubtless have influenced local councillors and even registered with MPs. But especially towards the nineties, with strengthening expenditure controls from the centre, the scope for local policy variation was narrowing steadily. Grass-roots

---

[8] Findings from ESRC-funded research into variations in childcare policy amongst British local authorities. See Vicky Randall and Kimberly Fisher, *Towards Explaining Child Daycare Policy Variations amongst the Local Authorities*, Institute of Social and Economic Research Working Paper 99:18 (Colchester: ESRC Centre on Micro-social Change, 1999). We speculated that the waning effect of party control might result also from the fact that through the 1980s and early 1990s the number of Labour-controlled councils was steadily growing and thereby including increasingly marginal cases.

initiatives have not been co-ordinated in any broader national or regional strategy, although local authorities *have* in many instances learned from one another's experience, discussed under-fives provision in collective forums, and sought to influence government through their associations. Advocacy at national level has mostly involved a painstaking and protracted process of trying to influence thinking in key institutions with access to central policy-making—in some ways a high-risk strategy. The headway made in some of these—the Labour Party, trade unions, local authority associations—by the end of the seventies seemed to count for nothing under the Conservative dispensation of the eighties, though if and when central government is convinced of the childcare case, centralization could make it easier to establish a national policy.

Centralization is linked to a further characteristic at odds with the liberal state model: the British state's considerable *capacity*, as manifest most strikingly in the last war. In the Introduction we noted Dunleavy's argument about the existence in Britain of an 'ungrounded statism':[9] the widespread acceptance, at least up to the 1980s, both at official levels and amongst the public at large, that government machinery would play a considerable role in policy implementation. That is to say, the actual application of liberal tenets has varied in relation to different policy areas and issues.

But finally we must return to the point made above that 'global' liberalism could mask potentially childcare-friendly social democratic elements. The fact is that in practice these social democratic elements have not necessarily and always been supportive of childcare. This in turn implies that liberalism is not the whole story but that wider gender interests and ideologies have to be invoked. The post-war British welfare system pursued redistributive policies in a number of fields that went well beyond what is usually understood by a liberal remit, to the extent that, for this period, Esping-Andersen and others have hesitated to include Britain in the liberal welfare state category. These policies, moreover, incorporated many central concerns of the organized labour movement (Esping-Andersen's 'mobilised working class', a key player in the genealogy of welfare states). But the overall welfare regime was heavily premised on the 'male-breadwinner' model: it was not imposed on trade unions but reflected, or at the least was heavily congruent with, their own assumptions. And these assumptions continued to influence attitudes to working mothers for a long time, both in the trade unions and in the Labour Party, with consequences for childcare policy.

---

[9] See p. 10 above.

'GENDERING' THE STATE

This takes us back to Ruggie's observation that the liberal approach has been 'particularly strong' in the case of childcare. Why has childcare been singled out for such 'orthodox' liberal treatment? True, liberal ideology, with its emphasis on the public–private divide, has been invoked in justification. But the categories of public and private are neither absolute nor self-evident: to the contrary, as with other such 'conceptual dyads', the very flexibility of the boundary between them makes them a valuable ideological instrument to legitimize policies whose actual determinants may be rather different.[10] Although the family has been conceived almost as the heart of the private sphere, this has not prevented state intervention in practice. Leaving aside the impact of policies, such as protective factory legislation, which indirectly helped to shape the character of family relations, already by the turn of the century measures had been enacted, for instance, to improve mothers' and children's health, to establish universal primary education, and to prevent cruelty to children. This suggests that childcare policy does not simply reflect the logic of liberal government; within the institutions of government themselves, there has been, if in varying degrees, a predisposition to see childcare through a more rigorously liberal lens.

In other words, at this point we are approaching the broader issue of how the state itself is 'gendered' in its composition, assumptions, and effects. As noted in the Introduction, Connell has coined the term 'gender regime' to describe the way in which the state embodies a set of power relationships between men and women, which is itself the pre-cipitate of its earlier gender history. In the case of childcare we can see this first and most starkly in terms of gender hierarchy. Men have dominated the highest decision-making levels impinging on the child-care question within government, political parties, the trade unions, and so forth; women have been hugely over-represented amongst junior office staff, secretaries, nursery nurses and nursery school teachers, and the clients of childcare provision. But this study has also demonstrated the extent to which the 'maternalist' assumption that the mother's primary and natural duty is to look after her child, and that as an exten-sion childcare is and should be a 'woman's issue', has been almost

[10] I am indebted to Alison Rowlands, a historian at Essex University, for an enlight-ening discussion on this point. For an excellent account of the inconsistencies and ambi-guities in liberal conceptions of public and private, see Susan Moller Okin, 'Gender, the Public and the Private', in David Held (ed.), *Political Theory Today* (Cambridge: Polity, 1991).

literally embodied in the political process, through a gender division of labour running virtually up to the top.

While systematic figures cannot be provided, the following examples already indicate how far men have been willing to cede key public, campaigning, and even decision-making roles to women players. We noted the role of the Women Inspectors of the Board of Education in 1905, the McMillan sisters, Miss Puxley and Miss Smieton in the respective Ministries of Health and Labour during the Second World War, and the Committee of the Medical Women's Federation at its end. When the issue of daycare was discussed in the TUC in the late forties and fifties, the speakers voicing different sides or aspects of the debate were all women. The commission of inquiry into primary education, established in 1964, was chaired by a woman, Lady Plowden.

In the early years this may doubtless have been empowering for the individual women involved. They found in childcare one policy arena where their participation and views enjoyed an unusual degree of legitimacy. However, the basis of this legitimacy was ambiguous in that it tended to presuppose their special understanding as women, and thus as actual or potential mothers, of the needs of children. Because they were women, the implicit expectation was that they would put children's interests above women's interests, or rather refuse to see the potential conflict of interests that resulted from the current way that childcare and employment were organized. This is not to say that the women in question all conformed to such expectations. But where disagreements arose the different arguments were articulated by women actors, thereby serving to distance male policy-makers from apparent responsibility for the outcome, just as at home, one assumes, they left that sort of thing to their wives.

This gender division of labour has persisted even as the childcare lobby has grown and the case for childcare in principle been more widely accepted. With few exceptions,[11] childcare experts and voluntary group activists have been female. It has been women in the Labour Party and the trade unions who have pushed the issue up the agenda. Within the Labour leadership, a succession of women have been given responsibility, as part of a wider brief, for childcare policy. Under the New Labour government, within the DfEE both the initial Childcare Policy Team and then the Childcare Unit were headed by women officers. At local level my impression is that this gendering is, if anything, more marked. This is not to denigrate the part that many women have played in advancing the childcare cause or to suggest that they should

[11] Two requiring honourable mention are Jack Tizard and Peter Moss.

resist such 'collusion' with male expectations—as I shall shortly argue, one could indeed have wished for a stronger 'femocrat' presence. But in this continued gendering of the childcare process we can perhaps see the extent to which, at some level, male decision-makers still feel that childcare is or should be women's responsibility, because it is women who become mothers.[12]

Second, we can consider the assumptions underpinning daycare policy. Ruggie has suggested that because in Britain the liberal emphasis on the public–private distinction has meant childcare was largely consigned to the private sphere, this left more scope for 'traditional' assumptions about women's mothering role in shaping how they were understood. That is, it was not so much that government promoted these assumptions as that it did not interfere with them. But this understates the extent to which government has itself actively espoused traditional or maternalist constructions and served to reinforce them through its childcare policies and other measures.

As already noted, up to the seventies at least, 'male-breadwinner' and maternalist assumptions were adhered to almost as strongly within those political institutions closest to a social democratic outlook, the trade unions and the Labour Party, as elsewhere. The tenacity of these assumptions within the labour movement has been of particular moment given the potentially redistributory character of childcare policy. Lowi and others identified producer groups as crucial actors in redistributory politics in the expectation that this would primarily be redistribution between classes. The support of such producer groups has helped to propel the childcare issue up the political agenda in Britain more recently and has contributed importantly to the success of child-care campaigns in Australia, Canada, and New Zealand. But in the early post-war years, the prevalence of a 'male-breadwinner' perspective actually made organized labour a barrier to change.

Focusing more directly on government, we note that under both Labour and Conservative rule there were repeated references in government circulars from the forties through to the end of the sixties, and in the Plowden, Seebohm, and Finer reports, to the mother's proper place at home with her children. Although the specific formulation shifted, admitted of increasing exceptions, and allowed for part-time attendance at nursery school, the ideal of the mother at home remained the informing vision. Here policy-makers were not so much asserting

---

[12] One further symptom of this unspoken assumption has been the continuing failure to tackle the issue of nursery nurses pay or to sort out the training 'muddle'. The implication is that child daycare, and still more childminding, are seen as an extension of women's natural mothering role, rather than constituting a 'proper job'.

the privacy of the family as breaching that privacy by pronouncing on the ideal form that relationships in the family should take and shaping policy with this in mind. Through their policies and discourse they were thereby contributing both to the range of practical options and to the legitimate ideals in terms of which mothers could frame and defend their self-understanding.

The growing number of working mothers and the growing impact of feminism made it increasingly difficult to voice the full-blown maternalist position that mothers should be at home looking after their children. By the late seventies the rhetoric had altered to one of 'choice' and, often quite disingenuously, to parents' rather than mothers' choice. In the eighties, the reaffirmation of liberal premises, especially the renewed emphasis upon the market, might seem sufficient to explain childcare policy. Even then, can it fully explain the extraordinarily low priority given to childcare matters, until they were almost forced upon government? Can it not be argued that a weaker, more implicit form of maternalism has continued to inform government policy?

FEMINISM—A MISSED OPPORTUNITY?

Given the prevalence of these assumptions amongst policy-makers, feminist interventions have been of great potential importance. Without doubt second-wave feminism in Britain has helped to change the normative context and terms in which childcare advocates have been able to make their case. It has also offered mothers an alternative discourse through which to frame and legitimize their childcare needs. Yet, contrary to the impression sometimes given in the media, and even in the movement's own literature, we have seen that direct feminist involvement in childcare politics has been quite limited and at national level emerged relatively late. The reasons for this reticence are complex and difficult to unravel. Certainly it has partly been a reflection of the context, the way in which childcare policy has been institutionalized, which chimes with feminist suspicion of the state and poses divisive class implications. But first, it has also stemmed from particular features of British second-wave feminism, notably the initial weakness of reformist or pragmatic strands. Second, the issue of childcare has raised problematic issues for feminism, above all perhaps as it touches on the ambiguous question of motherhood.

In face of the strength of the liberal state tradition, especially as reaffirmed and combined with the economic neo-liberalism of the Conservative government from 1979, feminists would always have had their work cut out for them, no doubt a deterrent in itself. Moreover in time, within the trade unions and Labour Party, women activists did help to raise childcare awareness, which is now feeding into government policy. But was an opportunity missed here after all? The experience, in particular, of femocrats in the childcare policy arena in Australia suggests that in Britain more could possibly have been achieved if, at the national level, feminists had mobilized more powerfully and earlier on the issue.

TIMING

This brings us to the final point, about timing. This is not simply that the development of childcare policy in Britain has been 'path-dependent', with events and (non-)decisions at one stage helping to determine options and constraints at a later stage, though this has been a central theme of the analysis. Childcare policy has also been affected by the way the different components shaping it have interacted over time. Of course such components are not necessarily discrete but may well reflect common underlying developments. Still, the precise timing has sometimes seemed to make a difference. For instance it has often been the case that pressure for daycare peaks just when public interest in nursery education has subsided, and vice versa. Perhaps the most fateful such 'coincidence' has been between the emergence of a more extensive childcare lobby and the arrival of Thatcherism. Although the need for childcare assistance was growing from the 1960s, if not earlier, only very slowly was this taken up by the organizations with an interest in children, trade unions, and the women's movement. By the mid- to late seventies, when some kind of lobby could finally be said to be emerging, first retrenchment under Labour, and then neo-liberalism's reassertion of the public–private rationale for leaving childcare to the family, voluntary organization, and the market, nipped it in the bud. Government's failure to act at that stage will in turn create enormous difficulties for a Labour government more seriously committed to change.

NEW LABOUR MEETING THE CHILDCARE CHALLENGE

On that inauspicious note we turn to developments in childcare policy since the Labour government came to power in May 1997. Labour under

Tony Blair has given childcare a much higher profile than hitherto. It featured prominently in the election manifesto,[13] and as early as July 1997 the Chancellor of the Exchequer, Gordon Brown, declared in his budget speech that childcare was to be 'an integral part of our economic policy'.[14] In May 1998, the government issued its Green Paper, *Meeting the Childcare Challenge*, which set out its underlying approach. Observing that 'childcare has been neglected for too long', for the first time in British history the government recognized the need for a national childcare policy. This was justified in terms both of gender equity and of supporting the family. The paper was critical of earlier governments for their excessive reliance on the private sector, arguing for a mixed economy of provision in which policy would be advanced through 'partnerships' between national and local bodies and, more specifically at local level, between a whole range of public, private, and voluntary agencies.

Before analysing this childcare policy and its consequences in greater detail, it needs to be related to policy developments in adjacent fields. These policies taken together need further to be set in the wider context of the government's policy priorities. And we must also consider the different political interests and pressures driving these policies.

It is noteworthy, first, that while the thrust of policy statements, and of many of the accompanying organizational changes, has been further to integrate educational and daycare components of childcare, there are respects in which the policies remain distinct. By the time of the General Election steps were already under way to extend the voucher scheme to all the local authorities. Labour repudiated the scheme but while its spokespersons would claim that subsequent policy developments owe nothing to the Conservative initiative and simply reflect what the party leadership already intended to do, there were significant elements of continuity with Conservative policy in the new government's early years programme. As early as June 1997, local education authorities were being asked to establish Early Years Partnerships with agencies in the voluntary and private sectors, in order to produce Early Years Development Plans that would demonstrate how all 4-year-olds in their area could be provided with a half-day nursery place by September 1998. These partnerships were supposed to be based on co-operation rather than the competitive ethos engendered by the voucher scheme. But while no longer taking the form of a voucher going directly

---

[13] Though the issue received little attention during the election campaign.
[14] Cited in Lisa Harker, 'A National Childcare Strategy: Does it Meet the Childcare Challenge?', *Political Quarterly* (1998), 249.

to parents, the sum of £1,100 was still to be available for the nursery education of each child of eligible age. In March 1999 a further target was announced of 50,000 places for 3-year-olds by the following September. I shall return to the consequences of this initiative for childcare, or more precisely daycare, policy, which are both complicated and still unclear. The main point here is that this policy preceded the childcare strategy, was fully funded, and required compliance. The new childcare partnerships were simply grafted onto the existing Early Years Partnerships.

Childcare strategy also needs to be seen in the context of wider economic and social policies. The concerns both with gender equity and with being 'family-friendly' should not be entirely discounted, as discussed below. But arguably they were largely important to the extent that they complemented these broader objectives and helped to make them acceptable to different sets of interests. Under John Major we saw that childcare was beginning to be identified not just negatively as an area for retrenchment but as capable of playing a more active role in the process of welfare state restructuring, by helping to bring the lowest-income families and especially lone parents off welfare. Labour criticized the ineffectualness of the childcare disregard, whose take-up was extremely limited. But rather than abandoning it, the effect of Labour's subsequent policies has been to take it further.

Labour, that is to say, is pushing forward the project of welfare state restructuring—Tony Blair prefers to call it 'welfare state modernizing'—as indeed must governments everywhere. But as the previous chapter has shown, such restructuring can take very different forms. Just to remind overseas readers, the present Labour government is the outcome of the growing ascendancy within the Labour Party of the political strand or faction that calls itself 'New Labour'. This has strenuously sought to dissociate itself from both traditional 'Old Labour' and the 'Democratic Left' which challenged it from the late seventies. Partly because the New Labour leadership has seemed to move the party in a centrist direction and also because the Prime Minister, Tony Blair, in particular appears to espouse much of the neo-liberal analysis of globalization and its economic implications, some critics have represented it as little different from the outgoing regime, as 'Thatcherism by other means'. This is to ignore an important shift of mood and emphasis.

Although by the mid- to late nineties overall rates both of employment and unemployment compared favourably with other European countries and average income had actually grown by 44 per cent from 1979, this had been accompanied by increasing economic and social polarization. This included a growing gulf between dual-earner house-holds and workless households, as well as within the ranks of the employed.[15] While there has been little attempt to reverse privatization and deregulation, and an electoral pledge not to increase income tax has limited opportunities for substantial redistributive measures, there is a genuine concern, symbolically marked by the setting up of a Social Exclusion Unit, to be more socially inclusive through policies aimed at redistributing opportunity.[16] One of the means through which this is to be achieved is education, and the decision to expand nursery education, while the culmination of a long-growing commitment within the party, evidently sits comfortably in this frame.

At the same time, the present government, like the last, has been anxious to reduce or at least contain welfare dependency. The way to reconcile these dominant concerns—cutting the welfare burden and social inclusiveness—is seen to be through increasing employment opportunity. Work brings not only enhanced financial independence but a new sense of social involvement and self-respect: 'work is central to the government's attack on social exclusion. . . . Work is not just about earning a living. It is a way of life'.[17] A central plank of government employment policy has been the 'welfare to work' programme,[18] a range of measures aimed at reducing welfare dependency through paid work, usually combined with in-work social security benefits, so as to over-come the 'poverty trap' in which pay for the lowest-paid jobs fails to compensate for loss of eligibility for social benefit. This has been pro-moted through a series of 'New Deals' for different social groups.

We have already noted that in Britain a higher proportion of lone parents are unemployed and living in poverty than in any other EC country, and this situation worsened during the period of Conservative rule.[19] One of the first and most important of these New Deals was

[15] Between 1979 and 1995/6 the income of the top decile of earners grew by 70% whilst that of the bottom decile fell by 9%. These and the preceding figures are taken from Diane Perrons, 'Labour Market Transformations and Employment Policies: The Organ-isation of Work, Care and Leisure in the UK', paper presented to the National Institute for the Working Life workshop on 'Labour Market and Social Policy—Gender Relations in Transition', Brussels, 1999.

[16] This is well discussed in Ruth Lister, 'From Equality to Social Inclusion: New Labour and the Welfare State', *Critical Social Policy*, 55: (1998), 215–25.

[17] Statement by Harriet Harman while Minister of Social Security, quoted in Lister, 'From Equality to Social Inclusion', 219.

[18] This programme is inspired in part by Clinton's 'workfare' reforms in the United States, though there is likely to be greater resistance in Britain to making participation compulsory. See Desmond King and Mark Wickham-Jones, 'From Clinton to Blair: The Democratic (Party) Origins of Welfare to Work', *Political Quarterly* (1999), 62–74.

[19] 'The percentage of lone parents living below half average income dramatically increased from only 19% in 1979 to 63% by 1995/6': Perrons, 'Labour Market Transfor-mations and Employment Policies', 4.

for 'lone parents', launched only a few months after coming into office, with pilot schemes introduced in eight areas initially and the programme extended nationally in October 1998. The 'deal', which was however targeted at mothers of school-age children, included the commitment to ensure accessible and affordable childcare.

New Labour's childcare policy has to be understood first and foremost in the context of these wider economic and social objectives. Childcare can be a means of helping mothers into work and out of economic dependency and social exclusion. It can also, incidentally, generate much new employment, though this is not an argument frequently deployed.

But we should not ignore the feminist influence on policy. Chapter 5 traced the growing influence of feminist childcare demands within the party. Following the 1997 General Election the number of women MPs virtually doubled and 101 of these were Labour. We do not have systematic information concerning Labour women MPs' views on childcare. Analysing data from the 1992 *British Candidate Study*, Norris found that women candidates attached somewhat greater priority than men to social policy issues, although when asked to identify the three most important policy questions facing the country, few volunteered childcare.[20] Childs's survey of 34 of the 65 new Labour women MPs focused on the broad issue of gender representation. She found a majority of them expected women's increased parliamentary presence to produce more informed debate and a policy agenda taking more note of women's concerns—Childs calls this the 'gender agenda'. To the extent that this agenda was itemized, childcare was one of the issues cited, though less frequently than domestic violence.[21] The subsequent conduct of 'Blair's babes' has been scrutinized and criticized but with few direct implications for childcare: since the government has launched its childcare strategy as promised, their commitment to the childcare issue has not really been tested. But it would be surprising if their presence made no difference at all to government's wish to be seen to honour its childcare pledge.

Childs found that Labour women MPs in general strongly supported the institution for Minister for Women. Under this arrangement, which replaced the earlier commitment to a full-blown Ministry for Women, the Minister for Women was to chair a new Cabinet sub-committee on women's issues, supported at the administrative level by a Women's

---

[20] Pippa Norris, 'Women Politicians: Transforming Westminster?', *Parliamentary Affairs*, 49: 1 (1996), 89–102.

[21] Sarah Childs, 'The New Labour Women MPs in the 1997 British Parliament and the Political Representation of Women', paper presented to the EPOP Conference, Manchester Business School, 1998.

Unit. The first appointee to this office was Harriet Harman. On the down side, she had to combine this responsibility with her job as Secretary of State for Social Security, possibly creating a clash of interest and certainly limiting the time she had available for it.[22] On the other hand Harman is a self-proclaimed feminist and long-standing champion of improved childcare provision. Childcare was swiftly pinpointed as one of the key issues the Unit would address.

Although by the time Labour took office, childcare was already seen as a necessary complement of economic policy, it had been Harriet Harman, while working as Shadow Chief Secretary to the Treasury in 1994, who helped to make the Shadow Chancellor, Gordon Brown, appreciate the connection.[23] Although responsibility for childcare resided largely within the DfEE, as Minister for Women, Harman sought to ensure there was no delay in producing the Green Paper. She also pushed for inclusion of a childcare allowance in the Working Families Tax Credit, discussed further below.[24]

Childcare has been presented by government as one of a number of 'family-friendly' measures aimed at making it easier to combine employment with family responsibilities. Trade unions have been prominent amongst those pressing for change, but business, particularly small businesses, have been less enthusiastic. Many feminists have also supported family-friendly policies, whilst at the same time being suspicious of the way they tend to be couched in terms that avoid reference to gender equality. The government has endorsed the EU Directives on working time and on part-time work. The Employment Relations (Fairness at Work) Bill, published in January 1999, incorporated provisions of the EU Directive on parental leave. It extended paid maternity leave from 14 to 18 weeks, covering 95 per cent of working women, and proposed establishing a new right to unpaid paternity leave as well as an additional three months, unpaid leave for mothers. These steps are an improvement, practically and symbolically, but still lag enormously behind policies in some other European countries. There has been particular criticism from a number of quarters (including the Prime Minister's wife[25]) of the failure to provide for paid leave—without it, it is argued, neither poorer mothers nor most fathers will feel they can afford to take time off. To repeat, then, considerations of gender equity

[22] In the event Joan Ruddock was appointed to support her as junior minister with responsibility for women but there was further indignation when it was announced that this post would be unpaid.

[23] See also Polly Toynbee, 'Wooing Women', *Guardian*, 18 Mar. 1999.

[24] Interview with Harriet Harman, 8 July 1999.

[25] Clare Dyer, 'Cherie Wants Paid Leave for New Dads', *Guardian*, 17 May 1999.

and the need for family-friendly employment have played some part in motivating and shaping childcare policy developments under Labour but they are not the driving force.

THE NEW CHILDCARE STRATEGY: FUNDING AND ORGANIZATION

With a clearer idea of the policy context of the childcare strategy we can consider details of its finance and implementation. Very little public funding, in addition to what is already being provided for nursery education places, will go directly into provision for under-fives, meaning daycare for children up to 3 years and 'wrap-around' care to top up statutory early years half-day provision for 3- to 5-year-olds. Public funding for daycare is to come through three main sources: a modest direct government subvention to the partnerships to help get them established and to conduct a childcare audit; a much larger amount of lottery money (£ 170 million) earmarked for after-school schemes; and, on the demand side, a still larger projected sum, through the Working Families Tax Credit coming on stream in October 1999. While the exact amount available through WFTC was for a time unclear it now appears that any mothers earning £14,000 or less will be entitled to £70 a week for childcare for one child or £105 for two. For mothers earning above that amount, the sum will 'taper' to nothing for those at incomes of £22,000 for one child and £30,000 for two. Though the rate of take-up cannot be predicted, this is potentially a very considerable subsidy. Initially there were fears that parents would use the money to pay those who had already been providing informal care but it was subsequently made clear that it could only be spent on officially registered forms of daycare.

The childcare initiative has been associated with considerable organizational change and has generated a great deal of activity nationally and locally. Before the Green Paper, in the autumn of 1997 an interdepartmental committee helped to identify the different areas to be covered in a national childcare strategy, which was then elaborated by a small childcare policy team within the DfEE, which by January had been upgraded to a Childcare Unit. Following publication of the paper, this unit was expanded until by January 1999 it included over 35 staff members; at the same time, from April 1998 most daycare responsibilities (excluding some for children in need) were transferred from the Department of Health to the DfEE, bringing childcare administration finally under one roof, and in the same division.[26] In fact the Childcare Unit and the Early Years Development Unit are cheek by jowl on the same floor.

At local level the combination of the early years and child daycare initiatives has triggered much reorganization of management structures to facilitate co-ordination. Often this has meant that childcare has been brought under the auspices of the Department of Education if it was not there already. It is understood that local authorities will take the lead in setting up and providing an agenda for, though not necessarily chairing, the partnerships. Having set up the early years partnerships, expanding them to encompass childcare has involved bringing in a few additional players such as representatives of childminders and the local New Deal for Lone Parents. The partnerships were required to submit local plans by February 1999, to consist mainly of an audit of childcare demand and supply; for some local authorities this meant a huge amount of work, for others much of the information was already accessible. In the event the DfEE judged all but two of the plans satisfactory.

It is much too soon to know how much difference the childcare strategy will really make. Whatever else may happen, it is a huge step forward that government has finally acknowledged the importance of childcare, as seen in terms both of child development and the needs of working parents. Processes have been set in train—rationalization and growth of childcare administration; systematic gathering of detailed information, nationally and locally, about the different forms of provision available and their relationship to childcare needs; greater dialogue and co-ordination between local providers; expansion of effective childcare demand—that should in turn generate a numerically stronger, better-informed, and better-resourced childcare lobby, more able to keep up pressure for change.

Inevitably there have been doubts and criticisms voiced from many quarters. For instance the Chancellor has been urged to extend tax relief for childcare to women whose salaries put them above the WFTC ceiling but whose childcare costs still consume a large share of their income.[27] Playgroups have been particularly hard hit by the new early years policy, because of 3- and 4-year-old children being 'mopped up' by primary schools in pre-reception classes to maximize school income. Although this problem was first attributed to the operation of the

---

[26] Interviews with Fran Greaves, DfEE Childcare Policy Team, 1 Oct. 1997, and Shirley Trundle, DfEE Childcare Unit, 19 Jan. 1999.

[27] Valerie Elliot, 'Childcare Costs "are Double Tax"', *Guardian*, 11 Mar. 1999.

voucher scheme, which led to the closure of 800 playgroups in 1997, it grew worse under Labour and the government twice felt obliged to provide grants to the Pre-school Alliance to help tide playgroups over until the WFTC arrangements came into effect.[28]

Here we will focus on three particular areas of concern. The first has already been broached—the way that daycare has been to an extent tagged on to the statutory Early Years Development provision. There is now much greater recognition of the need to integrate education and care; for instance a range of childcare providers, including day nurseries and playgroups, assuming they satisfy the educational criteria, have been able to participate in both the voucher scheme and subsequently the Early Years scheme.[29] However, in practice the real winners have been primary schools providing nursery classes, pre-reception, or simply reception classes. Nursery education, we have seen, has always been popular with parents. Now, following the government's new emphasis on curriculum content and phasing in primary as well as secondary education, many parents see nursery classes as the best way to ensure their child is well prepared for Key Stage 1. This obviously places other kinds of providers at a disadvantage in recruiting 4-year-olds, and increasingly also 3-year-olds.

From a daycare perspective, the problem is compounded by the fact that the early years provision is only for part of the day and during school term time. It is in no way geared to the needs of working parents. Ideally these two kinds of provision need to be offered within the same or adjacent institutional settings and dovetailed with one another. But such integration is difficult and costly to achieve.[30] Moreover, where it has been attempted the problem arises of reconciling differences in staffing arrangements, discussed further below.

Second, because the early years measures came first, were funded, and placed an obligation on local authorities to deliver, energies were bound to be concentrated on this target, especially where existing nursery education levels were low, with daycare a secondary consideration. In particular, because funding was for 4- and, more recently, 3-year-olds, much less attention has been paid to provision for children in their first three

---

[28] Rebecca Smithers, 'Threatened Children's Playgroups and Nurseries Win £500,000 Grant', *Guardian*, 17 Mar. 1999.

[29] One consequence has been inconsistency in the rules regulating such questions as educational standards and staff–children ratios, according to whether they stem from the 1989 Children Act or from DfEE requirements. Government has already recognized the need for 'a more integrated and consistent system of regulation for early education and daycare' and mounted a separate consultation exercise.

[30] Though government is helping to fund a series of Early Excellence centres that will offer a model—by 1999 there were 18 of these.

years (which in the absence of more generous parental leave provision has to include very young babies, since many mothers may not feel they can afford to stay out of work). Under a separate 'Sure Start' scheme, government is making funding available in 250 disadvantaged areas for a range of provision for under-threes including nursery childcare. Additional public investment in the supply of childcare for this age range will be strictly limited and confined to pump-priming in areas of 'market failure'.

One of the paradoxes of the childcare issue is that while governments from the mid-seventies at least have been exploring ways of facilitating 'low-cost provision', the growing body of experts in child development has argued not only for greater childcare provision but for the need to ensure its quality. This means ensuring that staff are adequately vetted and trained, that premises are suitable, and so forth; above all for day nursery provision for the youngest children, it means high staffing levels. These are all costly requirements, making it difficult to operate on a commercial basis unless high fees are charged. It is not at all clear how such high-quality childcare can be provided at a cost within the reach of most parents, without some significant element of public subsidy. The WFTC will generate demand but private nurseries, where these are available, may still be beyond many mothers' means. Clearly demand for registered childminders is likely to grow but this requires measures to ensure that they are sufficiently numerous and properly remunerated, trained, and supported.

The third set of concerns, then, focuses on the staffing of childcare. Again, staffing problems have long been recognized and are acknowledged afresh in the Green Paper. But the measures proposed are unlikely to resolve them. The Green Paper notes that childcare workers are often low-paid, and accordingly low in status, but can offer no more by way of remedy than the introduction of a national minimum wage.[31] The paper also recognizes that many existing childcare staff are unqualified, including an estimated 70 per cent of childminders and 2 per cent of pre-school workers. Implementing the childcare strategy will require a further massive recruitment drive, and indeed an extra £4 million was allocated for training childcare workers for the year 1998–9, but can this produce the numbers needed? Furthermore, as the paper points out, there is still great confusion regarding the equivalence and progression of different training qualifications. The onus is on the local partnerships to organize the training of their own childcare workers. Government has undertaken to consult with a range of awarding bodies with a view ulti-

---

[31] Initially, in 1999, set at £3.60 an hour.

mately to producing a 'climbing frame'. *If* this can be done it should certainly increase the attraction of childcare as a career and mitigate at least the continuing friction between nursery teachers and nursery nurses, but the ideal would probably be to create a single, integrated early years profession.[32]

THE CONTINUING IMPORTANCE OF CHILDCARE

The new childcare strategy is a far cry from early feminist demands for free universal public provision. Coming at a time when we are experiencing a growing 'crisis of confidence, not in the state but of the state',[33] it envisages a very limited direct role for government either as funder or provider. This is especially the case for under-threes, a serious shortcoming. Even so, this awareness should not prevent us from appreciating the extent of change under New Labour and the opportunity it presents for pressing childcare demands.

On the other hand policy development cannot simply be left to government. As outlined, the gender-equality and family-friendly dimensions of government thinking are far from secure.[34] Childcare should remain high on the feminists' agenda. Unfortunately they have given the childcare strategy a somewhat lukewarm reception. We do not yet have, as in the United States, an organized feminist grouping campaigning against redistribution in favour of families. But as we have seen, for some feminists government pledges of increased childcare provision have raised or confirmed suspicions that mothers are being increasingly put under pressure to go out to work, whether they want to or not. This was not helped by the coincidence of the New Deal for Lone Parents with reduction of the lone-parent benefit.[35]

However, the central fact about child daycare policy in this country is that there is still so little available. No doubt, mothers' childcare

---

[32] For a fuller discussion of these issues see Sally Dench, *Supporting Skills for Care Workers* (Brighton: University of Sussex Institute for Employment Studies, 1999).

[33] According to Freeden, New Labour is 'uncertain to what extent the state *can* innovate and provide, rather than facilitate and protect. . . . Instead, businesses, families, communities, voluntary associations—preferably anyone but the state—are entreated to set examples, take a lead and stamp their authority on social conduct': Michael Freeden, 'The Ideology of New Labour', *Political Quarterly* (1999), 42.

[34] Many have noted the government's reluctance, while pursuing a number of policies that will benefit women, to be in any way associated with feminism—the 'f' word. See for instance Anna Coote, 'It's Lads On Top at Number Ten', *Guardian*, 11 May 1999.

[35] Following legislation submitted to Parliament in Dec. 1997.

demands and preferences are complicated and varied, reflecting both their practical situation and personal inclination. No doubt, some mothers would prefer to stay at home, or to reduce their working hours.[36] What matters is that they should have a meaningful choice. A world in which parents work extended hours, leaving their small children for long days on end to the care of others, however excellent, is scarcely the ideal to which many of us would aspire. That ideal would entail shorter hours, more (genuinely) flexible work schedules, but above all, perhaps, much greater involvement in childcare by men, in the home where this is relevant but also outside it.

For the moment that ideal is exceedingly distant. Despite brief excitement over the appearance of 'New Man', available evidence suggests that on average men still spend the minimum of time with their own children.[37] Political organizations representing the interests of men or fathers, most notably Families Need Fathers, have campaigned on the issues of custody and child support but never on childcare or parental leave. The profession of childcare remains almost entirely female—variously estimated at 98 or 99 per cent. Men should of course be encouraged to take more interest: we should not freeze them out when they do. Initiatives like that of Sheffield Council, in one of whose day nurseries half the staff are men, are greatly to be welcomed. In the meantime, however, childcare remains overwhelmingly the mother's responsibility. While this may be welcome for many, it is to say the least unfair that in the absence of satisfactory childcare arrangements, women should be penalized, whether in terms of career, standard of living, or personal development.

Over the last decade many gender issues that for feminists once, seemed relatively straightforward have become more confused. While talk of post-feminism is certainly premature, much has been achieved, especially but not only for white, middle-class women. Our media now relay images of powerful and confident women—often irritatingly so—including mothers, and we hear of worrying symptoms of a 'crisis in mas-

[36] In those countries where rates of mothers' full-time employment are much higher, there has been some evidence that a growing number would like to reduce their working hours. One example is Denmark, where there is increasing public interest in shortening parents' working hours, although at the same time there remain long waiting lists for public childcare provision. See Lansted and Sommer, 'Denmark', in Moncrieff Cochran (ed.), *International Handbook of Child Care Policies and Programs* (Westport, Conn.: Greenwood Press, 1993).

[37] For instance, in 1997 an NSPCC survey of 1,000 children aged 8–15 found that they reported doing far fewer activities, whether inside or outside the home, with their fathers than their mothers. One in five could not recall sharing a single activity with their father in the previous week. Cited in Benn, *Madonna and Child*, 94.

culinity'[38] in boys' under-achievement at school and rising suicide rate. In this context the absence of substantial change in the childcare arena is the more remarkable but is also in greater danger of being over-looked. Childcare is one area in which, however complex its other dimensions, the gender issues still seem pretty transparent. It is one of the last and most crucial redoubts of vested male interest and as such has to remain a central issue for feminism.

[38] For an excellent discussion, see the introduction to the revised edition of Lynne Segal, *Slow Motion: Changing Masculinities, Changing Men* (London: Virago, 1997).

BIBLIOGRAPHY

Acker, Joan, 'Hierarchies, Jobs, Bodies: A Theory of Gendered Organizations', *Gender and Society*, 4:2 (1990), 139–58.

Adams, Carolyn Teich, and Winston, Kathryn Teich, *Mothers at Work: Public Policies in the United States, Sweden and China* (New York: Longman, 1980).

Altbach, Edith Hoshino, *et al.* (eds.), *German Feminism: Readings in Politics and Literature* (Albany, NY: State University of New York Press, 1984).

AMA (Association of Metropolitan Authorities), *Education Vouchers for Early Years: The State of Play* (London: AMA, 1996).

Ambler, John S. (ed.), *The French Welfare State* (New York: New York University Press, 1991).

Ariès, Philippe, *Centuries of Childhood* (London 2nd Harmondsworth: Penguin, 1986).

Arnot, Margaret L., 'Infant death, child care and the state: the baby-farming scandal and the first infant life protection legislation of 1872', *Continuity and Change*, 9:2 (1994), 271–311.

Ashford, Douglas, *The Emergence of the Welfare States* (Oxford: Basil Blackwell, 1986).

Association of County Councils and Association of Metropolitan Authorities, *Under-Fives* (London: Oyez Press, 1977).

Atkinson, Valerie, and Spear, Joanna, 'The Labour Party and women: Policy and practices', in Smith and Spear (eds.), *The Changing Labour Party*.

Attar, Dena, 'The demand that time forgot', *Trouble and Strife*, 23 (1992), 24–9.

Bacchi, Carol L., *Women, Policy and Politics: the construction of policy problems* (London: Sage, 1999).

Baker, Susan, and van Doorne-Huiskes, Anneke (eds.), *Women and Public Policy* (Ashgate, 1999).

Ball, Christopher, *Start Right: The Importance of Early Learning* (London: Royal Society of Arts, 1994).

Banks, Olive, *Faces of Feminism* (London: Martin Robertson, 1980).

Banting, Keith, *Poverty, Politics and Policy* (London: Macmillan, 1979).

Benn, Melissa, *Madonna and Child: Towards a new politics of motherhood* (London: Vintage, 1999).

—— 'Wandsworth—a cut above the rest', *Guardian*, 26 Feb. 1992.

Bergqvist, Christina, 'Still a woman-friendly welfare state?', paper presented to the Council of European Studies, Baltimore, 1998.

Blackstone, Tessa, *A Fair Start?* (London: Allen Lane, 1971).

Bock, Gisela, and Thane, Pat (eds.), *Maternity and Gender Politics: Women and the Rise of European Welfare States, 1880s–1950s* (New York: Routledge, 1991).

Bone, Margaret, *Pre-school Children and the Need for Day-care* (London: HMSO, 1977).

Borchorst, Anette, 'The State and the "Social Pedagogic" Universal Child Care Services—Danish Child Care Policy and Gender Equality', paper presented to the National Institute for Working Life workshop on 'Labour Market and Social Policy—Gender Relations in Transition', Brussels, 1999.

Boston, Sarah, *Women Workers and the Trade Union Movement* (London: David Poynter, 1980).

Brannen, Julia, and Moss, Peter, *Managing Mothers: Dual Earner Households after Maternity* (London: Hyman Unwin, 1991).

Braybon, G., *Women Workers in the First World War: The British Experience* (London: Croom-Helm, 1981).

Brennan, Deborah, 'Australia', in Cochran (ed.), *International Handbook of Child Care Policies and Programs.*

——*The Politics of Australian Child Care*, 2nd edn. (Cambridge: Cambridge University Press, 1998).

Brennan, Zoe, 'Mothers spurn chance of full-time childcare', *Sunday Times*, 9 Nov. 1997.

Breugel, Irene, 'Whose Myths Are They Anyway?', *British Journal of Sociology*, 47:1 (1996), 175–7.

——'Women's Employment, Legislation and the Labour Market', in Lewis (ed.), *Women's Welfare: Women's Rights.*

Briskin, Linda, and Yanz, Lynda (eds.), *Union Sisters: Women in the Labour Movement*, 2nd edn. (Toronto: Women's Press, 1985).

Broberg, Anders, and Hwang, C. Philip, 'Daycare for young children in Sweden', in Melhuish and Moss (eds.), *Day Care for Young Children: International Perspectives.*

Bryson, Valerie, 'Feminism and Common Sense', paper presented to the ESRC-sponsored seminar on 'Feminism: Theory and Practice', Bath University, 1996.

Castles, Frank, 'Needs-based Strategies of Social Protection in Australia and New Zealand', in Esping-Andersen (ed.), *Welfare States in Transition.*

——(ed.), *The Comparative History of Public Policy* (Cambridge: Polity, 1989).

Cawson, Alan (ed.), *Organised Interests and the State* (London: Sage, 1985).

Central Advisory Council for Education (Plowden), *Children and their Primary Schools* (London: HMSO, 1967).

Chamberlayne, Pru, 'Women and the state: changes in roles and rights in France, West Germany, Italy and Britain', in Lewis (ed.), *Women and Social Policies in Europe.*

Charlton, Val, 'The patter of tiny contradictions', *Red Rag*, 4 (1973), 5–8.

Childs, Sarah, 'The New Labour Women MPs in the 1997 British Parliament and the Political Representation of Women', paper presented to the EPOP Conference, Manchester Business School, 1998.

Cochran, Moncrieff (ed.), *International Handbook of Child Care Policies and Programs* (Westport, Conn.: Greenwood Press, 1993).

Cockburn, Cynthia, 'Equal Opportunities: The Short and Long Agenda', *Industrial Relations Journal* (1989), 213–25.

Cohen, Bronwen, *Caring for Children: the 1990 Report* (Edinburgh: Family Policy Studies Centre, 1990).

——and Fraser, Neil, *Childcare in a Modern Welfare System* (London: Institute for Public Policy Research, 1991).

Colley, Susan, 'Free Universal Day care: the OFL Takes a Stand', in Briskin and Yanz (eds.), *Union Sisters: Women in the Labour Movement*.

Committee on Local Authority and Allied Social Services (Seebohm), *Report of the Committee* (London: HMSO, 1968).

Committee on One-parent Families (Finer), *Report of the Committee* (London: HMSO, 1974).

Community Relations Council, *Who Minds? A Study of Working Mothers and Childminding in Ethnic Minority Communities* (London: Community Relations Council, 1975).

Connell, R. W., 'The state, gender and sexual politics', *Theory and Society*, 19:5 (1990), 507–44.

Coote, Anna, 'It's lads on top at Number Ten', *Guardian*, 11 May 1999.

——and Campbell, Bea, *Sweet Freedom* (London: Picador, 1982).

——Harman, Harriet, and Hewitt, Patricia, *The Family Way* (London: Institute for Public Policy Research, 1990).

——and Hewitt, Patricia, 'The Stance of Britain's Major Parties and Interest Groups', in Moss and Fonda (eds.), *Work and the Family*.

Coulter, Angela, *Who Minds about the Minders?* (London: Low Pay Unit, 1979).

Cowley, Sue, 'Thatcher's nurseries—expansion or containment?', *Red Rag*, 4 (1973), 3–5.

CPRS (Central Policy Review Staff), *Services for Young Children with Working Mothers* (London: HMSO, 1978).

Cullen, J., 'Nurseries', in Wandor (ed.), *The Body Politic*.

David, Miriam, 'Day Care Policies and Parenting', *Journal of Social Policy*, 11:1 (1982), 81–91.

——and New, Caroline, *For the Children's Sake* (London: Penguin, 1985).

Davies, Sonja, *Bread and Roses* (Masterson, NZ: Fraser Books, 1984).

Davin, Anna, 'Imperialism and Motherhood', *History Workshop Journal*, 5 (1978), 9–65.

Deakin, Nicholas, and Page, Robert (eds.), *The Costs of Welfare* (Aldershot: Avebury, 1993).

——and Parry, Robert, 'Does the Treasury have a social policy?', in Deakin, and Page (eds.), *The Costs of Welfare*.

Delphy, Christine, 'Mothers' Union?', *Trouble and Strife*, 24 (1992), 12–19.

Dench, Sally, *Supporting Skills for Care Workers* (Brighton: University of Sussex Institute for Employment Studies, 1999).

Department of Education and Science, *Better Schools*, Cmnd. 9469 (London: HMSO, 1985).

Department of Education and Science, *Education in Schools: A Consultative Document*, Cmnd. 6869 (London: HMSO, 1977).

——*Starting with Quality* (London: HMSO, 1990).

Dex, Shirley, and Rowthorne, Robert, *Parenting and Labour Force Participation: the Case for a Ministry of the Family*, ESRC Centre for Business Research Working Paper No. 74 (Cambridge: Cambridge University Press, 1997).

——Walters, Patricia, and Alden, David M., *French and British Mothers at Work* (London: Macmillan, 1993).

DHSS (Department of Health and Social Security) and DES (Department of Education and Science), *Low Cost Day Provision for the Under Fives* (London: DHSS, 1976).

Douglas, Gillian, 'Family Law under the Thatcher Government', *Journal of Law and Society*, 17:4 (1990), 411–26.

Drucker, Henry, *et al.* (eds.), *Developments in British Politics*, 1st edn. (Basingstoke: Macmillan, 1983).

Duchen, Claire, *Women's Rights and Women's Lives in France, 1944–1968* (London: Routledge, 1994).

Duncan, Alan, Giles, Christopher, and Webb, Steven, *The Impact of Subsidising Childcare* (Manchester: Equal Opportunities Commission, 1995).

Dunleavy, Patrick, 'The United Kingdom: Paradoxes of an Ungrounded Statism', in Castles (ed.), *The Comparative History of Public Policy*.

——*et al.* (eds.), *Developments in British Politics 4* (Basingstoke: Macmillan, 1993).

——and Rhodes, Rod, 'Beyond Whitehall', in Drucker *et al.* (eds.), *Developments in British Politics*, 1st edn.

Dyer, Clare, 'Cherie wants paid leave for new dads', *Guardian*, 17 May 1999.

Dyhouse, Carol, 'Working-class mothers and infant mortality in England, 1895–1914', *Journal of Social History*, 12:2 (1978), 248–67.

Edwards, Maud, 'Towards a third way: women's politics and welfare policies in Sweden', *Social Research*, 58:3 (1991), 677–705.

Edwards, Rosaline, *Beginnings: the Department of Health's New Under-Fives Initiative 1989–1992* (London: National Children's Bureau, 1992).

Elliot, Valerie, 'Childcare costs are "double tax"', *Guardian*, 11 Mar. 1999.

EOC (Equal Opportunities Commission), *I Want to Work . . . but What about the Kids?* (Manchester: EOC, 1978).

——*The Key to Real Choice* (Manchester: EOC, 1990).

Erikson, Robert, *et al.* (eds.), *The Scandinavian Model: Welfare States and Welfare Research* (New York and London: M. E. Sharpe, 1987).

Esping-Andersen, Gøsta, 'After the Golden Age?', in Esping-Andersen (ed.), *Welfare States in Transition*.

——*The Three Worlds of Welfare Capitalism* (Cambridge: Polity Press, 1990).

——(ed.), *Welfare States in Transition* (London: Sage, 1996).

——and Korpi, Walter, 'From Poor relief to Institutional Welfare States: the Development of Scandinavian Social Policy', in Erikson *et al.* (eds.), *The Scandinavian Model: Welfare States and Welfare Research*.

European Commission Childcare Network, *Childcare in the European Communities 1985–1990* (Brussels: Commission of the European Communities, 1990).

European Commission Network on Childcare and Other Measures to Reconcile Employment and Family Responsibilities, *A Review of Services for Young Children in the European Union 1990–1995* (Brussels: EC Directorate General V, 1996).

Eyken, W. van der, *The DHSS Under-fives Initiative 1983–1987: Final Report* (London: DHSS, 1987).

Fagnani, Jeanne, 'Who should take care of the child? The ambiguities of French family policy', paper presented to the National Institute for Working Life workshop on 'Labour Market and Social Policy—Gender Relations in Transition', Brussels, 1999.

Ferguson, Sheila, and Fitzgerald, Hilda, *Studies in the Social Services*, History of the Second World War: Civil Series (London: HMSO and Longmans, Green and Co., 1954).

Ferree, Myra Marx, 'Making Equality: the Women's Affairs Offices in the Federal Republic of Germany', in Stetson and Mazur (eds.), *Comparative State Feminism*.

Firestone, Shulamith, *The Dialectic of Sex* (London: Paladin, 1970).

Franklin, Bob (ed.), *The Rights of Children* (Oxford: Basil Blackwell, 1986).

Franzway, Suzanne, 'Childcare', in Franzway, Court, and Connell, *Staking a Claim*.

——Court, Dianna, and Connell, R. W., *Staking a Claim* (Cambridge: Polity Press, 1989).

Fraser, Derek, *The Evolution of the British Welfare State*, 2nd edn. (London: Macmillan, 1984).

Freeden, Michael, 'The Ideology of New Labour', *Political Quarterly* (1999), 42–51.

Freeman, Gary, 'National Styles and Policy Sectors: Explaining Structured Variation', *Journal of Public Policy*, 5:4 (1985), 467–96.

Frost, Nick, and Stein, Mike, *The Politics of Child Welfare* (London: Harvester Wheatsheaf, 1989).

Gardiner, Jean, *Gender, Care and Economics* (London: Macmillan, 1997).

Garrett, Myra, 'Girls and boys come out to play', *Red Rag*, 5 (1975), 6–8.

Gathorne-Hardy, Jonathan, *The Rise and Fall of the British Nanny* (London: Hodder and Stoughton, 1972).

George, Vic, and Taylor-Gooby, Peter (eds.), *European Welfare Policy* (London: Macmillan, 1996).

Gibson, Anne, 'Women in the Trade Unions: Present and Future Policy on Equal Opportunities', paper presented to the Political Studies Association Women's Group Conference, Bedford College, London, 1980.

Gieve, Katherine, 'Rethinking feminist attitudes towards mothering', *Feminist Review*, 25 (1987), 38–45.

Ginn, Jay, *et al.*, 'Feminist fallacies: a reply to Hakim on women's employment', *British Journal of Sociology*, 47:1 (1996), 167–74.

Gittins, Diana, *The Child in Question* (London: Macmillan, 1998).

Gordon, Linda (ed.), *Women, the State and Welfare* (Madison, Wisc.: University of Wisconsin Press, 1990).

Gormley, William T., *Everybody's Children* (Washington, DC: Brookings Institute, 1995).

Gornick, Janet C., Meyers, Marcia K., and Ross, Katherine E., 'Supporting the Employment of Mothers: Policy Variation across Fourteen Welfare States', *Journal of European Social Policy*, 7:1 (1997), 45–70.

Haas, Linda, *Equal Parenthood and Social Policy* (New York: State University of New York Press, 1992).

Hakim, Catherine, 'Five feminist myths about women's employment', *British Journal of Sociology*, 46:3 (1995), 429–55.

—— 'The myth of rising female employment', *Work, Employment and Society*, 7:1 (1993), 97–120.

Hall, Catherine, *White, Male and Middle-class: Explorations in Feminism and History* (Cambridge: Polity, 1990).

Hall, Peter A., and Taylor, Rosemary C. R., 'Political Science and the Three New Institutionalisms', *Political Studies*, 44:5 (1996), 936–57.

Hantrais, Linda, 'Women, Work and Welfare in France', in Lewis (ed.), *Women and Social Policies in Europe*.

Harding, Lorraine Fox, *Family, State and Social Policy* (London: Macmillan, 1996).

Harker, Lisa, 'A National Childcare Strategy: Does it Meet the Childcare Challenge?', *Political Quarterly* (1998), 458–63.

Harrop, Anne, and Moss, Peter, 'Working parents: trends in the 1980s', *Employment Gazette*, 102:10 (1994), 343–52.

Hayward, Jack, 'Mobilising private interests in the service of political ambitions: the salient elements in dual French policy style', in Richardson (ed.), *Policy Styles in Western Europe*.

—— 'National Aptitudes for Planning in Britain, France and Italy', *Government and Opposition*, 14:1 (1979), 397–410.

Heidenheimer, Arnold J., Heclo, Hugh, and Adams, Carolyn Tech, *Comparative Public Policy*, 3rd edn. (New York: St Martin's Press, 1990).

Held, David (ed.), *Political Theory Today* (Cambridge: Polity, 1991).

Hendrick, Harry, 'Constructions and Reconstructions of British Childhood: An Interpretative Survey', in James and Prout (eds.), *Constructing and Reconstructing Childhood: Contemporary Issues in the Sociological Study of Childhood*.

Heron, Elisabeth, 'The mystique of motherhood', *Time Out*, 21–7 Nov. 1980.

Hevey, Denise, *The Continuing Under-fives Training Muddle* (London: VOLCUF, 1986).

Hewitt, Margaret, *Wives and Mothers in Victorian Industry* (London: Rockliff, 1958).

Hewitt, Patricia, and Matinson, Deborah, *Women's Votes: the key to winning* (London: Fabian Society, 1989).

Hobson, Barbara, 'Feminist Strategies and Gendered Discourses in Welfare States: Married Women's Right to Work in the United States and Sweden', in Koven and Michel (eds.), *Mothers of a New World*.

Hogwood, B. W., and Gunn, L., *Policy Analysis for the Real World* (Oxford: Oxford University Press, 1984).

Holland, Joy (ed.), *Feminist Action 1* (London: Battle Axe, 1984).

Holliday, Ian, 'Organised Interests after Thatcher', in Dunleavy *et al.* (eds.), *Developments in British Politics 4.*

Holmes, Martin, *The First Thatcher Government, 1979–1983* (Brighton: Wheatsheaf, 1985).

House of Commons Education and Employment Committee, *The Operation of the Nursery Voucher Scheme* (London: Stationery Office, 1997).

House of Commons Employment Committee, *Mothers in Employment* (London: HMSO, 1995).

Humphries, Jane, and Rubery, Jill, 'Recession and Exploitation: British women in a changing workplace, 1979–1985', in Jenson, Hagen, and Reddy (eds.), *Feminization of the Labour Force.*

Huttunen, Eeva, and Turunen, Merja-Mararia, 'Finland', in Cochran (ed.), *International Handbook of Child Care Policies and Programs.*

Immergut, Ellen M., 'The Theoretical Core of the New Institutionalism', *Politics and Society*, 26:1 (1998), 5–34.

James, Alison, and Prout, Alan (eds.), *Constructing and Reconstructing Childhood: Contemporary Issues in the Sociological Study of Childhood* (London: Falmer Press, 1997).

Jenson, Jane, 'The modern women's movement in Italy, France and Great Britain: differences in life cycles', *Comparative Social Research*, 5 (1982), 341–75.

—— 'Representations of gender: policies to "protect" women workers in France and the United States before 1914', in Gordon (ed.), *Women, the State and Welfare.*

—— 'Who Cares? Gender and Welfare Regimes', *Social Politics*, 4:2 (1997), 182–7.

—— and Sineau, Mariette, *Mitterrand et les Françaises: Un rendez-vous manqué?* (Paris: Presses de la Fondation Nationale des Sciences Politiques, 1995).

—— Hagen, Elisabeth, and Reddy, Ceallaigh (eds.), *Feminization of the Labour Force* (Cambridge: Polity, 1988).

Jordan, Grant, and Richardson, Jeremy, 'The British Policy Style or the Logic of Negotiation?', in Richardson (ed.), *Policy Styles in Western Europe.*

—— —— *Government and Pressure Groups in Britain* (Oxford: Oxford University Press, 1987).

Joshi, Heather, 'Sex and motherhood as handicaps in the labour market', in Maclean and Groves (eds.), *Women's Issues in Social Policy.*

Jowell, Roger *et al.* (eds.), *British Social Attitudes: the Fifth report* (London: Gower, 1988).

Jowell, Roger *et al.* (eds.), *British Social Attitudes: the 12th report* (Aldershot: Dartmouth, 1994).

Judd, Judith, 'Education Policy Rifts Revealed', *Independent*, 12 Mar. 1996.

Judith Judd and Tran Abrams, 'Tories could extend voucher scheme to all school pupils', *Independent*, 7 Oct. 1995, 8.

Kamerman, Sheila B., and Kahn, Alfred J., 'Child care and privatization', in Kamerman and Kahn (eds.), *Privatization and the Welfare State*.

——— (eds.), *Family Policy: Government and Families in Fourteen Countries* (New York: Columbia University Press, 1978).

——— (eds.), *Privatization and the Welfare State* (Princeton, NY: Princeton University Press, 1989).

Katzenstein, Mary Fainsod, and Mueller, Carol (eds.), *The Women's Movements of the US and W Europe* (Philadelphia: Temple University Press, 1987).

—— and Skjeie, Helga (eds.), *Going Public* (Oslo: Institute for Social Research, 1990).

Kavanagh, Dennis, and Seldon, Arthur (eds.), *The Thatcher Effect: A Decade of Change* (Oxford: Oxford University Press, 1989).

King, Desmond, 'The establishment of work-welfare programmes in the United States and Britain: Politics, ideas, and institutions', in Steinmo *et al.* (eds.), *Structuring Politics*.

—— and Wickham-Jones, Mark, 'From Clinton to Blair: The Democratic (Party) Origins of Welfare to Work', *Political Quarterly* (1999), 62–74.

Koven, Seth, and Michel, Sonya (eds.), *Mothers of a New World* (London: Routledge, 1993).

Land, Hilary and Parker, Roy, 'United Kingdom' in Kamerman and Kahn (eds.) *Family Policy*.

Langsted, Ole, and Sommer, Dion, 'Denmark', in Cochran (ed.), *International Handbook of Child Care Policies and Programs*.

Leira, Arnlaug, 'The "Woman-friendly" Welfare State?: the Case of Norway and Sweden', in Lewis (ed.), *Women and Social Policies in Europe*.

Lenoir, Rémi, 'Family Policy in France since 1938', in Ambler (ed.), *The French Welfare State*.

Leprince, Frédérique, 'Day care for young children in France', in Melhuish and Moss (eds.), *Day Care for Young Children*.

Lewenhak, Sheila, *Women and Trade Unions* (London: Ernest Benn, 1977).

Lewis, Jane, 'Gender and the Development of Welfare Regimes', *Journal of European Social Policy*, 2:3 (1992), 159–73.

—— 'Gender and Welfare regimes: Further Thoughts', *Social Politics*, 4:2 (1997), 160–77.

—— 'Models of equality for women: the case of state support for children in twentieth-century Britain', in Bock and Thane (eds.), *Maternity and Gender Politics*.

—— *The Politics of Motherhood* (London: Croom-Helm, 1990).

—— *Women in Britain since 1945* (Oxford: Blackwell, 1992).

——(ed.), *Women and Social Policies in Europe* (Aldershot: Edward Elgar, 1993).

——(ed.), *Women's Welfare: Women's Rights* (Beckenham: Croom-Helm, 1983).

Liddington, Jill, and Norris, J., *One Hand Tied Behind Us: the Rise of the Women's Suffrage Movement* (London: Virago, 1978).

Lister, Ruth, 'From equality to social exclusion: New Labour and the welfare state', *Critical Social Policy*, 55 (1998), 215–25.

Liz, 'Games Children Play', *Shrew*, 3:2 (1971), 6–8.

Lovenduski, Joni, and Randall, Vicky, *Contemporary Feminist Politics* (Oxford: Oxford University Press, 1993).

Lowi, Theodore J., 'American Business, Public Policy, Case-studies and Political Theory', *World Politics*, 16:4 (1964), 677–715.

——and Ginsberg, Benjamin, *American Government: Freedom and Power* (New York: W. W. Norton, 1996).

Lukes, Steven, *Power: A Radical View* (London: Macmillan, 1974).

McCarthy, Michael, *The Politics of Welfare* (London: Croom-Helm, 1986).

McCrate, E., 'Gender Differences: the Role of Endogenous Preferences and Collective Action', *American Economic Review*, 78:2 (1988), 235–9.

Maclean, Mavis, and Groves, Dulcie (eds.), *Women's Issues in Social Policy* (London: Routledge, 1991).

MacLeod, Donald, and Carvel, John, 'Major to fulfil nursery pledge with voucher plan', *Guardian*, 14 June 1995.

Manchester City Council, *1995–96 Children Act Review* (Manchester: Manchester City Council, n.d.).

Marchbank, Jennifer, 'Agenda-setting, Policy-making and the Marginalization of Women', unpubl. Ph.D. diss., University of Strathclyde, 1994.

Marquand, David, *The Unprincipled Society* (London: Jonathan Cape, 1988).

Marsh, David, and Rhodes, Rod, 'Policy Community and Issue Networks: Beyond Typology', in Marsh and Rhodes (eds.), *Policy Networks in British Government*.

————(eds.), *Implementing Thatcherite Policies: Audit of an Era* (Buckingham: Open University Press, 1992).

————(eds.), *Policy Networks in British Government* (Oxford: Oxford University Press, 1992).

——and Tant, T., *There is no alternative: Mrs Thatcher and the British Political Tradition*, Essex Papers in Politics and Government, No. 69 (Colchester: Department of Government, Essex University, 1989).

Mawty, R. I., 'Childminding and Social Change', *Social Services Quarterly*, 48 (1974).

May, Helen, 'Changing Policies, Changing Politics: Early Childhood Care and Education in New Zealand', in Pflaum and Pignatelli (eds.), *The Yearbook of Bank Street College of Educational Thought and Practice*.

——*The Hand that Rocks the Cradle* (Department of Early Childhood, Waikato University, 1993).

Melhuish, Edward, and Moss, Peter (eds.), *Day Care for Young Children: International Perspectives* (London: Routledge, 1991).

Meltzer, Howard, *Day care services for children* (London: HMSO, 1994).

Millar, Jane, 'Mothers, workers, wives: comparing policy approaches to supporting lone mothers', in Silva (ed.), *Good Enough Mothering?*

'More than minding', *Shrew*, 3:2 (1971), 6–8.

Moss, Peter, 'Day Care Policy and Provision in Britain', in Moss and Melhuish (eds.), *Current Issues in Day Care for Young Children*.

——and Fonda, Nickie (eds.), *Work and the Family* (London: Maurice Temple Smith, 1980).

——and Melhuish, Edward (eds.), *Current Issues in Day Care for Young Children* (London: HMSO, 1991).

——Mooney, Ann, Munton, Tony, and Stantham, June, *Local Assessment of Childcare Need and Provision*, Research Report RR72 (London: Department for Education and Employment, 1998).

Muir, Annette, 'Laissez-faire parenthood?', *Red Rag*, 3 (1973).

Murray, Charles, *The Emerging British Underclass* (London: Institute of Economic Affairs, 1990).

Myrdal, Alva, and Klein, Viola, *Women's Two Roles* (London: Routledge and Kegan Paul, 1956).

National Commission on Education, *Learning to Succeed* (London: William Heinemann, 1993).

Norgren, Jill, 'In Search of a National Child Care Policy: Background and Prospects', *Western Political Quarterly*, 34:1 (1981), 127–42.

Norris, Pippa, 'Women Politicians: Transforming Westminster?', *Parliamentary Affairs*, 49:1 (1996), 89–102.

Norvez, Alain, *De la naissance a l'école*, INED, Travaux et Documents, Cahier no 126 (Paris: PUF, 1990).

Oakley, Ann, 'Feminism and motherhood', in Richards and Light (eds.), *Children of Social Worlds*.

O'Connor, Julia, Orloff, Ann Shola, and Shaver, Sheila, *States, Markets, Families* (Cambridge: Cambridge University Press, 1999).

Okin, Susan Moller, 'Gender, the Public and the Private', in Held (ed.), *Political Theory Today*.

Ostner, Ilona, 'Slow Motion: Women, Work and the Family in Germany', in Lewis (ed.), *Women and Social Policies in Europe*.

Owen, David, 'Foreword', in DHSS and DES, *Low Cost Day Provision for the Under-Fives*.

Parton, Nigel, *Governing the Family* (Basingstoke: Macmillan, 1991).

Pedersen, Susan, *Family, Dependence and the Origins of the Welfare State: Britain and France, 1914–1945* (Cambridge: Cambridge University Press, 1993).

Pence, Alan, 'Canada', in Cochran (ed.), *International Handbook of Child Care Policies and Programs*.

Perrigo, Sarah, 'Women and Change in the Labour Party', *Parliamentary Affairs*, 49:1 (1996), 16–29.

Perrons, Diane, 'Labour market transformations and employment policies: the organisation of work, care and leisure in the UK', paper presented to the National Institute for Working Life workshop on 'Labour Market and Social Policy—Gender Relations in Transition', Brussels, 1999.

Pettinger, Rudolf, 'Germany', in Cochran (ed.), *International Handbook of Child Care Policies and Programs*.

Pflaum, Susanna W., and Pignatelli, Frank (eds.), *The Yearbook of Bank Street College of Educational Thought and Practice* (New York: Bank Street College, 1993).

Phillips, Deborah, 'Day care for young children in the United States', in Melhuish and Moss (eds.), *Day Care for Young Children*.

Phillips, Melanie, *The Sex Change State* (London: Social Market Foundation, 1997).

Pierson, Paul, *Dismantling the Welfare State?* (Cambridge: Cambridge University Press, 1994).

Pinchbeck, Ivy, and Hewitt, Margaret, *Children in English Society*, vol. ii (London: Routledge and Kegan Paul, 1973).

Pringle, Mia Kellmer, 'A Policy for Young Children', in DHSS and DES, *Low Cost Day Provision for the Under-Fives*.

Pugh, Gillian, 'Closing Remarks', in *Services for Under Fives: Developing Policy and Practice*, report on NES/NCB Conference, July 1988.

——'An equal start for all our children?', unpubl. Times Educational Supplement/Greenwich Lecture 1992.

——*Services for Under-Fives: Developing a Co-ordinated Approach* (London: National Children's Bureau, 1988).

Randall, Vicky, 'Comparative Childcare Policy and the Public–Private Divide', in Baker and van Doorne-Huiskes (eds.), *Women and Public Policy*.

——'Feminism and Child Daycare', *Journal of Social Policy*, 25:4 (1996), 485–505.

——and Fisher, Kimberly, *Towards Explaining Child Daycare Policy Variations amongst the Local Authorities*, Institute of Social and Economic Research Working Paper 99:18 (Colchester: ESRC Centre on Micro-social Change, 1999).

Rich, Adrienne, *Of Woman Born* (London: Virago, 1977).

Richards, M., and Light, P. (eds.), *Children of Social Worlds* (Cambridge, Mass.: Harvard University Press, 1986).

Richardson, Jeremy (ed.), *Policy Styles in Western Europe* (London: Allen and Unwin, 1982).

Riddell, Peter, 'Cabinet and Parliament', in Kavanagh and Seldon (eds.), *The Thatcher Effect: A Decade of Change*.

Riley, Denise, 'War in the Nursery', *Feminist Review*, 2 (1979), 82–108.

——*War in the Nursery* (London: Virago, 1983).

Riley, Susan E., 'Caring for Rosie's Children: Federal Child Care Policies in the World War II Era', *Polity*, 26:4 (1994), 655–75.

Robinson, Olive, 'The changing labour market: growth of part-time employment and labour market segregation in Britain', in Walby (ed.), *Gender Segregation at Work*.

Rodgers, Barbara N., 'Family Policy in France', *Journal of Social Policy*, 4:2 (1975), 113–28.

Roseneill, Sasha, and Mann, Kirk, 'Unpalatable choices and inadequate families', in Silva (ed.), *Good Enough Mothering?*

Rowbotham, Sheila, *The Past is Before Us* (London: Penguin, 1990).

Ruggie, Mary, *The State and Working Women: A Comparative Study of Britain and Sweden* (Princeton, NJ: Princeton University Press, 1984).

——'Workers' Movements and Women's Interests: The Impact of Labor–State Relations in Britain and Sweden', in Katzenstein and Mueller (eds.), *The Women's Movements of the US and W Europe*.

Ruin, O., 'Sweden in the 1970s: policy-making becomes difficult' in Richardson (ed.), *Policy Styles in Western Europe*.

Rutter, Michael, *Maternal Deprivation Reassessed* (London: Penguin, 1972).

Sainsbury, Diane, *Gender, Equality, and Welfare States* (Cambridge: Cambridge University Press, 1996).

Sawer, Marion, ' "Femocrats in Glass Towers?" The Office for the Status of Women in Australia', in Stetson and Mazur (eds.), *Comparative State Feminism*.

Schattschneider, E. E., *The Semi-sovereign People: A Realist's View of Democracy in America* (Holt, Rinehart and Winston, 1960).

Segal, Lynne, *Is the Future Female?* (London: Virago, 1987).

——*Slow Motion: Changing Masculinities, Changing Men*, revd. edn. (London: Virago, 1997).

Shaw, Marion, 'The 53rd TUC Women's Congress', in Holland (ed.), *Feminist Action 1*.

Short, Clare, 'Women and the Labour Party', *Parliamentary Affairs*, 49:1 (1996), 17–25.

Silva, Elizabeth Bortolaia (ed.), *Good Enough Mothering?* (London: Routledge, 1996).

Sly, Frances, 'Mothers in the labour market', *Employment Gazette*, 102:11 (1994), 403–13.

Smart, Carol, 'Deconstructing motherhood', in Silva (ed.), *Good Enough Mothering?*

Smith, Harold L., 'The Womanpower Problem in Britain during the Second World War', *Historical Journal*, 27:4 (1984), 925–45.

Smith, Martin J., and Spear, Joanna (eds.), *The Changing Labour Party* (London: Routledge, 1992).

Smithers, Rebecca, 'Threatened children's playgroups and nurseries win £500,000 grant', *Guardian*, 17 Mar. 1999.

Somerville, Jenny, 'The New Right and family politics', *Economy and Society*, 21:2 (1992), 93–128.

Spitzer, Robert J., 'Promoting Policy Theory: Revising Arenas of Power', *Policy Studies Journal*, 15:4 (1987), 675–89.

Steedman, Carolyn, *Childhood, Culture and Class in Britain: Margaret McMillan 1860–1931* (London: Virago, 1990).

Steinmo, Sven, Thelen, Kathleen, and Longstreth, Frank (eds.), *Structuring Politics* (Cambridge: Cambridge University Press, 1992).

Stetson, Dorothy McBride, and Mazur, Amy (eds.), *Comparative State Feminism* (London: Sage, 1995).

Summerfield, Penny, *Women Workers in the Second World War* (London: Croom-Helm, 1984).

Sylva, Kathy, 'Educational Aspects of Day Care in England and Wales', in Moss and Melhuish (eds.), *Current Issues in Day Care for Young Children*.

Taylor-Gooby, Peter, 'The United Kingdom: Radical Departures and Political Consensus', in George and Taylor-Gooby (eds.), *European Welfare Policy*.

Teightsoonian, Katherine, 'Neo-Conservative Ideology and Opposition to Federal Regulation of Child Care Services in the United States and Canada', *Canadian Journal of Political Science*, 26:1 (1993), 97–121.

Thane, Pat, *Foundations of the Welfare State*, 2nd edn. (London: Longman, 1996).

Thelen, Kathleen, and Steinmo, Sven, 'Historical institutionalism in comparative perspective', in Steinmo, Thelen, and Longstreth (eds.), *Structuring Politics*.

Thomson, Katarina, 'Working mothers: choice or circumstance?', in Jowell *et al.* (eds.), *British Social Attitudes: the 12th report*.

Tizard, Barbara, 'Introduction', in Moss and Melhuish (eds.), *Current Issues in Day Care for Young Children*.

Tizard, Jack, 'Ten Comments on Low Cost Day Care for the Under Fives', in DHSS and DES, *Low Cost Day Provision for the Under-Fives*.

——Moss, Peter, and Perry, Jane, *All Our Children* (London: Temple Smith, 1976).

Toynbee, Polly, 'Working Women', *Guardian*, 18 Mar. 1999.

TUC (Trades Union Congress), *Charter on Facilities for Under-5s* (London: TUC, 1979).

——*TUC Report* (London: TUC, various years).

Vickerstaff, Sarah, 'Industrial Training in Britain: The Dilemmas of Neo-Corporatist Policy', in Cawson (ed.), *Organised Interests and the State*.

Walby, Sylvia (ed.), *Gender Segregation at Work* (Milton Keynes: Open University Press, 1988).

Wallsgrove, Ruth, 'Thicker than Water', *Trouble and Strife*, 7 (1985), 26–8.

Wandor, Micheline (ed.), *The Body Politic* (London: Stage 1, 1978).

Watson, Sophie, 'Unpacking "the state": reflections on Australian, British and Swedish feminist interventions', in Katzenstein and Skjeie (eds.), *Going Public*.

Weber, Eugene, *Peasants into Frenchmen* (Stanford, Calif.: Stanford University Press, 1976).

White, Cynthia, *Women's Magazines 1693–1968* (London: Michael Joseph, 1970).

Wilding, Paul, 'The Welfare State and the Conservatives', *Political Studies*, 45:3 (1997), 716–26.

Williams, Fiona, *Social Policy: A Critical Introduction* (London: Polity, 1989).

Wilson, Elizabeth, *Only Halfway to Paradise: Women in Postwar Britain, 1945–68* (London: Tavistock, 1980).

——*Women and the Welfare State* (London: Tavistock, 1977).

Witherspoon, Sharon, 'Interim Report: A Woman's Work', in Jowell *et al.* (eds.), *British Social Attitudes: the Fifth Report.*

Yudkin, Simon, *0–5: A Report on the Care of Pre-School Children* (London: National Society of Children's Nurseries, 1967).

ALL ENTRIES REFER TO UK
UNLESS OTHERWISE STATED